Life on Quaker Road

History, Stories & Goodwillie Genealogy

COMPILED BY DIANE GOODWILLIE

**Stories by Ruth Cornett
& John Ross Goodwillie**

2005

© Copyright 2005 Carol Diane Goodwillie.
All rights reserved. No part of this publication may be reproduced, stored in a retrieval system, or transmitted, in any form or by any means, electronic, mechanical, photocopying, recording, or otherwise, without the written prior permission of the author.

Prepared with technical assistance from Bill Lewis, Peter Meyler, Ruth Lechte, Diane Potter, Joyce and Joan Dinnin, Jane Allen, Hugh & Sally Goodwillie and Anne Miller.
Maps, Photographs and drawings courtesy of Earl Plato, Alan L Brown, the Welland Public Library Local History Collection, the Archive Collection of the Welland Historical Museum, Germantown School, Pocantico Hills School, Ontario Ministry of Culture and Recreation, Barnet Historical Society, Committee for Anglophone Social Action, Municipal Council, Municipality of Welland, Ontario Ministry of Agriculture and Food, Fitzsimmons Collection of the Hockey Hall of Fame, Diane Potter, Sandy Stokes, Kim Rapp, Karen Kalashnik, Adrienne Roy. All other photographs provided by J.R.Goodwillie, D.Goodwillie, and Ruth Cornett.
Design and layout by Steve Cook Nambour Queensland Australia.
Most photos scanned by Talat Mehmood of Pro Photos Fiji.

Front cover photos: John Allan and Luella Page Goodwillie c. 1890; Goodwillie house and silo, 1975.
Back cover photos from top left: Farming on Quaker Raod c. 1930. The young Goodwillie family visits Niagara Falls c. 1912. The Goodwilie family in their McLaughlin-Buick at the Welland Firemen's Parade. c. 1914. John Allan loved racing with Sox. Goodwillie family behind the Quaker Road farmhouse. c. 1916. Pretend marriage among the Goodwillie vineyards. c. 1913.

Note for Librarians: A cataloguing record for this book is available from Library and Archives Canada at www.collectionscanada.ca/amicus/index-e.html
ISBN 1-4120-7024-4

Printed in Victoria, BC, Canada. Printed on paper with minimum 30% recycled fibre. Trafford's print shop runs on "green energy" from solar, wind and other environmentally-friendly power sources.

Offices in Canada, USA, Ireland and UK
This book was published *on-demand* in cooperation with Trafford Publishing. On-demand publishing is a unique process and service of making a book available for retail sale to the public taking advantage of on-demand manufacturing and Internet marketing. On-demand publishing includes promotions, retail sales, manufacturing, order fulfilment, accounting and collecting royalties on behalf of the author.

Book sales for North America and international:
Trafford Publishing, 6E–2333 Government St.,
Victoria, BC v8t 4p4 CANADA
phone 250 383 6864 (toll-free 1 888 232 4444)
fax 250 383 6804; email to orders@trafford.com
Book sales in Europe:
Trafford Publishing (uk) Ltd., Enterprise House, Wistaston Road Business Centre,
Wistaston Road, Crewe, Cheshire cw2 7rp UNITED KINGDOM
phone 01270 251 396 (local rate 0845 230 9601)
facsimile 01270 254 983; orders.uk@trafford.com
Order online at:
trafford.com/05-1935

10 9 8 7 6 5 4 3 2 1

Preface

For years the Goodwillie family has heard about my 'redoing Auntie Ruth's book'. The original ten copies of Auntie Ruth Cornett's 1973 **Old Time Stories Of The Farm** are highly valued. But before publishing for a broader audience, edits and the addition of new material were needed. Trying to find the time to focus on the project has been a problem for me. However, retirement from my South Pacific women's rights and environment work plus Auntie Ruth's generous bequest motivated and enabled me to bring the book to its conclusion.

Visits to Goodwillie haunts and genealogy websites have uncovered new facts. For example the Municipality of New Carlisle in the Gaspé, Quebec shed light on Joseph Goodwillie's community activities and the Teague genealogy of his wife, Mary Ann. Bill Lewis, Welland historian, Peter Meyler author of *A Stolen Life: Searching for Richard Pierpoint*, and others have reviewed the historical details. The book has benefited from many comments, family contributions and Internet information.

Auntie Ruth and my father, John Ross, through his book, **The Goodwillies 1590 - 1986: Four Hundred Years of Family History** provided 95% of the book's material. These two storytellers, no longer with us, are acknowledged as authors since without their efforts the book would not exist. Content and style of the original stories has been retained but some editing has been done for reader understanding. Referring to North American First Nations and African Americans as 'Indians' and 'Coloureds' is not meant to be disrespectful but rather reflects the language used in the original manuscripts.

Most of the photos are original family heirlooms, previously unpublished, although others, acknowledged elsewhere have been added to help interpret the stories. Kevin McCabe and Lynn Prunskus from Brock University have been most helpful. I thank all for their help and contribution to this project.

As Ruth Cornett said about her stories: "I don't pretend to be much of a writer ... I have enjoyed doing this and hope you will all look back and remember with a bit of nostalgia the fun and work that took place at the farm."

For me it is an act of love to unite and make more widely available Goodwillie records and stories. For those in the Welland area and especially those living in their suburban houses on the old Goodwillie farm, I hope you will touch base with the spirits, understand sacrifices and enjoy privileges associated with your homes. For my own family, and especially new generations emerging, may we remember our roots and grow in tolerance and in joy of the wide world around us.

It is with special love and thanks that I dedicate this book to Ruth Cornett and John Ross Goodwillie.

Diane Goodwillie

September 2005

Diane with Scottish ancestors.   *John Ross Goodwillie and Ruth Cornett.*

Contents

Introduction

Section One: Links to Quaker Road

Chapter One: Neutrals and Other First Nations

Names for the Neutral and Iroquois Nations; The Downfall of the Neutral Nation; First nations Involvement in European Conflicts; Legend of the Grasshopper War; Port Colborne Burial Ground; European Settlers Encounter Canada's First Nations; First Nations Help Laura Secord.

Chapter Two: Pioneer Stories of Indigenous People

Memories of a Young Norwich Settler; Indians Acts of Kindness; Pumpkins Save the Day; Mrs. Hagar's Embarrassment; Always be Prepared – Masterman Ready;

Chapter Three: Slavery and Africans in the Niagara Peninsula

Niagara Leaders Support Black Freedom; Slavery and African Americans in the Niagara Peninsula; Black History and Quaker Road

Chapter Four: Wildlife and Settling into the Land

The Wolves

Chapter Five: Goodwillie and Page Family History

The Goodwillie Name; Goodwillie Scottish Origins; Migration and Loyalist Leanings; New Carlisle, Quebec; New Carlisle's Unique and Historic Plans; Early Justice and Jury Duty in 1790; To Barnet, Vermont and Back to Canada; The Move to Quaker Road; Children of Joseph Junior; Hiram in Norwich and Welland; First Thorold Vineyard and Fruits Bottled Under Glass; Notes from Various Royal Tours to Canada; The Canning Business Expands; The Pages of Quaker Road.

Section Two: Quaker Road Stories

Introduction: Who Wrote the Farm Stories?

Grandma Stover- Always Ready to Tell Old Stories; Auntie Ruth Goodwillie Cornett – A Writer and Story Teller; John Ross Goodwillie – The Genealogist

Chapter Six: The Goodwillie Farm and Surroundings

The Farmhouse; Our Surroundings; Building the House; A 1980 visit to the Farmhouse; The Main Floor of the Quaker Road House; The Opening of the Safe; The Kitchen and Pantry; Water Supply for the House; Upstairs; Gas and Electricity; Playing in the Yard; The Graperies, Orchards and Bush; The Barns; Farm Fun and

Children's Adventures; The First Farm Radio; Farm Dogs; Easter Eggs; Boating on the Pond-The S.S. Artusa; Hockey on the Farm Pond; Curling in Welland; Sleigh Rides and the Dance; Paul Jones Dance; Halloween Party; The Sunday School Picnic;Washing Clothes, Milking and Other Chores; The Power of Fire; Walnuts, Hickory Nuts and Chestnuts; Cutting Ice; Making Ice Cream; Courting and Marriages; Fonthill Bank Manager's Quarters.

Chapter Seven: Horses, Roads and Cars

The Drive Shed at the Farm; Gyp- Runaway Racing Horse; Sox- the Handsome and Smart Horse; Frightening Donkeys and Mad Dogs; Dick- the Faithful Horse; Charlie's Horse and Pete's First Summer Job; The Gravelling of Quaker Road; The First Car; Niagara Falls Picnic; Daredevils at Niagara Falls.

Chapter Eight: Local Happenings: School, Parties and Events

School Days; School Work; Games at School and Lunch; School Holidays; Arbor Day; Valentines Day; 24th of May; Frog Hunting; 24th May-Spring Planting; School Days; The Sunday School Concert; Christmas at the Farm; Summers and End of the World War; Long Beach Cottage.

Chapter Nine: Farming and Fruit Canning Factory

Community Harvesting; Slaughtering the Meat; The Sawmill; The Factory-Early Beginnings; The Expanding Goodwillie Factory; Fruit Harvesting and Canning Work; Family Work in the Factory; Selling Peach Pits; Picking Grapes; The Farm Factory Moves to Welland.

Chapter Ten: Last Days on the Quaker Road Farm

After Father's Death; Electro-Metals Company; Fruit Picking During the War; TB Takes it Toll; Selling the Quaker Road Farm; Postscript.

Section Three: A Brief Family History

Timeline of Relevant Events;
First Five Generations of Goodwillies Born in Scotland;
Goodwillie Emigrants from Scotland to North America;
Descendants of Joseph and Mary Ann Teague Goodwillie;
Descendants of John Allan and Luella Page Goodwillie.

Appendix

Endnotes
Notes and References on Illustrations and Graphics
References and Further Reading
Index

Introduction

This book focuses on stories, events and activities originating from the 1870s Goodwillie farmhouse on Quaker Road, near Welland, Ontario. Included are local legends and anecdotes about indigenous men and women, early black refugees and white pioneer settler encounters with wolves and Canada's First Nations. Day-to-day incidents are told about the farm, now a Welland suburb, and the fruit canning factory developed by the Goodwillie family in the period between 1880 and 1928. A glimpse is given of a sawmill located near Ridgeville, summer cottage life at Long Beach and family connections in Wainfleet and Norwich Townships.

Life on Quaker Road identifies Goodwillie history that originated in Fife, Scotland where stone ruins on Goatmilk Farm are thought to be the home in the 1600s of Goodwillie ancestors. The book includes Loyalist land allotments recorded in New Carlisle in the Gaspé region of Québec. Mention is also made of the Goodwillie Museum in Barnet, Vermont, where the secret chamber of the 1790 Goodwillie House was thought to be a refuge for black refugees on the Underground Railroad. Genealogy charts trace the Quaker Road Goodwillie lineage from 1590 to the present day.

It is hoped the book will give the general public as well as teachers and students a more complete picture of the history of Quaker Road and its surroundings. Trying to understand the complex relationships of the first people in the Niagara peninsula and their dealings with black and white settlers has been a challenge. Iroquois, French, Dutch, and English accounts reveal bias, omission and misunderstandings. Early black history in the Welland area commonly overlooked has also been included. For example, how many know that slavery existed in Niagara peninsula or that there was an army unit of black soldiers stationed at Port Robinson in the 1840's?

The Goodwillie stories convey relationships and passions. Alexander McCall Smith in his recent book, **In the Company of Cheerful Ladies** said: *"A life without stories would be no life at all. [Stories bind us one to another], the living to the dead, people to animals, people to the land."*

While unintentional errors or omissions are my responsibility, any gaps can be filled by your imagination. I hope you will enjoy delving into the adventures and everyday life of the Niagara peninsula, and especially life on the Quaker Road farm, around the turn of the 20th century.

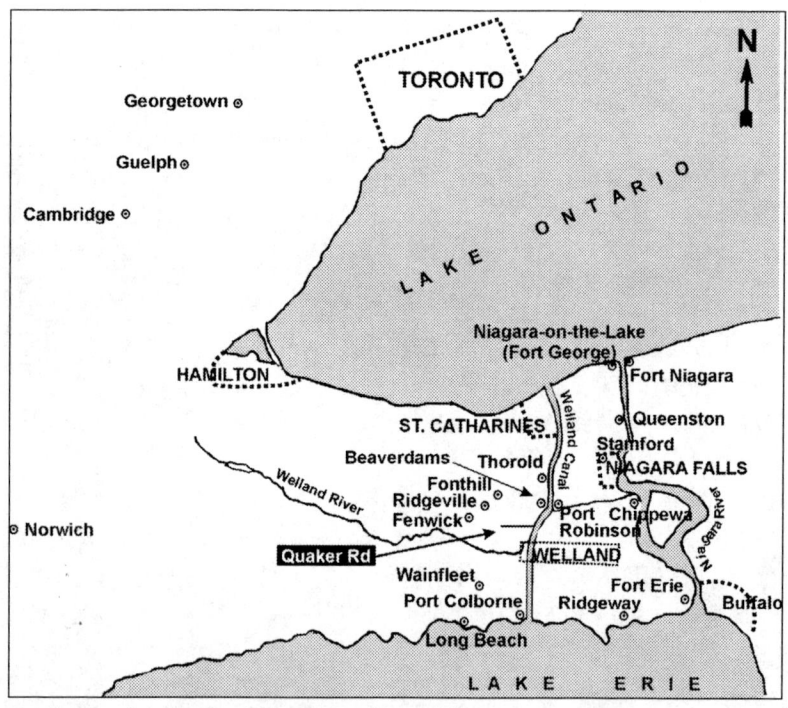

Quaker Road and areas of importance (Goodwillie)

SECTION ONE

Links to Quaker Road

Map of Iroquoian and Algonquin Settlements circa AD 1615 (O'Brien. The Pre History of South Central Ontario)

CHAPTER ONE

Neutrals and Other First Nations

For more than 7,000 years humans have lived in southern Ontario, and, for at least one thousand years people have moved through Welland's Quaker Road district. Archeologists have discovered sites revealing the prehistory of the first inhabitants but accurate understanding of the early history of southern Ontario prior to the European invasion is difficult. Much has been lost, ignored or misinterpreted.

In Ontario, separate tribes or nations evolved from two main language groups, Algonquian[1] and Iroquoian. The attached map points out the various Nations identified in the early 1600s.

The territory of the Algonquian nomadic fishers and trappers existed in Ontario's mid north, the St. Lawrence River basin and beside the Atlantic Ocean. Agriculture was difficult and the clans relied on fishing and hunting more than farming. Men were the leaders and the heads of family. Territorial hunting rights were passed from father to son. Algonquian speakers included the Mississauga of the Ojibway Nations (Chippewa in the USA)[2], the Algonquin, Delaware and the Mi'kmaq.

Iroquoian speaking nations lived communally in more permanent settlements and were farmers and traders. Iroquois oral history reveals that by about 900 A.D. corn was cultivated. By between 1100 and 1500 A.D. a League of Iroquois nations was formed which used diplomacy and political unity to advance their cause and keep things under control.[3] Included in Iroquoian language groups were the Iroquois (made up of Seneca, Cayuga, Mohawk and others), Neutral, Huron, Petun, Erie and many others.

Iroquois men and women had definite roles. Women were respected, maintained ownership of the land and homes, and exercised a veto power over any Council action that might result in war. The Iroquois Nations provided models for peace-building confederacies which later influenced writers of the American Constitution and those advocating for women's rights[4].

Names for the Neutral and Iroquois Nations

After exploration in the Niagara peninsula, in 1640, the French Missionary, Father Brébeuf noted that the people lived in 40 villages with a minimum population of 12,000 persons, including 4,000 warriors.

These people were known by several names but are most commonly referred to as the Neutrals, a term introduced by the early French explorers. The Hurons called them Attawandaron meaning 'those

Villages of Iroquoian longhouses provided shelter and protection for many people. (Germantown Elementary School)

that speak a little differently'. The Seneca and Huron often referred to both the Erie and Neutral people as the 'Cat Nation'. Other nations from the Iroquoian language group, such as the Hurons, Erie, Neutrals, who settled in southern Ontario referred to themselves collectively as the Wendat 'dwellers or villagers on a peninsula'. New York State was the homeland of the people self-named the Haudenosaunee Confederacy, or the 'People of the Long House,' but called Iroquois by the French.[5]

The First Farmers in the Niagara Peninsula

Some Neutral villages had women rulers but men filled most leadership positions. People of the Neutral nation lived in villages consisting of bark wigwams and communal long houses. They dressed in furs and skins and were the original Niagara peninsula farmers and traders. They made oil by boiling sunflower seeds in water then skimming off the floating oil with wooden spoons. Surplus tobacco was traded for skins, furs, and porcupine quills and quillwork with the northern Algonquin peoples.

Ontario's first farmers tended crops of maize (corn), beans, and pumpkin. (O'Brien, The Pre History of South Central Ontario)

French missionaries commented that although the Neutrals had few tools, they developed good farming practices. For example they planted about ten seeds in small hills and continued to plant so that they would have three or four years of supply in case of bad weather, poor fruiting or loss of seed stock. To clear land, trees were destroyed by carefully trimming lower branches, burning them at the base, thereby effectively ring-barking the tree. Net and spear fishing and skilled hunting practices were used, for example deer were slaughtered after being driven into pens via a triangular shaped funnel made from hedges.

At this time, Beaverdams was the hub of a network of trails stretching in all directions to St. Davids, Chippawa, Queenston, Hamilton and the head of the lakes. The major native trail in the Niagara peninsula was the Iroquois Trail from Queenston to Hamilton, which was thought to be a part of a longer trail from Albany, New York to St. Louis, Missouri and perhaps further west. The old Highway Eight, now St. Paul's Street, St. Catharines is part of the Iroquois Trail. Quaker Road also was thought to be a route used by Canada's first nations.

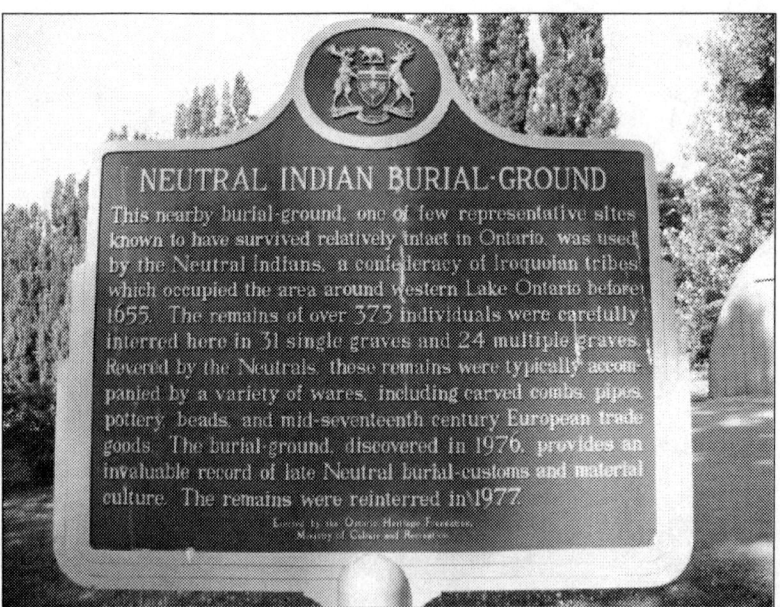

Neutral Burial Ground near Grimsby are marked by a Government Plaque. (Photo used with permission from Alan L. Brown)

Three large Neutral villages in the Niagara peninsula were believed to be at Point Abino, near Ridgeway and Crystal Beach, Beamsville and Niagara Falls, a word derived from the Ongniaahra pronounced *OH-NEE-AH-GAH-RA* meaning the strait or 'Thunder of Waters'. Burial grounds have been found at Grimsby, and Port Colborne.[6]

The Downfall of the Neutral Nation

The name 'neutral' can be misleading, as these people were not necessarily peaceful. Because they did not take sides in the wars between northern Huron groups and other Iroquois nations to the south, the French considered them uninvolved or impartial and hence the name.

One written report of actual warfare, in 1643, noted that 2,000 warriors of the Neutrals attacked a large, fortified Algonquin village in central Michigan. After ten days of fighting, the village was overrun, and 800 prisoners captured. Women and children were taken back to the Neutrals' villages, but male warriors were killed and the old men blinded and left to wander aimlessly in the woods.[7]

Members of the Iroquois League of Nations, the Mohawks and Senecas were sometimes known as 'Keepers of the Western Gate'. They lived to the south and east of Lake Erie, in present day New York State. Seneca people were great conquerors, highly skilled at warfare. They used alliances with Dutch colonials to obtain guns and were fierce opponents to any other tribe who tried to resist their takeover.

Jealousy and rivalry between various Nations exploded into a series of attacks that led to the elimination of all Neutral settlements in the Niagara peninsula by 1650. During fighting, in the 1640s, the Neutral nation maintained a non-alignment policy. They did not discourage Iroquois and Huron war parties to slip through their territory to attack each other's villages. The Iroquois blamed the Neutrals for permitting this, and, after diplomatic efforts failed to force the Neutrals to surrender Huron people hiding in their land, the Iroquois, attacked the Neutrals. By 1650 all Neutral villages on the north shore of Lake Erie were completely destroyed although some

The Neutrals were known to be aggressive, even when they visited each other's villages for trade. (Drawing by Neil Reichelt, courtesy Earl Plato)

Neutral people escaped or were taken slaves. It is thought that some Neutral members ended up by 1667 in Wisconsin, Pennsylvania, and particularly in La Prairie (Caughnawaga or Kahnawake) just south of Montreal.

During the American Revolution, the Mississauga Nations, Algonquian speakers, supported the British. After the American Revolution, the Mississauga Indians settled along the banks of the Chippawa River and by 1788, nearly 600 Mississauga Indians lived at Queenston.[8] This is how the Township of Thorold recorded the events:

"Neutral country was avoided by superstitious Indians for a long time. Much later the Mississauga tribes of the Chippewa or Ojibway nation settled the district. It is from these Indians that we got the name 'Chippawa'. [an earlier name for the Welland River] ... These Mississaugas continued to occupy the Thorold Township area until it was ceded to the British Government in will on May 22 1784, and in deed on December 7, 1792. The treaty signed in 1784 defined the boundaries of the Mississauga lands, and the second treaty signed in 1792, provided for the sale of all the Indian lands between lakes Erie and Ontario to the British--who wanted it for their Loyalists---for the sum of 1,180 pounds. Most of the Indians [six of the Iroquois language groups] moved to a reservation on the banks of the Grand River although a few married and remained in the Thorold Township."[9]

First Nations Involvement in European Conflicts

Contact between Canada's indigenous people and explorers, missionaries and traders added to troubles facing the native populations. Inter tribal jealousies and poor health increased with European fur trading. For example in the early 1600s, the Huron population in the north was reduced by more than 50% from European introduced diseases/epidemics such as measles and smallpox. First Nations aligned and fought battles with various European groups, for example the Huron tribes sided with French missionaries and fur traders during the rivalries between the French and British. The Dutch settlers provided arms to the Iroquois Confederacy in Upstate New York. Some tribes stayed neutral, but as many as 13,000 from different Iroquois nations sided with the British during the Revolutionary Wars. Similarly during the War of 1812-14, most indigenous people sided with Britain and Canada. Laws were changed and land initially reserved for the indigenous people was traded or bought by the British government, thereby limiting the lifestyles of Canada's original people.

Indian Legends and Stories

Many stories of the fierce battles of inter-tribal rivalry, and of missionary and settler encounters with Indians have been passed down through the generations. Interpretations were often biased against the Indians, the term commonly used for Canada's First Nations. The accuracy of details varied. Some of these stories were based on lessons that parents wanted their pioneer children to learn.

One lesson about extreme violence is linked in history to legend called *The Grasshopper War*. It is told that of a clash between children for the possession of a grasshopper that led to inter-tribal war, ambushes, raids, and mass destruction. The first written publication of the story, in 1886, attributed the legend to the Delaware Indians (part of the Lenni Lanape Nation) living in today's states of Pennsylvania, and New Jersey where Richard Howell was governor from 1793-1801. His granddaughter, Mrs.

Neutral or Attawandaron Hunter. (By Neil Reichelt, courtesy Earl Plato)

Jefferson Davis, later wrote a *grasshopper war* commentary when vacationing in Port Colborne in 1903. At that time, the discovery of human remains from a battle was suggested to be from Huron and Iroquois (Neutral nations) conflict in the Niagara peninsula.

Legend of the Grasshopper War

Lillian Arnold Lopez

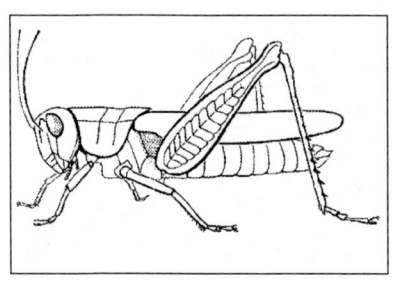

An innocent grasshopper was the cause of conflict. (T. S. Sechrist)

In the wilds of old New Jersey, before the white man came, the Lenape took up the land ... Two tribes liked to visit back and forth whenever they could. The braves would hunt together. The wives gossiped and carried out household tasks while the children played outside.

During a visit, one boy glimpsed a streak of green and caught the biggest grasshopper that he had ever seen. He laughed with glee while playing with the new pet he had found.

When a gang of other children gathered round, he showed off its agility to their admiring eyes. However, one lad, filled with envy, wore a scowl upon his face - 'shouldn't it be his grasshopper? It was found in his home place!' In haste, he snatched the insect, thus setting off a feud.

Like a chain reaction, a free-for-all ensued. All the young people joined in the fray, attacking one another - each one taking sides, of course, with his own tribal brother. The women rushed from the teepees when they heard screams fill the air. They took part also, and soon were pulling out each other's hair.

The braves returning from hunting later on found the injured, spent and bleeding huddled on the ground. Both tribal chiefs swore vengeance, and this epic tale of woe saw the guests who'd come in friendship stagger down the path as foe. What had started off as child's play ended in a trail of gore and is recorded in their annals as the big 'Grasshopper War.' [10]

Port Colborne Burial Ground

From 1888 to 1933, wealthy Southerners, their white guests and servants (most of whom were black) escaped the hot humid summers of Memphis Tennessee to a summer place overlooking Lake Erie on the edge of Port Colborne. The Humberstone Club, also known as Southern Comfort, was located along an old Indian trail now named Tennessee Avenue. It consisted of over twenty houses, two tennis courts, a casino and central dining hall. Whole families travelled by train from the southern states to spend the summer months near the cool waters of Lake Erie. A one man cheese making operation by Mr. Kraft was part of the Club's service. In later days his operations became the international conglomerate of the same name.[11]

Soon after the first houses were built, in 1890, the community decided to place a flagpole at the bend of the road near the entrance near their Casino. The excavation in this sandy hilly place uncovered the remains of about 500 of the area's first inhabitants. Buried copper kettles, pottery, pipes, and wampum beads were later distributed to museums in Toronto, Buffalo and Memphis, Tennessee.

Referring to this large burial ground, in 1903, the 76 year old widow, Mrs Varina Jefferson Davis, recalled *The Grasshopper War* legend and suggested the burial may have resulted from quarrels initially between Hurons and Iroquois when meeting for a harvest feast. Mrs. Davis, a gracious woman of strong individuality, rare good sense with an unusual gift of conversation published her thoughts on the grasshopper legend.[12] Her writing revealed some remaining southern bitterness about the American Civil War:

Mrs Varina Jefferson Davis, 1884, as a young bride. Her grandfather was Governor of New Jersey. Her husband was the President of the former Confederate States of America during the Civil War. (Photo in Public Domain)

"Like the Hurons, the Americans feel neither regret nor pity for the sad fate of the brave men who once owned this splendid continent ... what will be the verdict of the coming race, how many of the wars waged with Berserker fury by fighting men of the past will posterity adjudge to have been 'Grasshopper Wars'?"[13]

European Settlers Encounter Canada's First Nations

The breakup of the First Nations' power along with expanding European interests and colonial wars enabled new pioneer settlement in the Niagara area.

The war that ended French rule in North America (1756-1763) gave Canada's First Nation people exclusive use of a great block of land including all of Ontario. The Royal Proclamation of 1763 prohibited all white settlement.

However the Quebec Act of 1774 which aimed at solidifying Upper and Lower Canadian settler's allegiance to Britain lifted restrictions to European settlement leaving indigenous people with few land rights. The Treaty of Paris in 1783, gave no recognition to the supportive role of the indigenous *first* landowners. It formally ended the American colonial opposition to Britain and provided British recognition to America as an independent nation.

Peace and the possibility of new land resulted in massive migrations from Europe and the United States in the 1780s and 90s. This paralleled much negotiation and final surrender of native land to the British in 1792. A newly appointed Governor Simcoe, supported by Elizabeth Simcoe, an observant and intelligent wife, promoted lucrative offers to pioneer settlers which included 200-acre free grants to all who would establish farms and swear an oath of British allegiance. This open invitation to cheap land (known to be fertile) brought many young adventurers from America as well as British Loyalist, military personnel, and African Americans fleeing discrimination and persecution against them.

Throughout the 1800s pioneers continued to encounter native people. However gradually settlers displaced the First Nations

Birch Bark teepee and Chippewa Indians from Rama Reserve near Simcoe 1876? (Toronto Public Library, John Ross Robertson Collection)

people. For example, when the construction of the Welland Canal began in 1824, there were several families of indigenous people living in wigwams on both sides of Chippawa Creek. But the rowdy canal workers were fond of annoying and mistreating the natives, and they soon withdrew to the Six Nations Reserve on the banks of the Grand River.[14]

Defending the British Colony

Records show that indigenous people helped defend the British Colony against American invasion during the War of 1812 - 14. Plaque 129[15] located in Queenston Ontario verifies Canada's first nations involvement during the War of 1812-14.

INDIANS AT QUEENSTON HEIGHTS
October 13, 1812

Warriors of the Six Nations of Iroquois (Mohawks, Oniedas Onondagos, Cayugas, Senecas, Tuscaroras), mainly from the Grand River, fought as allies of the British in this historic battle with the Americans. Speaking distinctive dialects and with different religious beliefs, these Indians were drawn together for the battle by John Norton, a resourceful and courageous commander. Norton, a man of Cherokee and Scottish ancestry, was a Mohawk (Teyoninhokarawen) by adoption. With John Brant (Ahyouwaeghs), the youngest son of Joseph Brant (Thayendanegea), and John Bearfoot, a veteran of the American Revolutionary War, the Iroquois fought for their own survival as a people and in support of the British.

First Nations Help Laura Secord

Colonial settlers' defense of Upper Canada included brave women such as Laura Secord with her courageous journey to Beaverdams, to warn Lieutenant Fitzgibbon[16] of American soldiers' plans to attack. In June 1813, Laura travelled alone from St. Davids, [although she started from Queenston with another female relative] through the St. Catharines area until at DeCew Falls she met up with Iroquois warriors who supported British defence of Canada:

"Afraid she might meet one of the American units on the main road, Laura Secord [a 37 year old housewife with five small children and a wounded husband at home] chose the Swamp Road, despite the wolves and rattlesnakes common to the area. On this road, she lost one shoe, then the second at Twelve Mile creek. It had been an extremely rainy season and the Twelve Mile Creek was so swollen that the bridge had been swept away. Laura Secord found a fallen tree trunk and using it as a bridge, she crawled carefully over the raging waters.

Suddenly she was startled to find herself in the midst of an Indian encampment, where, no doubt, the Indians were equally surprised to find a white woman. They did not speak English and it was difficult to make them aware of her mission. Finally she was able to convince the chief that it was important that she be taken to see Lieutenant Fitzgibbon without delay."[17]

> **THIS MONUMENT HAS BEEN ERECTED BY THE GOVERNMENT OF CANADA**
>
> **TO LAURA INGERSOLL SECORD**
>
>
>
> **WHO SAVED HER HUSBAND'S LIFE IN THE BATTLE ON THESE HEIGHTS OCTOBER 13th. 1812.**
>
> **AND WHO RISKED HER OWN IN CONVEYING TO CAPT. FITZGIBBON INFORMATION BY WHICH HE WON THE VICTORY OF BEAVERDAMS**

This stone monument (#58) is located in Queenston Heights.[18]

CHAPTER TWO

Pioneer Stories of Indigenous People

While indigenous people were recoiling from disrespect and the overrunning of their lands, the great difference between European and First Nations cultures, belief systems, and practices led many Europeans to be frightened by 'Indians'. In the 1780s and 90s indigenous people continued to move about the land. Pioneer settlers often feared visits by 'Indians' and pioneer stories created in the 1800s reflected these reactions. The following accounts from pioneer perspectives show their attitudes and beliefs about the First Nations people.

Memories of a Young Norwich Settler

The Norwich & District Archives has documented Loyalist pioneer experiences. Here are excerpts from an account by Moses Mott who in 1810 as a boy of 12 accompanied his family travelling to a new home in Norwich from New York State.[19]

"When we came to the Genesee River, where the city of Rochester now stands the country was quite new with very few settlers. A number of men with teams had just come to repair the bridge as we came to it. They said we had better stop and settle there, that Canada was a cold place, with but few white settlers and most of them had squaws for wives.

Drawing of Niagara Falls. (by Neil Reichelt, courtesy Earl Plato)

... After starting in we met an Indian richly dressed in Indian costume, with much jewelry and wampum about him supposed to be a great man in his tribe. He was the first being of that kind we youngsters had ever seen, and it made us keep pretty close to the old folks."

... We came along by the Falls and stopped and took a look at them. The road along the bank was good, but when we turned toward where St. Catharines now stands, the roads were horrible nearly all the way to the Grand River. Some small streams had no bridges, others had old, rotten ones. Then we would get stuck in mud holes at times, and had to be pried out and have a double team pull us through. We saw where a few white people had settled along the road and came across a Indian village or two between Niagara and where we crossed the Grand River which we had to ford, for there was no bridge or ferry boat. [The road referred to was likely the Iroquois Trail and the ford may have been at present day Brantford]"

... During the war [1812-14] there were but few settlers scattered through the woods and plenty of Indians hunting all over the place. Sometimes the settlers felt afraid the Indians might do them injury as we often saw them with their faces painted in streaks of red and black, and acting somewhat fierce, but they never harmed any settlers or their property in the least, probably because there was no whiskey at that time that they could get drunk on."

Indian Acts of Kindness

Indian knowledge of herbal medicine, ways to soften furs for clothes, produce sugar from maple syrup and a variety of other survival techniques helped new white settlers endure the difficult conditions. Indian knowledge of terrain and their allegiance to the British contributed greatly to the survival and success of the new country. For example the Township of Thorold notes that during the 1789 'Hungry Year' when frosts destroyed crops and food was scarce, a group of Indians called on one starving family in the Niagara district. The family whose only food was small portions of corn meal mixed with oxen blood offered to share their dwindling supply but when the Indians saw the sad state of their family, they gave them bread made from bean flour instead of taking from them. They also told the settlers that pork and dried beans could be obtained from the military stores at Fort George [at Niagara-on-the Lake].[20]

Pumpkins Save the Day

Goodwillie grandchildren loved this story told by Grandma Sarah Stover who would explain: "when this happened, [presumably 1845-55 in Norwich, Ontario] I was just a little girl and your Grandpa [Hiram Goodwillie] was just a little boy. I didn't even know your Grandpa at that time."[21]

The winter was about half over and Mother wanted Father to go to town for some groceries, sugar, tea and such. Most of the food we ate was grown right on the farm but some supplies had to be bought.

Vegetables grown in summer were dried or canned for the winter months. Carrots, apples, turnips, potatoes and such were stored in what we called a pit or a large hole dug partly into the ground and well rounded over the top with straw and dirt. It had to be well covered so that the winter cold would not penetrate and freeze things. We didn't have freezers or refrigerators in those days but vegetables kept very well all winter or until used up.

For meat there was always a cow and perhaps several pigs to be slaughtered. The meat was salted, smoked, pickled or frozen in an outside shed. There was always something on hand for

Pete with Grandma Sarah, Mother Luella, Father John Allan Goodwillie about 1915-1917. (Cornett)

our own use or in case visitors arrived unannounced. Father used to say: "Not one speck was wasted except the squeal".

Mother and Father hitched the horse to the buggy and left for town real early in the morning. It was quite a long drive to town and the roads were not very good. There wasn't any pavement then. When it rained the roads were a sea of mud but in the summer and fall usually they were dry and dusty.

This was a day in late October. We were excited about bringing in the pumpkins from the garden and making faces on some of them for Halloween. We made faces off and on most of the day after the folks had left, seeing who could make the wickedest looking ones. It was a lot of fun and helped make the storing of the pumpkins a little more interesting.

Our house and barns were quite close together with a pointed log fence surrounding them. The fence was not much protection from intruders but at least visitors had to come in by the gate and couldn't climb over very easily.

The day soon passed and we began to watch for Mother and Father. They didn't come home and didn't come home, and we children, four of us who were alone, were beginning to get worried.

We had heard funny noises outside the fence and on peeking over saw six or seven Indians with painted faces and feather head-dress, and carrying bows and arrows. They didn't look friendly to us.

While we had never before had any trouble and were on good terms with any neighboring Indians, in those days one never quite knew for sure what would happen. Father had told us very firmly that we were never to open the gates to anyone.

It got very dark and still our parents were not in sight. The Indians were very noisy, running around and yelling and once in a while pounding on the gate. We were really frightened. What should we do?

My brothers lit a bonfire thinking that would scare the Indians away but they continued to make a big hullabaloo outside the fence. The look of the fire gave the boys an idea. We were instructed to bring all the pumpkin jack-o-lanterns to one spot. Candles were fastened in each one and we somehow managed to fix each pumpkin head on the end of a pole, and stacked in *various places. Now we were ready.*

We would poke a lantern over the fence, first on one side of the yard then the other side. We ran from side to side of the stockade as fast as we could and always jabbing up those lanterns over the fence.

(A. Roy)

I am sure those Indians got the shock of their lives. They were very superstitious and to see those fiery faces popping over the fence must have certainly startled them. We kept up our yelling and putting the fiery spooks over the fence until there was a sudden quiet outside.

We cautiously peaked over the fence just in time to see the last Indian running into the woods. It was a good thing for we were all desperately tired by that time.

Not long afterwards when the last Indian had disappeared, Mother and Father came driving out the woods on the other side of the farm. They thought all the lights were for them but when we told them all our exciting happenings they were very glad that among the four of us, we had been smart enough to outwit our enemies. The Indians never came back around our farm.

Mrs Hagar's Embarrassment

In the spring of 1793 the Hagar family, Jonathon and wife Azubah who had come from New Jersey settled in the Beaverdams [Ontario] area. By 1861, other family members, Jonathon and Frank Hagar lived about a quarter of a mile from the Goodwillie home on Quaker Road. This story is told of one brave pioneer woman's encounter with local indigenous people.[22]

[Like many in the Niagara peninsula, the Hagar family] built a stockade of long poles planted in the ground in an upright position, leaving a few loopholes through which a gun could be inserted in case marauders attacked them.

One time a band of troublesome Indians came by and although Azubah Hagar was a crack shot with the gun she decided prudence was the better part of valour. She took her children to the stockade where she peeked through a loophole while the Indians ransacked the house.

The Indians made no attempt to molest the family. But when the Indians left the Hagar home Azubah was appalled to find the chief wearing the possessions that had most appealed to him, her corset was draped around his middle and on his head was her best Sunday to meeting bonnet, backwards.

Lacrosse was a sport created and played by First Nations.
(by Neil Reichelt, courtesy Earl Plato)

Always Be Prepared - Masterman Ready

This tale may be a form of cautionary tale invented by settlers. Grandma Stover Goodwillie regularly recounted the adventure and Ruth Cornett captured it in writing:

Once upon a time, there were a few families who decided to move out of the village and settle in the country. They knew they would have to cut trees and clear the land and had been warned the Indians were not too friendly. But these people decided to go anyway as they would eventually have their own little farms and be more independent.

They packed their belongings, clothes, bedding and essential household utensils. Then these were loaded into the farm wagons. After driving many miles for several days they finally came to a lovely spot beside a river which was high and dry with good soil. They decided this was the place to start building. Of course the trees had to be cut down and clearings made for their cabins but all worked hard in order to prepare for the cold weather.

The women did the cooking, made soap out of lye and wood ashes, spun wool into yarn and wove it into dress material. They washed and ironed and did all the usual things to help and keep things neat and tidy. Each child had a chore to do and parents emphasized that children were depended upon and must do as they were directed.

The men worked in the woods cutting and chopping early and late until it felt that all was fairly safe. First they built a stout stockade, which enclosed a good-sized piece of land so they could build their house within it. They did this for protection against any troublesome Indians. They had not been bothered all summer but knew that roving bands of Indians were in the neighborhood.

The first winter in this sort of settlement was pretty hard. The food was scarce and very ordinary and they were thankful to have enough when they went to bed. When spring came everyone was thankful they had survived the long hard winter but an unspoken fear always hung over the settlement.

A man called Masterman Ready took command of the settlement and everyone in the district knew him. He was well respected for his knowledge, leadership and careful preparations.

Water within the stockade had to be brought from the river that was just a short distance away. Joe and Johnny had been told that they must fill the water barrels just inside the gate filled each day. It was a big job and a very important one but Joe and Johnny were big enough to carry the pails of water. Boys their size could manage. It helped make their arms strong and taught them responsibility.

The water had to be brought within the stockade during the daylight hours. It was too dark to go to the river at night and if there were Indians around they usually would not show themselves during daylight. The water in these barrels were for emergency only and rarely used, but they had to be fresh all the time.

One-day Johnny's mother was doing the washing and needed lots and lots of water. She called to Johnny to get some from the river but Johnny was tired. If the barrels were full why bother to go to the river. It would save him a lot of hard work and he could fill the barrels the next day without anyone knowing.

So he carried all the wash-water to his mother from the emergency barrels. No one saw him do it and he figured he was pretty smart. Johnny's mother thought he has been pretty quick but she had a lot of things on her mind.

During the night there was a lot of yelling outside the stockade. Masterman Ready and his friends jumped out of bed and rushed outside the cabins to look over the stockade. They were shocked to see a large crowd of Indians screeching, waving their tomahawks and running to and fro.

Fortunately the sturdy logs pointed on the top of the stockade kept out the attackers. The gates were well braced on the inside but Masterman Ready knew that they were in a dangerous situation.

All the men had guns and ammunition but it wouldn't last too long. The men would shoot whenever they could see anything but it was very dark. No-one knew how long the Indians might stay so they had to be careful with the use of ammunition.

When morning came the small band of pioneers counted about twenty-five Indians who had full war paint and feathers. Their canoes were drawn up on the river bank and although quieter, they were still very much on the alert to shoot their arrows if anyone should poke so much as a head over the walls.

It was summertime and soon the sun shone hot and bright. Worried and frightened, the settlement inside was very quiet, but watchful and busy. The Indians did not go away.

On the morning of the second day, Masterman Ready went to the water barrels to see how the water was holding out. Only three small pails of water were left. Where had all the water gone in just one day? He called Joe and Johnny to him: "Did you fill those barrels and keep them full?" "Yes we did," they said."

"Are you sure? Did you use any after filling?" Johnny knew what had happened. He squirmed and although very frightened he admitted taking the water to his mother's washing and not refilling the barrels. He had planned to do it later in the day.

Poor Masterman Ready. What could he do? The people had to have water and anyone venturing to the river in daylight could be captured by the Indians and probably killed. He warned the people to stop using water.

Finally Masterman Ready decided he would have to go to the river under cover of darkness. Even if he could only bring in one pail full it would help. He would have to take the chance of running very fast while the other men distracted the Indians. They would all die of thirst if not from Indians.

When darkness fell, and it was a very dark night for there wasn't a moon, Masterman Ready very cautiously opened the gate, a pail on each hand. The other men closed the gate quickly and quietly. Then they started making lots of noise on the far side of the fort. The Indians, thinking the men were coming from there, ran over to that side.

During the commotion Masterman Ready ran as fast as he could. He scooped the pails full of water and was almost back to the gate when the enemy saw him. They knew they had been tricked. They yelled and screeched. The arrows flew but Masterman Ready managed to get back inside the gate. However, an arrow had hit him.

In the meantime the Indians seemed to get discouraged and after more yelling in frustration, they got in their canoes and went away. No one ventured too far from the fort or a few days but the Indians were never seen again.

Masterman Ready wasn't hurt too badly and after a while he was able to carry on his everyday work. When Johnny saw all the trouble he had caused in not doing his regular chores and trying to get out of a little bit of work, it taught him a lesson. No one ever had to tell Johnny a second time to carry out any little jobs he had to do. I'm sure he grew up to be a very fine man, like Masterman Ready who was the hero of the settlement.

(by Neil Reichelt, courtesy Earl Plato)

CHAPTER THREE

Slavery and Africans in the Niagara Peninsula

Slavery did exist in Canada, first with the French, then with the British. A large number of African people came to the Niagara area as slaves and servants of American Loyalist settlers. At that time there were no laws against slavery in Canada. Relationships between black slaves and indigenous people were more egalitarian but some such as Mohawk leader Joseph Brant had black slaves.[23] One of the first recorded blacks to live in Ontario, or Upper Canada, was Sophia Burthen. She was born in New York State and sold to Brant as a child in the 1770s, before the American Revolution.

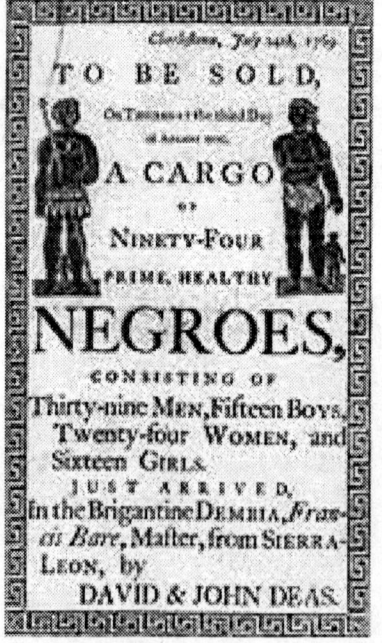

To provide land for the American refugees, the government gave Loyalists generous land grants, military positions and permission to bring slaves. In 1791, residents living in the Niagara district owned approximately 300 slaves, more than any other part of the province. Lieutenant

Colonel John Butler, a respected wealthy farmer in the Queenston area and a former commander of British and Indian troops during the American War of Independence, in 1793 placed an advertisement in a Niagara paper giving a $5.00 reward for the return of his "negro man servant named John". Six of the original 16 members of the elected Legislative Assembly owned slaves.[24]

Niagara Leaders Support Black Freedom

Governor Simcoe was the driving force behind Canada's first anti-slavery legislation to halt the use and importation of slaves. During his term of office, slavery was limited by an Act of Parliament of 9 July 1793. A slow trickle in the 1820s turned to a flood of black refugees in the 1850s especially after the American passage of the Fugitive Slave Act in 1850 that enabled slave hunters to pursue runaways anywhere in America. By 1861, it is estimated that more than 40,000 blacks had moved into Canada but in the 35 years following the American Civil War, 60-75% of the black migrants left Canada to reunite with their African American families south of the border.[25]

African Americans joined with others in Ontario to fight for the rights of black freedom seekers. For example, Mary Ann Shadd (later Cary) a teacher in Chatham was the first African American woman in North America to edit a weekly newspaper 'the Provincial Freeman'. Through teaching, lecturing and producing her paper, and later as a lawyer, she promoted equality, integration and tolerance.

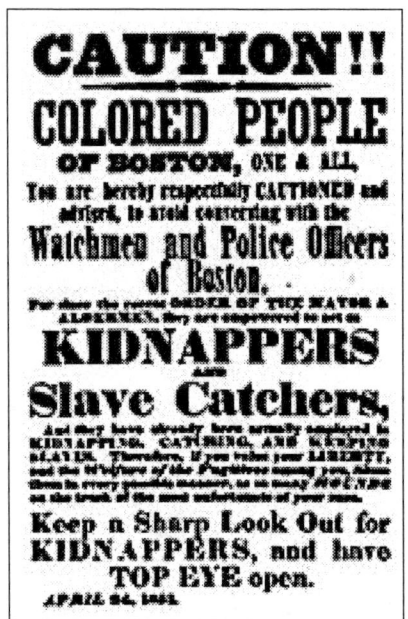

Those black people who slipped away from plantations were followed and if caught were severely punished. Families left behind were beaten or persecuted, so runaways

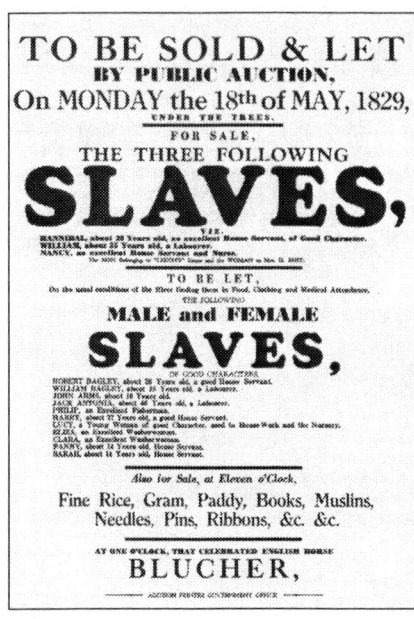

had to be bold and brave. If they succeeded in escaping, freedom was reached through a secret chain of safe houses leading to northern USA and Canada, known as the 'Underground Railroad'. Harriet Tubman, an escaped slave, helped more than 300 people escape many to St. Catharines where local citizens assisted ex-slaves. At the height of her activities a price of $40,000 was posted on her head by a group of slave-owners. William Merritt, instigator of the Welland Canal and mayor of St. Catharines also was an abolitionist and helped form the interracial Refugee Slaves' Friends Society.

In ten years Harriet Tubman (left) led over 300 people to Canada. (public domain & D. Hill)

Slavery and African Americans in the Niagara Peninsula

Slavery was legal in Upper Canada until 1834 but it was not popular ,yet prejudice and discriminatory practices against African Americans existed in the Niagara Peninsula. Competition for jobs by Irish and English immigrants, and attitudes by former American slave owners, who vacationed or moved to Niagara, resulted in forms of racism. For example some hotels excluded blacks, and education was often segregated. A separate, inferior school for black children in St. Catharines began in 1846 and continued until 1883 when black pupils were integrated into the community schools of St. Catharines.

A black Military Corps, loyal to Britain, fought in the War of 1812 and the Rebellion of 1837. Between 1840 and 1850, the Corps assisted in road building and keeping peace along the construction route of the Second Welland Canal. By 1850 the Coloured Company as it was commonly referred to was disbanded. Many members settled throughout the Niagara Peninsula forming close links with the Underground Railroad and helping refugees it brought into the Niagara area.

Black History and Quaker Road

With the Coloured Company stationed at nearby Port Robinson Quaker Road residents would have been familiar with them. The black troops were used to suppress a famous disturbance between the Irish Catholics and Protestants near St. Catharines.

For Sale

A Negro Slave 18 years of age, stout and healthy, has had the small-pox and is capable of service, either in house or out door. The terms will be made easy to the purchaser, and cash received in payment. Enquire of the printer. Niagara Nov 28th 1802. [26]

Indian Slave

All persons are forbidden harboring, employing or concealing my Indian slave called SAL as I am determined to prosecute any offender to the utmost extent of the law, and persons who may suffer her to remain on their premises for the space of half an hour, without my written consent, will be taken as offending and dealt with according to the law. (signed) Charles Fields [26]

Black soldiers, given the status and power to keep law and order, humiliated and angered the mainly white, uneducated European Canal workers, who scorned the blacks. While inactive during a strike, they marched on black troops stationed at Port Robinson. The priest of the canal workers, Father MacDonagh galloped up on his famous black horse, drew a line of truce between the black troops and canal workers, threatened them with ex-communication from the Church if they overstepped the boundary, then rode into the crowd distracting and dispersing them.[27]

Whether Quaker Road people were active in the Underground Railroad is an intriguing question. Most families living in the area were Quakers who believed in temperance, equality for women, caring for the poor and homeless, and abolition of slavery. Other Presbyterians, Methodists and Baptists had religious leaders who advocated temperance, and civil and religious rights.

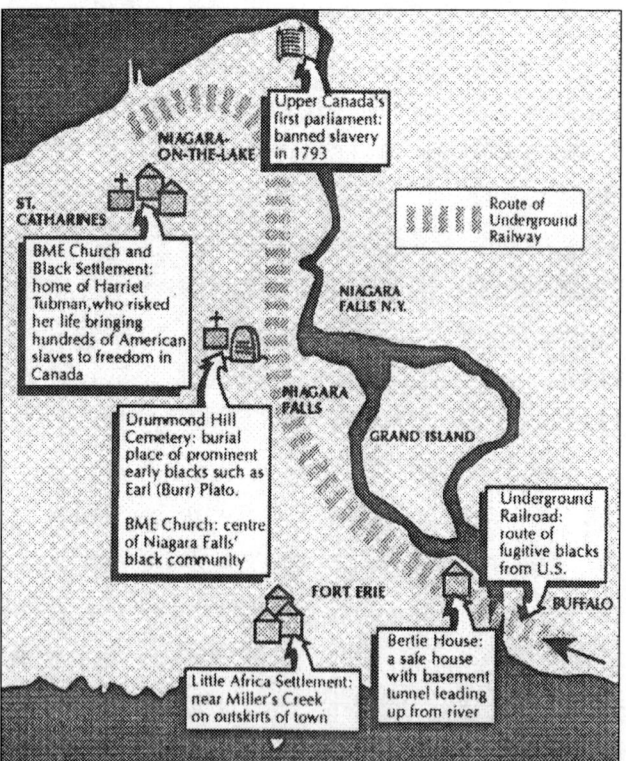

The Freedom Trail in the Niagara peninsula. (Grant Smith, Niagara Falls Review)

The Goodwillies and other Quaker Road families had links to Vermont, which in 1777 became the first state to prohibit slavery. In fact, one of Quaker Road's first settlers, Joseph Goodwillie had a brother, the Rev. David Goodwillie, who was a prominent Presbyterian minister in Barnet Vermont. His house built in 1790-1791 (now a museum) included a tiny cupboard close to the fireplace, thought to be a safe secret hiding place for escapees.

It is well documented that Niagara Peninsula towns of Fort Erie and St Catharines played central roles in black migration into Canada. The Norwich and Georgetown areas also were a destination for many escapees.

In the mid 1800s two Goodwillie brothers, Hiram and Charles Harmon lived in the Norwich area while their father, mother and other family members lived on Quaker Road, in Wainfleet, Fonthill and Georgetown. Grandma Sarah Stover Goodwillie's Quaker relatives, for example Frederick Stover, had helped found the colony of free blacks at the Wilberforce Settlement north of London Ontario. And the first Wilberforce ministers came from New Hampshire, on the eastern border of Vermont.

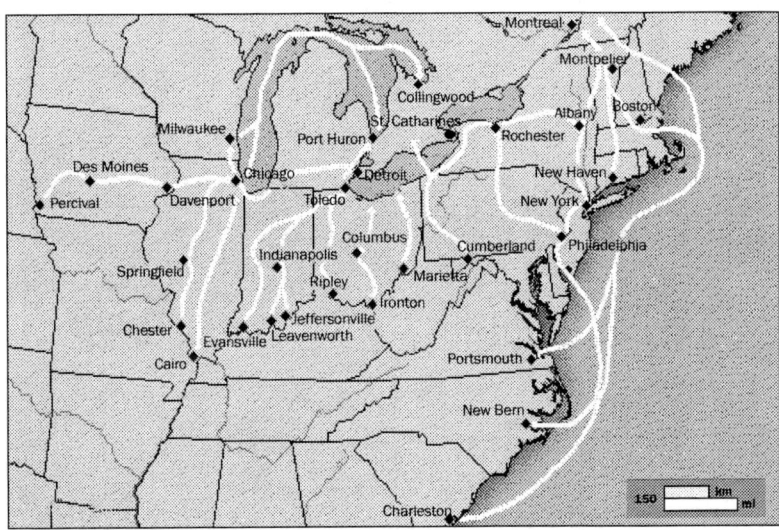

Map showing escape routes used by the Underground Railroad.
(Pocantico Hills School)

Although the main route taken by most African Americans escaping through Vermont and the New England states was to Montreal, it is possible Barnet people directed escaping blacks to family members on Quaker Road and beyond to the Georgetown and Norwich area. The Otterville area, south of Norwich was the site of an African Methodist Episcopal Church School, and Cemetery. And this part of Ontario was a terminal for many former slaves travelling via the Underground Railroad.

Nothing is documented. But it appears that the Welland Quaker Road families could easily have provided assistance, temporary housing and support to the refugee black population passing through from Buffalo and Niagara Falls and onwards.

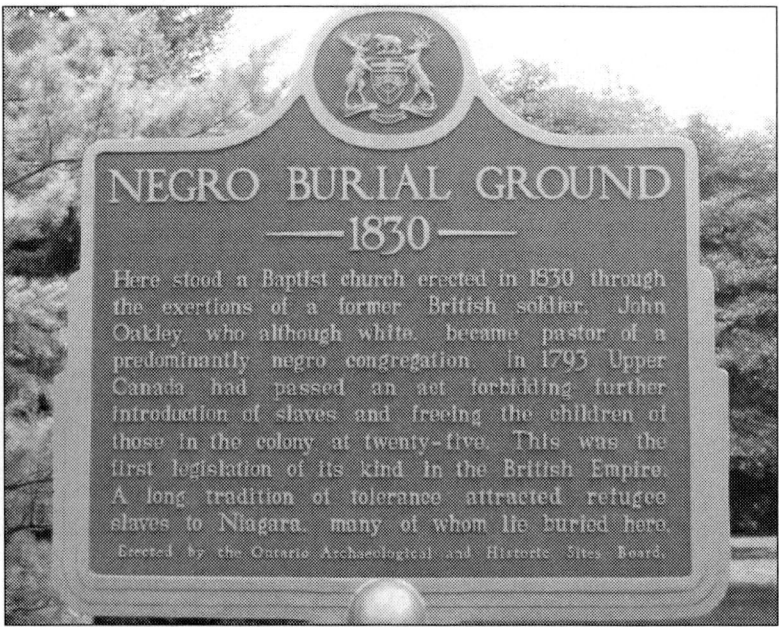

Plaque of Niagara on the Lake Negro Burial Grounds (Courtesy Alan L Brown)

CHAPTER FOUR

Wildlife and Settling into the Land

Pioneers settlers lived under constant threat of danger from wild animals. The barn was almost as important as the house because without it the settlers might lose what little livestock they had. Wild animals were mentioned in several Welland documents.

"Bears and wolves abounded. By the testimony of men still living [in 1887] it is an undoubted fact that the packs of wolves were at one time so numerous and so daring that it was unsafe for children to attend school without an armed escort. People have lain awake at night in their log houses while packs of wolves, wild with hunger, were howling round the farm-yard, sniffing at the crevices for the smell of human flesh, or striving to penetrate with tooth and claw the outbuildings where the cattle were secured. [Welland County's last recorded payment in 1850 was 12 pounds or approximately $60.00 for seven wolf-scalps].... The bears were not at all so dangerous to human life ... but would damage the crops, take a stray pig, a cow, a hive of bees, a field of grain, a patch of corn."[28]

And

" ... The pioneers built sturdy rail fences, and planted a fruit tree in each fence corner. When harvest time came they did not pick the fruit from the outside branches, believing that this fruit should be left to the poor. ... The uncleared sections of the township gave shelter to deer, bears, wolves, lynxes and an occasional panther. Beaver and otter were abundant in the

small streams.... The northwest section of the township was a rattlesnake-infested low-lying swamp."[29].

The following story is taken from Mary Goodwillie Young, a cousin's memoirs who moved from Barnet, Vermont to near Georgetown, Ontario in the 1820s:

One morning they found a wolf in one of the corners of the sheep pen, and the old bell sheep [the lead sheep with a neck bell] in another corner. [The wolf] had crawled in between the poles, and worried all the rest and was not able to get out again. Another time a bear walked off with a pig.... One time we heard a great bellowing of the cattle in the woods and went to see what was the matter with them and a wolf had bitten the cow and calf. The oxen and other cattle surrounded them and brought [the injured cattle] home.[30]

As the woods were cleared away and more people moved into the district, the wolves gradually went farther and farther back into the North. Sums of money given by the government for killing wolves (bounty) were available if skins were taken to government headquarters. Needless to say the farmers were all glad to kill the animals to collect that money and gradually wolves just disappeared, moving further into the country where fewer people were living.

This next story may have originated in Norwich. Grandma Sarah Stover and her husband Hiram Goodwillie were farmers and settlers in the Norwich, Ontario area before moving to Quaker Road in about 1867. It represents the life and times of all new settlers in the Niagara area.

The Wolves

as told by Grandma Stover Goodwillie

Once upon a time Grandma and Grandpa lived on a little farm, away out in the country surrounded by woods. Grandpa had done some clearing and would eventually get the whole farm cleared but at that time he hadn't many fields free from stumps and trees.

No road existed, just a narrow track or path through the woods, only wide enough to allow a horse and buggy, or sleigh, to pass between the trees. In the Spring it was muddy. It was dusty in the summer. In winter when deep snow made the road difficult going until a good track had been patted down, people didn't do too much travelling.

One winter day Grandma told Grandpa she really needed some supplies from the store. She wanted sugar, tea, flour some pieces of material, thread and a whole list of things. Grandpa said he needed some things too and agreed to drive the horse and cutter into town the next day.

The next morning he got up earlier than usual, for it was a long drive into town and he did not want to get home after dark. He hadn't told Grandma that he had heard wolves howling in the distance a couple of nights before. He knew he had lots of time to go and come before dark and wolves didn't usually bother in the daytime.

After a hearty breakfast prepared by Grandma, Grandpa hitched up the horse to the cutter and was ready to go to town. Grandma tucked a soapstone foot warmer beside his feet. She got the big fur robe out for him as it was a bitter cold day. Away he went at a good clip down the road between the trees. He was soon out of sight.

It was a nice bright day and with the sleigh bells jingling merrily and the horse in good fettle he really enjoyed the drive to town. The town was only a few small houses, a blacksmith shop and a general store. It was not too much to get excited about but it was the nearest place to shop.

All went well, Grandpa had a nice visit in the store with some of his neighbors whom he hadn't seen in a long time. He bought all the groceries, the piece goods, thread, a new axe and a nice sharp saw for cutting trees and so on.

Grandpa had been so busy he didn't realize how much time he had spent just visiting until suddenly he remembered he had that long drive home and should make it before dark if possible. He was a bit worried but thought there would be a full moon and the sky was clear. The horse had rested while he had done his shopping so all would be well. He hurriedly said his goodbyes, got in the cutter and tucking the robe around himself carefully started on his return trip.

The horse jogged along at a nice even pace and Grandpa began to think he had worried for nothing. A bit over half way home, the sun went down and it got very dark. The moon came up soon and was big, round and bright but with the road running between the tall trees was rather dark and spooky with lots of long dark shadows and only glimmers of the moonlight showing between the trees.

Suddenly Grandpa heard the long drawn "Whooooooo" of a wolf howling. "Whoooooo, Whooooo", it had such a bone chilling sound Grandpa wished he hadn't spent so much time visiting. If only he were closer to home.

The horse heard the howl too. He pricked up his ears and looked around as much as to say "did you hear that?".

Soon there was another long drawn out howl, a little closer this time, and yes, there seemed to be more than one howl. There must be a pack of wolves travelling together, as they usually did.

Grandpa slapped the reins and urged the horse on faster. The horse needed no urging for it was smart and knew they had better get home as fast as they could.

Grandpa looked back over his shoulder and sure enough outlined against the snow in a patch of moonlight he could see several wolves. They were still quite a way back but not far enough to suit Grandpa. He spoke to the horse and slapped the reins again and they fairly flew over the snow.

The sleigh bounced and slewed from side to side and several times almost upset. That would have been disastrous. They just had to outrun those pesky wolves.

The howls came closer and closer until finally Grandpa could see the wolves easily and counted six animals. He knew he needed to do something to stop them, if possible. If he could he slow them down a little bit, that might help.

He reached down and threw one of his precious parcels of groceries behind in the snow. There, he thought, maybe they will stop and give us more time. The wolves pounced on that parcel and soon tore it to bits, fighting among themselves to get at it. This did delay them a little so when they started to get close again Grandpa threw another parcel behind.

He threw another and another parcel to the wolves and each time the horse gained a little. Soon Grandpa could see a light in the window of the house still a distance away. They still had some distance to go and Grandpa realized he had run out of parcels. All his lovely groceries, piece goods and supplies were gone to those pesky wolves. There was only one more thing he could toss to them and that was the fur robe so finally he threw that too.

The wolves took a little longer over the robe as they tore it to shreds. It was just enough. With a little extra spurt of speed, the horse and cutter flew inside the barnyard gate and they were safe at last. The wolves wouldn't come too close to buildings.

It was a good thing they were home for the poor horse was exhausted what with fright and the frantic gallop over the snow for such a long distance.

Grandma had been getting more and more worried. When it got so late and no sign of the travellers she was afraid, and then she also heard the wolves howling so she knew something was wrong. She hurried and put lights in the two front windows. However candles in those days did not throw enough light to keep the wolves from coming near the house.

Grandpa got over his fright and then got angry with himself and those miserable wolves. He had lost all his purchases, not to speak of the money they cost. He would also have to make that long trip another day. He gave the horse a good rub-down and a good feed of hay and oats and made sure the barn door was shut securely so the horse would be safe for the night. Then he went in to tell Grandma what had happened.

Grandma was so glad to see Grandpa was safe and sound that she didn't really care about losing the groceries - too much - but she would surely like to get her hands on those pesky wolves and give them what for.

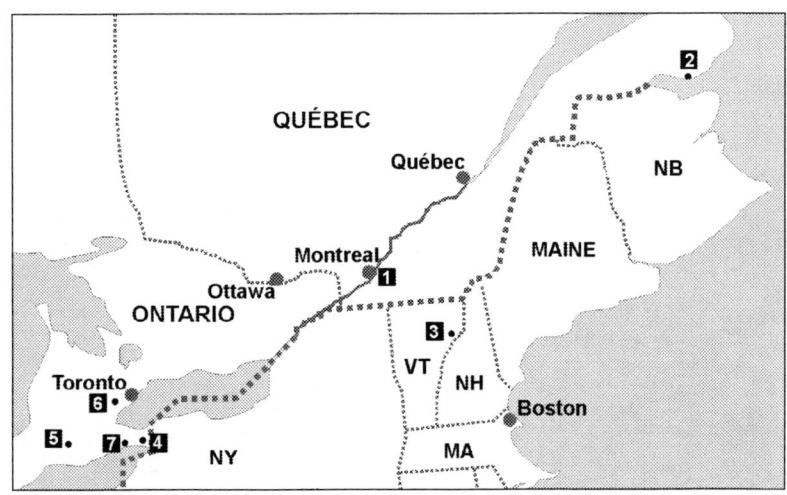

Map showing Goodwillie areas of settlement.
1 - Montreal, Québec; 2 - New Carlisle, Québec; 3 - Barnet, Vermont;
4 - Welland, Ontario; 5 - Norwich, Ontario; 6 - Georgetown, Ontario;
7 - Long Beach, Ontario; (D.Potter)

CHAPTER FIVE

Goodwillie and Page Family History

Few are familiar with the early life and times of people living on Quaker Road. Among the pioneer families the Pages and Goodwillies at the turn of the 20th century were prominent community leaders, farmers and industrialists. The streets named Goodwillie and Page Drive honour their family contributions to the Quaker Road district. Other Welland Streets such as Hellems Avenue and Beverley Crescent were named after Goodwillie family members.

The new Goodwillie home was completed 1906 and built on the 1870s farm house foundation. (Cornett)

Vineyards behind the children provided the first grapes in Thorold c 1913. Children from left: Pete, Doris Wills, Ethel Gaylor, Bill, Jack Goodwillie. (Cornett)

Who knows for example that the Goodwillie vineyards were the first on Quaker Road and probably in Thorold Township? One of the first fruit preservation industries in the Welland area started at the Goodwillie farm and produced Goodwillie's fruits 'picked and packed in the same day'. These were marketed throughout Canada, the USA, Europe and the West Indies and even served to British Royalty.

The Page brothers had several farms in the area and George Page enjoyed horse racing to the extent that he established a private race track north of the Goodwillie homestead. For 100 years First Avenue was known as Page Road in memory of the Page family who settled at the corner of Page (now First Ave.) and Quaker Road.

Welland's remaining Goodwillie legacy from these two families is the large farmhouse, today number 209 Quaker Road. On the western side is the the smaller Goodwillie farmhands' house. Both

Welland Street signs remember various Goodwillie family relations: Hellems, Goodwillie, Page. (D. Goodwillie & S. Stokes)

are found on Quaker Road between First Avenue and Niagara Street. This chapter gives a brief outline mainly of the Goodwillie, but also the Page family history in North America.

The People's Press

GREATER • WELLAND • EDITION

Whole Number 660,   May 23, 1911

H. Goodwillie and Son, Canners

THE NIAGARA PENINSULA is known the world over as the garden of Canada, and the firm of H. Goodwillie and Sons has done much to demonstrate this fact to the outside world by shipping their products of fruit in glass all over the globe.

This business was established twelve years go by Mr. John Goodwillie, who has had many years of experience both in fruit growing and fruit canning, and it bears the distinction of being the oldest house in Canada to pack fruits of canning consistency in glass. They do not make jam. [Jam making was started after 1911].

Only native fruits of Canada are used or packed in this establishment and all fruits that are used are packed while the fruit itself is actually in season. On no account are these dried and held over for packing purposes at a less busy season.

Besides his own products Mr. Goodwillie's cannery affords a large market for the fruits of the section.

The orchards in which his fruits are grown comprise 180 acres of land, it is probably one of the most beautiful sights to be seen in this neighbourhood, particularly when the trees and berry bushes are in bloom. The entire plant is conducted on a scientific and sanitary basis throughout, and in order to further secure cleanliness the work is all done by day labour. Over one hundred hands are employed in the factory alone, and the methods and formulas used in every department of this institution by the management, enable them not only to market their goods from coast to coast in Canada but they can compete and have created a demand for their products in Great Britain, Europe and the West Indies.

Mr. John Goodwillie is a well known man aside from the farm he has won through his business, for he was born in Welland county in 1863 ... He served several terms in the Thorold township council and has also been a member of the school board continuously for the past eighteen years. Every movement has been one of progress with Mr. Goodwillie, until he has reached his present position of commercial prominence.

The Goodwillie Name

In the past, the name of Goodwillie has been spelled Goodwilly, Goodwille, Goodwelly, Goodwooly and Goodwill. One Scottish reference book states the name originated in Fife in the 12th century with a Clan MacDuff association.[31] Most likely the origin of the name resulted from some outstanding characteristic of the individual. 'Good' was a derivative of 'God' and possibly came from a motto of 'God Willing' which was shortened to Goodwillie or one of the other spellings.

Goodwillie Scottish Origins

Looking across the Firth of Forth, north from Edinburgh Castle, one can see the rolling hills of Fifeshire across the bay. The city of Kirkcaldy is located on the Firth and further east is the famous St. Andrew's Golf Club.

In 1751, Joseph, the first Goodwillie to emigrate to America was born in the little town of Leslie, close to the family farm in Tanshall, Fifeshire Scotland. Within ten kilometers is Kinglassie Church where the final resting places of Joseph's family date back to the 1700s.

Possibly a Fife 12th Century name, the Goodwillie family was associated with the Clan Macduff, which had a red and blue tartan with the motto of 'God Assists'. (J.R. Goodwillie)

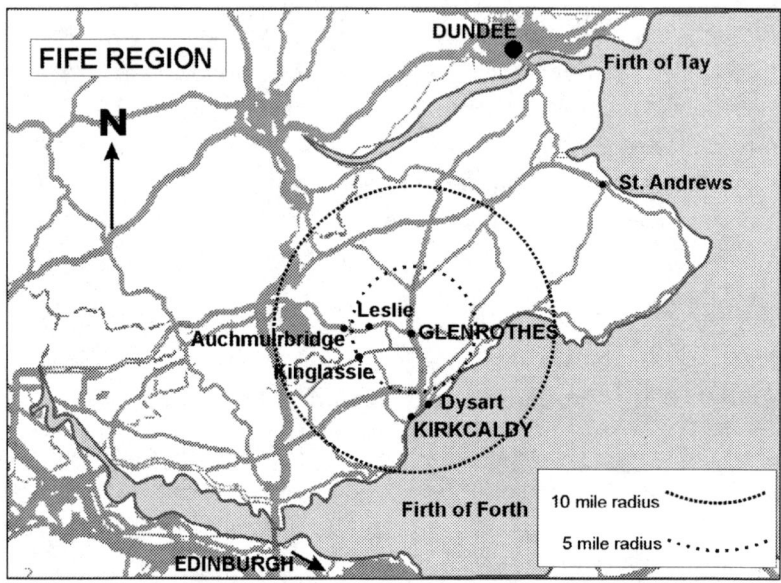

The Kingdom of Fife: Kinglassie, Glenrothes (Tanshall) and Leslie were important sites of Goodwillie activity in Scotland. The larger map above shows distances from Glenrothes. (Glenrothes Devt. Corp in Goodwillie)

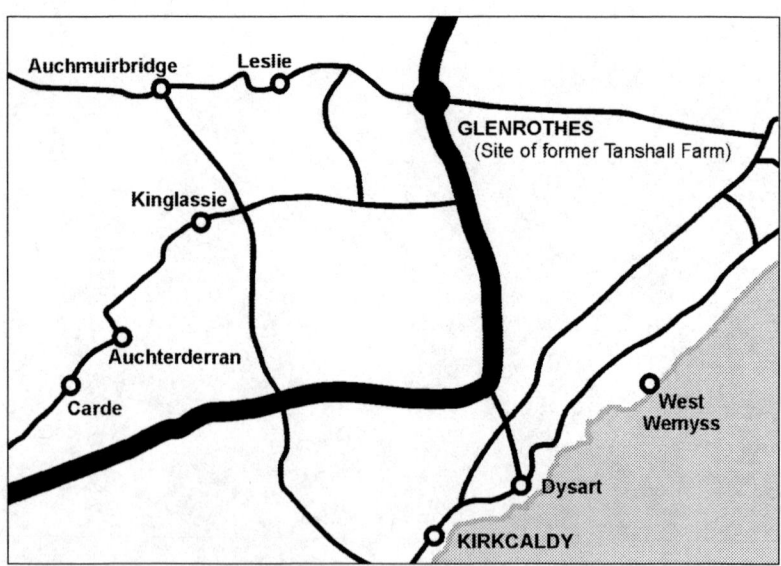

Old maps and church records note many 'Goodwillie' references in the area. After the Second World War, the original Tanshall Goodwillie farmhouse was demolished, replaced by townhouses and Tanshall School, part of a new "economic growth" city called Glenrothes.

Migration and Loyalist Leanings

How can we grasp the complex stories of life over two hundred years ago? About 1773, at age 22 Joseph Goodwillie left his Scottish home, tramped around the Mohawk Valley, New York probably working as a blacksmith. By June 1777 not far from Albany, New York, he joined Ebenezer Jessup's Loyal Rangers. No one knows if a land grant offered to those joining was more of an incentive than loyalty to the British Crown.

Joseph fought in the Battle of Saratoga, which was a major loss for Britain and a turning point for American Independence. Along with over a thousand soldiers, Joseph was taken captive. Most prisoners were taken south, but Joseph was confined to an Auburn or Albany prison. He managed to escape with some others and travelled north to rejoin Jessup's forces and loyalist refugee settlements in the Montreal area. For five years, from 1778 to 1883 he continued doing army engineering projects, clearing woodlots, and providing garrison duty.

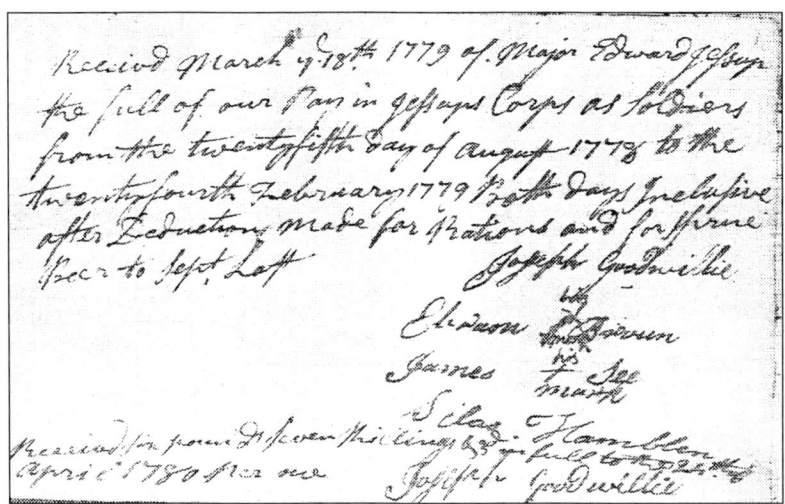

This document copied from Captain Edward Jessup's Corps shows the first recorded signature of Loyalist Joseph Goodwillie dated 1779. (Goodwillie)

Above: Ancient stone ruins on Goatsmilk Farm, near Glenrothes across from the Fife/Leslie Airport Scotland could possibly be the tradesmen's houses where the oldest known Goodwillie patriarch James (c. 1590-95) and his son David (baptized 1627) were blacksmith and farmer. (D. Goodwillie)

Above left: Goodwillie ancestors worshipped and were buried here in Kinglassie Church near Leslie, Glenrothes and Kirkaldy, Scotland. In the 12th century, the parish, known as 'Gaytmylkshire', was conferred to the Monastery of Dunfermline and assigned to Kinglassie by James IV in 1501. (D. Goodwillie)

Above right: Lying in the Kinglassie Church grounds is the dust of David Goodwillie Jr. b. 1665, his wife Elizabeth Dewar and son James Goodwillie, b 1709. They were the father and grandparents of Rev David and Joseph who migrated to America. (D. Goodwillie)

Left: Farm buildings on the original Goodwillie Tanshall Scottish farm, now Glenrothes. 1930 (David Rae in Goodwillie)

Right: Town houses in Glenrothes built on Keith Drive replace the Goodwillie's Tanshall farm. (D. Goodwillie)

New Carlisle, Quebec

The disbanded military from Jessup's Corps could choose to resettle in New Carlisle or the area around Kingston Ontario. Most Loyalists from the refugee camps in Québec had chosen the latter since little was known about the area of the Gaspé region of Québec. However Joseph must have been anxious to get settled, and in the spring of 1884, joined 315 Loyalists to take up land in New Carlisle, a settlement near Paspébiac on the north side of the Baie de Chaleur.

The passengers were checked off as they boarded and rations were allotted for the period from June first to the end of August. Joseph's 85 passenger square-rigged brigantine, the St. Peter, was one of four ships, and four whaleboats headed for the Baie de Chaleur. The voyage was rough with gale winds causing ship damage and the destruction of the whaleboats but after three weeks all arrived at Bonaventure. Moving onwards they disembarked at Paspébiac, a low sandy beach with shallow marshy lagoons in front of heavily forested higher areas. In 1534 Jacques Cartier had encountered the Mi'kmaq Nation in this area which later became a French trading post and francophone fishing village.

Joseph, a single man at age 33 had little farming or fishing experience and no tools for blacksmithing, even if there had been any business. But he was given several blocks of town and farm land in the New Carlisle (birthplace of Quebecois politician René Lévesque, Provincial Premier from 1976-1985). Early pioneering life and conditions were very difficult with nothing but grim prospects for the future.[32]

Left: New Carlisle's beach and extensive wetlands with hills behind.
(D. Goodwillie)

Right: Typical houses used by Quebec's Mi'kmaq people displayed at Gaspeg, the Mi'kmaq Cultural Centre.
(D. Goodwillie)

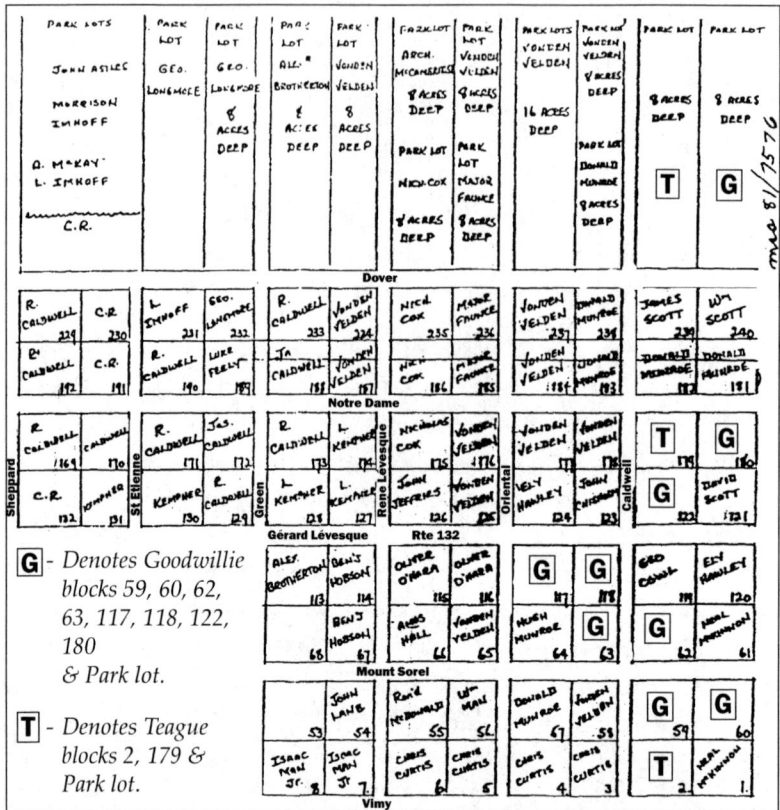

Sketch map of present roads with Loyalist town lots allocated in 1784 as researched by Committee of Anglophone Social Action (CASA) and others.

New Carlisle's Unique and Historic Plans

In early August 1784, 170 men drew lots for the newly surveyed town and country acreage. Gaspé's Lieutenant Governor Nicholas Cox writing to Governor Haldimand noted: "Mr. O'Hara left here the 11th [of August] heartily tired, and I believe will never undertake to survey land for the Loyalists again".

The technique of land division, thereafter known as the Haldimand plan, was used for all subsequent Canadian land distribution by the crown. Two hundred and twenty years later New Carlisle continues to follow the 1785 plans refined by William Vondenvelden.

The New Carlisle Municipality holds maps showing the original Loyalist land grants. Stately Hamilton House, built in the 1800s just

Present day Hamilton House in New Carlisle, soon to provide an art gallery, tea room and bed and breakfast accommodation, is most likely located on part of Joseph Goodwillie's original lots. (D. Goodwillie)

after Joseph left Quebec, currently occupies one of Joseph's town blocks. The Lease ownership of Lot 118 on the corner of Highway 132 [Rte. Gérard Lévesque] and Caldwell Street remained in the Goodwillie name until 1900.

Loyalists Anxiety About New Settlements

Felix O'Hara after the 1784 survey of New Carlisle wrote to the Governor:

"After exploration of the neighbouring site to Paspébiac, I attempted to find the most convenient location for a town. But to convince all the disgruntled people of the enumerable natural advantages would cost me more patience and time than I ever imagined. Nevertheless, they were now determined to provide a hand to help with the settlement of this place. I laid out the town according to a parallelogram in response to the demands of the loyalists, even though I would have preferred a square model."

"Their motive is to take in the beach and the marsh that lies before it and I humbly think the request was not unreasonable...Next I undertook to find out how much farm land would be sufficient to accommodate the people... this I found impossible as the people seem to drop in daily. I therefore took three leagues in front by four leagues in depth – this gives an area of 69,120 acres subdivided into hundred acre lots."[33]

Early Justice and Jury Duty in 1790

Joseph spent ten years establishing a farm. He engaged in community activity and started a young family with Mary Ann[34], the daughter of Jacob Teague, a Dutch Loyalist from Fifeshire who in 1775 had settled at the American colony called German Flats, Mohawk River. Joseph held land in town plots beside Mary Ann's father Jacob Teague. His son, Andrew was given 100 acres in lot 57 while Joseph occupied nearby farm lot 55. The Teague male line seems to have died out by 1830, but the female line still exists in the original area.[35]

With the climate, isolation, and lawlessness, it is understandable that many early settlers moved on. Lieutenant Governor Cox clearly worried about law and order in Paspébiac and in the new settlement even before people occupied the New Carlisle land. He wrote to Governor Haldimand in 1784:

"I need not explain to your Excellency my difficulty and trouble with the Loyalists. You know them better than I do. I must beg you will have compassion on me and appoint or allow me to appoint two or three Justices of the Peace for the town only. Some of the disbanded soldiers are very bad men, but when they see a civil authority over them it may keep them in awe. Without a civil or military force, thefts, murders, and all kinds of licentiousness will go on this winter. Mr. O'Hara goes from hence tomorrow to lay out the town and as soon as I hear from him I intend sending the men to build cabins for the reception of their families."[36]

Joseph Goodwillie was five foot eight inches tall and of slight build, an artisan [blacksmith] who was able to read and write. Records show that the community [New Carlisle] even had jury duty in 1790

New Carlisle (left) and the Paspébiac National Historic Site which demonstrates early fishing enterprises (right) are worth a visit. (D. Goodwillie)

and Joseph was appointed one of 12 male jurors in a 1790 case where Oliver O'Hara, Deputy Collector and Officer of his Majesty's Customs for New Carlisle, filed a complaint against Azariah Pritchard. During the American Revolution, Azariah had been charged with treason because of his continued loyalty to the King and eventually abandoned his grist mill and home, raised a contingent of soldiers for the British Army and was made a captain in the King's Rangers. After coming to Canada, he remained in the King's secret service and became Captain of the Liberty, one of four ships bringing Loyalists to New Carlisle in 1784. He was accused of 'knowingly and willfully making use of a counterfeited certificate of British Registry which was of five hundred pounds sterling value.' Azariah denied the accusation. Tried by the jury in July 1790, the accused, Azariah, was acquitted of the charge. The court was dismissed and Oliver O'Hara, the Plaintiff, had to pay a certain sum of money.

To Barnet, Vermont and Back to Canada

Family, religious ties and the possibility of better farmlands lured Joseph to move one last time. In 1792, Joseph received news that his older brother, the Reverend David Goodwillie had moved from Scotland to Vermont. Shortly after Joseph made the long voyage to meet up with a brother he had not seen for twenty years.

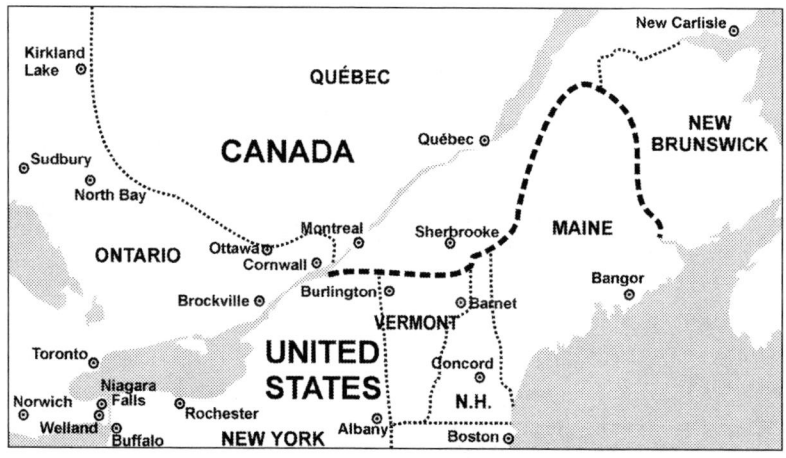

Map showing the location of New Carlisle Quebec and Barnet Vermont. Joseph fought in New York State, escaped to Montreal, moved to New Carlisle Quebec as a loyalist and finally joined his brother in Barnet Vermont. (Goodwillie)

The Rev David's house, where a secret cupboard was thought to hide escaping slaves. It is now the Goodwillie Museum. (Courtesy Barnet Historical Society)

A decision was made. After acquiring land and working for nine years to provide a home for his family in Canada, Joseph, his wife and 3 children moved to Barnet, in northern Vermont, where his brother, David, was a well loved minister and respected community leader.

The Reverend David's house built circa 1790 in classic Cape Cod style is now a community museum. David, his wife, Beatrice, (nee Henderson) Joseph and Mary Ann are buried in the nearby church cemetery.[37] How ironic for Joseph to fight against the Americans when a young man and then at age 42, change locations and spend the rest of his life on a farm in the newly independent USA.

Another twist of fate led several of Joseph's children to move to Ontario in the early 1800s. About 1818, Joseph's namesake and son joined waves of people heading for the cheap lands of Niagara Peninsula. He married Elizabeth Hellems whose family was of German and Loyalist origin, and after whom Welland's Hellems Avenue is named. Mathias Hellems had moved from Pennsylvania

Diane Goodwillie wearing a Goodwillie's t-shirt looks at Barnet Vermont graves of two of Loyalist Joseph Goodwillie's unmarried children, Mary Ann and James Goodwillie. They lived their lives in Barnet and kept in touch with their brother Joseph Junior who established the Quaker Road farm. 1998. (R. Lechte)

via a Mennonite scheme and had received 600 acres of land around Welland, much of which was later used for the Welland Canal.[38]

The Move to Quaker Road

Pioneering must have been in the Goodwillie blood. Working as a carpenter most likely from Wainfleet Township, Joseph Junior made furniture and walnut coffins (which sold for $10.00) as well as worked on farms. Joseph and Elizabeth (or 'Eliza') had five of their eight children before they were able, in 1836, to purchase 100 acres of Lot 227 on the north side of Quaker Road in Thorold Township.[39]

While the 1837 Rebellion led by Mackenzie was developing, newspapers were established. Joseph became the 'general agent' for the Welland Herald, today the Welland Tribune, which was published in Fonthill and issued each Thursday costing 10 to 17 shillings per year.

Tragedy struck in 1837, when the family house burned down. Rebuilding the following year, Joseph used planks twenty-six inches

Elizabeth Hellems Goodwillie, wife of Joseph Junior with third oldest son, Levi Goodwillie (J.R. Goodwillie)

wide and three inches deep. He took precautions against fire by including stone thimbles with the split log beams, covered with plaster. The Goodwillie family occupied this house until it was sold to Orin Bemis and the family in 1852 purchased for 125 pounds (approximately $625.00), the west half of Lot 231 on the opposite, southern side of Quaker Road. Later, Joseph added the adjacent Lot 232 to create a farm of 130 acres, which became the Goodwillie homestead for the next three generations.

By about 1867, Canada's year of confederacy, Joseph had convinced son number four, Hiram to move back to the family home from Norwich.

Joseph purchased 100 acres for 400 pounds on Quaker Road 30 March 1836. Copy of the Registration of Sale of Lot #227 from Isaac Willson to Joseph Goodwillie. Witnessed by Smith Hill and Jacob Gainer. (Goodwillie)

With the return of family members and the birth of a new granddaughter, Phoebe, a new Goodwillie house was built in the 1870s[40] on the southern side of Quaker Road, where it stands today as number 209. However few would recognize the original farm house from the 14 room 1905 renovated giant now flanked by a housing subdivision and located east of First Avenue down a long driveway off Quaker Road.

Children of Joseph Junior

Six sons and two daughters were born to Joseph and Elizabeth. The Quaker Road farm was passed on to son number four, Hiram who in about 1867 had re-established his young family on the property to help with its management.

George W.B Goodwillie, the first son of Joseph (Jr.), married Margaret Hilton. They owned a farm in Wainfleet, most likely the first location of father Joseph when he arrived from Vermont (Lot 14 Concession 5 or 6, Wainfleet Township). Although George died young, some of his children were incredibly long living. One of his sons, Charles Harmon Goodwillie lived to 101 and the daughter of Charles Harmon, Margaret Cullen lived in Niagara Falls to 105. Although the family moved from the farm, George's son/s continued ownership of the Wainfleet property until at least 1876 as identified in the Welland County Historical Atlas. Margaret remarried Francis Stokes but the family remained closely linked to Joseph and the Goodwillie Family.

Apparently George's premature illness before his death prompted a death-bed will. Joseph Goodwillie, George's father, and a neighbour were executors. He bequeathed to his children (one not yet born and the other only one year old at his death) the farm. He also provided for his wife. "It is my will that should my widow marry again she shall from that time only have the benefit of one third of the yearly income from my farm ... and my executors are hereby required to take care ... from destroying or selling any timber on this property". Was this an economic consideration or the beginnings of environmental awareness?[41]

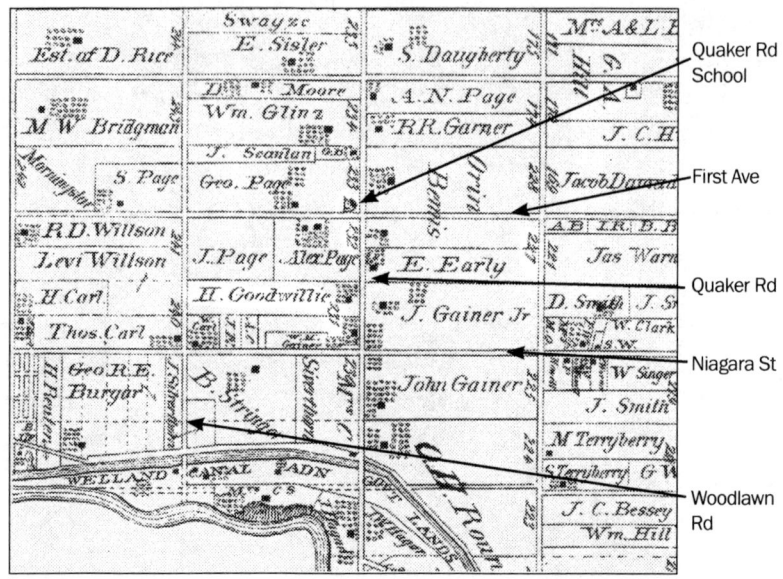

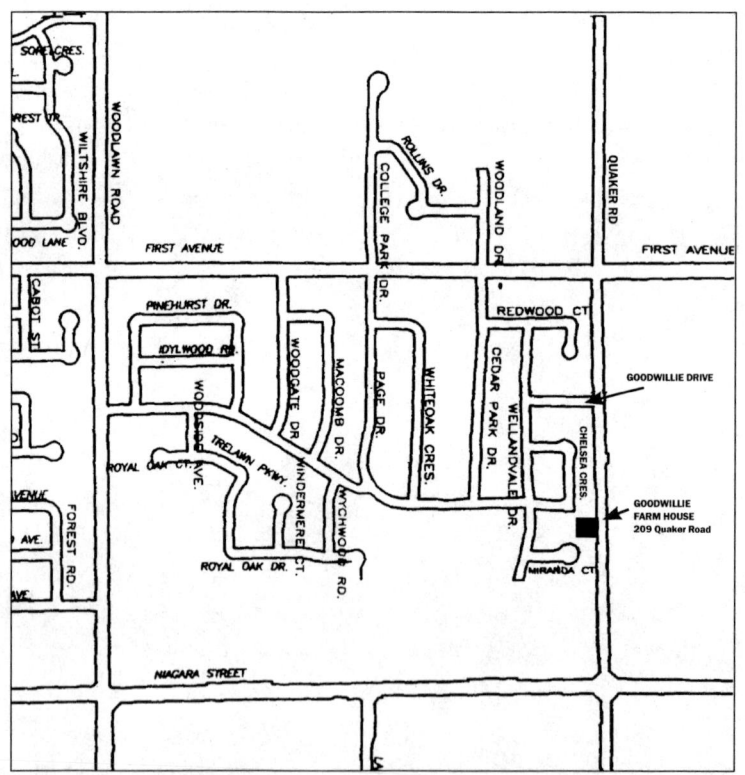

Quaker Road and First Avenue in 1876 and 2004. (Page & City of Welland)

Other sons and daughters of Joseph moved off the Welland property establishing their own farms, businesses, joining the army and becoming church pastors and missionaries.

Hiram in Norwich and Welland

As a young man, (before 1850) Hiram, Joseph's fourth son, ventured west to the Norwich area to seek his fortune. He was able to purchase 50 acres of land in 1858 and in 1862 married Sarah Stover whose family name was used for the main street of Norwich.

After refusing to go back to the Quaker Road farm several times, Hiram, wife Sarah, and 3-year-old son, John Allan, returned to Welland in about 1867. Finally in the 1870s Hiram must have decided to permanently reside on Quaker Road and sold his Norwich land to his older brother, Charles Harmon.

Harold and John Allan eventually transformed the Quaker Road property and established a business empire, and took advantage of expanding markets, improved transportation and a bumper fruit crop. They formed 'H Goodwillie and Son, Growers of Fine Fruits Packed in Glass'.

The Quaker Road home was built about 1880. The man on left is Hiram and the boy on the right most likely John Allan. (Cornett)

First Thorold Vineyard and Fruits Bottled Under Glass

From about 1867, Hiram with his father Joseph, and eventually his son John Allan Goodwillie, born 1867, worked side-by-side to build up the family farm. Over time it changed from general farming to fruit production and market gardening.

Edwin Morris of Fonthill, George Stone of Rochester, NY and William Wellington of Toronto formed a nurserymen business known as Morris, Stone and Wellington. H. Goodwillie and Son signed a commercial agreement with them dated December 1881. It showed that the Goodwillie family took advantage of the offer to purchase improved fruit stock from the nearby Fonthill Nurseries. The nursery contract provided explicit terms for the division of the stock and care and maintenance of the fruit for example: "on the 1st day of April 1887 the said grape vines [400] shall become the property of Hiram Goodwillie and on the 1st day of April 1893 the said trees [pears and plums] shall likewise become the property of the Second Part".

Site of the former Fonthill Nurseries (1837-1968)

Managed over the years by

D'Everardo & Page; Edward Morris & Co; Morris, Stone and Wellington, and Wellington and Davidson

Considered one of the largest nurseries in Canada at the turn of the century, this enterprise shipped nursery stock via agents throughout North America. With its origins in the Pelham Nursery Co., the home grounds of the Fonthill Nurseries contained 195 acres, but encompassed other farms for a total of more than 700 acres, where over 250 local residents were employed in peak seasons. Also the site of many local festivities, the nurseries were well known for their prize winning shire horses, lush gardens and beautiful scenery.

A plaque located at 1292 South Pelham St. in Fonthill. Erected by the Pelham Historical Society –2004

The H. Goodwillie and Son fruit canning factory on Quaker Road Farm used lots of firewood. (Goodwillie)

These types of agreements led to the growth of many fruit producing farms in the region. For the Goodwillies it enabled them to produce quality vineyards and improved berries and tree crops of apple, pear, plums and quince which were sold at local markets in Welland, St. Catharines, Toronto and Buffalo.

The excess produce from the Goodwillie farm and others in the area led to market saturation, spoilage and lowered prices. About the same time, new bottling technology was introduced and refrigeration enabled fruit to be stored for a longer period.

About 1886, Hiram and John A. decided to take advantage of the situation and started to preserve fruits under glass. This was the beginning of a thriving fruit canning factory, initially located on the Quaker Road farm. Women handled the fruit preparation and preservation. The women laborers were collected from the Welland area by a type of 'Democrat wagon', a horse driven flatbed buggy with a high seat in front, padded benches along the sides, four wooden wheels, a roof and drop down curtains in case of poor weather. It must have been a slow and uncomfortable journey to and from town. Later Welland's first gasoline truck, a 3-ton Packard was purchased in about 1910. In addition to transporting workers, it was used for picnics, parades, church outings etc.

Fruit was delivered to the factory from neighbourhood farms as far away as Fonthill, Beamsville, Stamford and other places. Wooden boxes were labeled 'Home Industry - glass canned by H. Goodwillie and Son' and advertisements stated: 'Picked and Packed in the Same

Advertising for Goodwillie products during the 1920s. Some said Grace Goodwillie Northcote was used as the model for the girl's drawing. (Goodwillie)

In 1911 this 'democrat wagon' transported canning factory staff to the farm from Welland and surroundings. (Cornett)

Day' and 'Goodwillie's - Just Like Mother's'. The canned fruits and jams were marketed all over Canada as well as in Great Britain, Europe and the West Indies. Like E.D. Smith products, it was even served to Royalty on the Transcontinental Railway.

Notes from various Royal Tours to Canada

"At Niagara, [1860] Albert, Prince of Wales, horrified his entourage who stopped him from taking up the offer of aerialist Blondin [Jean Francois Gravelot] to wheel him in a barrow across the [Niagara] Falls on a wire...."

"In 1901 the Prince of Wales at sixty became King Edward VII and the first great event of his reign for Ontario was a tour by the Heir to the Throne, Prince George and his wife... When the Duke and Duchess arrived in Toronto, a quarter of a million people greeted them." (source: Loyal She Remains)

"The story is told of a visit made to the area by George V when he was a Prince. While touring the Agriculture Fair, he reached out to touch some fruit, when someone slapped his hands. His host felt badly about it and took the Prince to a farm where he could touch all the fruit he wanted.

Upon seeing so much of it the prince exclaimed, "I wish my grandmother could see this" (meaning Queen Victoria). To which the jovial farmer replied, "Why don't you bring the old lady around" (source: Michael, Township of Thorold.)

The Canning Business Expands

John Allan Goodwillie continued to expand business ventures. He inherited the estate when Hiram died in 1903. A sawmill in Ridgeville (Pelham) about five miles from the farm kept the male workers employed over the winter months. John A. purchased wood lots, logged and timbered the wood and sold boards in the local area mainly for house building.

When the inventory of milled wood became too high, John started buying building lots in Welland and built houses for sale or rent. Several such houses were built on Dorothy and Burgar Streets. This timber was also used to build a family cottage "Goodvilla" at Long Beach (Wainfleet Township). Later, in the 1940s, Tim (Harold Hiram), John's oldest son, who had no children of his own, helped develop a new subdivision in Welland, where he established the house for

The new factory built about 1912 on the corner of Burgar and Hagar Streets in Welland with the Goodwillie name on the chimney. The factory was later used by Martin's Dairy. (J.R. Goodwillie 1958)

himself and his wife Grace (nee Schooley). Beverly Crescent was named after his sister Mary Haist's newly born granddaughter [Beverley Pierce Warner] although the recent book on Welland Street names claims it was named after Bill Maudsley's daughter.

(S. Stokes)

Final Days of the Goodwillie Canning Factory

Expansion and the need to be closer to factory workers, led to the establishment of a new Welland factory employing over 100 workers. It was built on the corner of Hagar and Burgar Streets in about 1912/13. If continued, the business would have rivaled today's E.D. Smith Company. However, in 1922, at the peak of the business's success, John A. died suddenly aged 59.

Of the eight children, the four boys were all under the age of 20, so it was decided to sell the factory. Mrs. Luella (nee Page) Goodwillie carried on farming with the help of her oldest son Tim. Another

The four Goodwillie boys were born after the four girls. All boys were given nick names From left, Luella, John Allan holding Pete (John Ross), Bill (Hugh Allan), Jack (Donald Brock) and Tim (Harold Hiram) with friend and Muriel Crow at Niagara Falls c. 1912-13. (Cornett)

The present Goodwillie House at 209 Quaker Road dates back to 1870 but was renovated and extended about 1905. (D.Potter)

tragedy struck when the 25 year old son and potential farm manager, Hugh Allan ('Bill'), died suddenly of TB in 1932. The farm was eventually sold in 1938 for about $35,000.00 to John McKinnon and in 1940 to the Faragalli family who lived there until 1952. In January 1980, the 'restored farmhouse and three car garage' was listed in the Welland Tribune News for sale at $158,000.00. It is now a private house on one and a half acres of the original farm.

Lifestyles and values alter – the passing of one hundred years has seen the coming of indoor plumbing, telephones, and automobiles. A century ago the stately Goodwillie farmhouse on Quaker Road was built complete with seven bedrooms, marble fireplaces, indoor plumbing etc. Many happy times and some sad ones occurred. The next chapters relate these times from the perspective of two of John Allan's children, Ruth Cornett (nee Goodwillie) and John Ross Goodwillie. Sadly, since both have passed away, we cannot query or learn more about their memories.

Selling the farm in 1938 was the end of Goodwillie family's presence on Quaker Road. (1929 photo. Cornett)

The Pages of Quaker Road

Between Quaker and Woodlawn Road off First Avenue is Page Road. It honours an early Loyalist settler Alexander Jeno Page, his sons, daughters and especially his granddaughter, Hattie Luella who married John A. Goodwillie in 1890. This book tells the stories from Luella and John Allan Goodwillie's farm on Quaker Road at the turn of the 20th century.

Alexander Page's ancestors came from England to Massachusetts in about 1675 eventually settling in Ryegate, Vermont, close to Barnet where the Goodwillie family eventually located. Born in 1806, the seventh child of a family of thirteen, Alexander at about 20 years of age, walked to the Niagara area. He settled on Lot No. 232 at the corner of Quaker Rd and what is now known as First Avenue North. Alexander and his family were devout Baptists and strong community members who contributed to the Quaker Road School and usually won prizes in the Agriculture Fair.

Many marriages took place between farm families on Quaker Road. In 1890 Luella Page married the boy next door, John Allan Goodwillie. In earlier days when the neighbouring Page brothers and Garner

Luella Page (left) with cousins and Grandparents Alexander and Edith (nee Young) Page at farmhouse opposite school house on Quaker Road. The building was used as a extra school classroom in 1920-22 and burned down about 1922-4. (Cornett)

boys were friends, Luella's mother, Jane Page married L.V. Garner, a well-known auctioneer and wholesale hay dealer who later moved to the USA.

Alexander Page died in November 1890. This was shortly after, Luella, the granddaughter that he raised, was married to J.A. Goodwillie. Alexander's wife Edith (nee Young) died in July 1892 about a year after her first great granddaughter, Iva, was born.

Two houses, one frame and the other brick were joined by the traditional woodshed and built on the Page property (Lot 232). With the coming of electricity, the power line was to cut across the property close to the house and destroy the many beautiful shade trees. The family agreed to sell the entire property and move to Welland.[42]

The power company bought some of the land and eventually J.A. Goodwillie bought the rest with the result that the powerlines went right through the Goodwillie farm. The Page's brick house was left empty for some time until it was added to the Quaker Road School S.S.#5 to provide a classroom for the junior grades. This building later burned down about 1924.

Hattie Luella page, grand-daughter of of Alexander Page. 1890. (Goodwillie family)

John Allan Goodwillie married Hattie Luella Page, thus cementing friendships between the two families. (Cornett & Goodwillie)

SECTION TWO

Quaker Road Stories

INTRODUCTION

People in the Farm Stories

Ruth Cornett wrote the stories but Grandma Sarah Stover Goodwillie told the wolves and First Nation stories of the previous section. She and her husband Hiram Goodwillie moved from Norwich to Welland in 1868 and gradually took over the management of the Quaker Rd. farm.

Grandma always wore dark dresses and a frilly white apron with large pockets. (Cornett)

Grandma Stover – Always Ready to Tell Old Stories

Grandma Stover was sixty when Ruth Cornett, the youngest girl in the family, was born. Here is Ruth Cornett's description of Grandma Stover:

"Women in those days seemed older. Of course anyone over twenty as far as we were concerned had 'had it'.

Grandma was a tall comfortably built woman with a pink and white complexion. Her hair was white and drawn straight back on either side into a tight little knot at the nape of her neck. When she went on a visit, or to Quaker Church, she always wore a black widows bonnet with a long flowing black veil at the back. It was very smart at that time. I always thought she looked very elegant, and she did.

I don't remember Grandpa so she had been a widow several years by the time these happenings took place. When my older sisters, Iva, Mary and Grace were young, Grandfather always had morning and evening devotions before and after the day's work was done.

Battenburg lace made by Grandma Sarah Stover. (Goodwillie)

Grandma did a lot of reading of the Bible but she was never too tired to tell stories of which she had a never ending supply. She was always on hand to advise or confide in and sort of pinch hit for Mother who of necessity was a very busy person.

I remember Grandma best as she sat in a big leather chair by a bright sunny window with a large basket of mending beside her, mostly heavy work socks. The boys and Father in those days wore heavy 'socks and rubbers' [rubber boots] during the winter. She also made beautiful fine duchess and Battenburg lace which took many prizes at the local Fall Fair."

Auntie Ruth Goodwillie Cornett – A Writer and Story Teller

Ruth was the only one of eight children who did not have a second name, nor was there any precedent for the name Ruth.

When Ruth was about eight years old, (about 1909) she contracted infantile paralysis, or polio, which struck young people in the summer months and often left lasting disabilities. Some summers it reached epidemic proportions until 1950 when the Salk vaccine was developed.

Ruth Cornett was one of four Goodwillie girls. From left Iva Secord, Grace Northcote, Ruth Cornett, Mary Haist. About 1915-1917. (Cornett)

Ruth Goodwillie Cornett on Old Dick. (Cornett)

Ruth's right leg was affected. Diagnosis and treatment in her time was slow and ineffective. She had to go to Buffalo, New York, for operations in order to prevent her foot from turning completely sideways, or even backward, as the paralysis had killed the inner muscle of the leg. There were many trips back and forth to Buffalo and she endured much suffering. The conductor would carry her on and off the train and she would go with her mother to the hospital by taxi. At home, the neighbouring children brought homework and helped her with her schooling. Eventually, she overcame and outgrew the paralysis, but had to wear leg braces for several years. After public school, she was able to walk to Welland to attend high school and later still, she took up dancing, lawn and alley bowling and lived to carry on a normal life with only a slight impairment.

Ruth completed high school, took a business course and became purchasing manager of Welland's Electro-Metallurgical Company where she worked for eight years. She married Jack Cornett on 21 March 1931 and after living on the farm for a while, they moved to Toronto. Ruth had arranged to continue working at the Metals after their marriage but because of the Depression, the company gave notice that all married women had to be laid off. It was a measure intended to ensure that at least one member of each family had employment; however, it was a financial blow to the newlyweds.

Ruth had no children but continues to be fondly remembered by all. From the eight Goodwillie children born before 1911, only four offspring remain with the name of Goodwillie, Diane and Hugh and two of his three children Lynne, and Jon. However other family members whose names changed with marriage have vivid memories of Auntie Ruth. Here is what one niece, Jane Goodwillie Allen, had to say about Ruth Cornett:

"Auntie Ruth was always very generous and kind. She was interested in what you and your family were doing. If she didn't hear from you, she would call out of the blue…just to talk. She was also a source of information about what the rest of the family was doing. She was the 'Matriarch' of the extensive Goodwillie family.

Lower left: Ruth Cornett with Jennifer and Jane Allen, Standing: Pete, Ruth and Diane Goodwillie. (Goodwillie)

My memories of Auntie Ruth are mostly around her house at 46 Old Mill Road. Growing up in Toronto, we would often go to her place for a visit. I remember Uncle Jack Cornett, smoking a pipe. He would spend hours trying to keep the pipe going.

Boxing Day Goodwillie gathering 1985. Auntie Ruth (seated centre) with Goodwillie, Dinnin, Cousins, Shepherd, Pierce, Warner family members. (J.R. Goodwillie) [43]

There weren't a lot of things to do at Auntie Ruth's. I remember the wooden marble game where you had to try and get rid of all the marbles except the one in the middle. The second generation of cousins would spend most of their time upstairs watching TV and playing games and developing strong family ties. My children remember the bottom drawer of the secretary in the dinning room. It contained all of the kids toys like pick up sticks and barrel of monkeys.

In later years Auntie Ruth started a Christmas Eve tradition with the Cousins, Dinnins and Goodwillies. All the families would get together at her house for an order of Chinese food for dinner. In our family we still have a Chinese meal during the Christmas period but nowadays the extended family tries to arrange a pot luck dinner on Boxing Day. [Family ties are also maintained through summer visiting between the Long Beach cottages: my mother's Payne cottage, which we Goodwillies own and the Goodwillie cottage, a five minute walk down the beach, owned by Auntie Iva Secord's grandchildren, the Dinnin's]."

John Ross Goodwillie – The Genealogist

The last Goodwillie to be born on the Quaker Road farm was John Ross known as 'Pete' but always called 'Ross' by his mother. It was said 'the parents could not agree on names for the Goodwillie boys so Father decided to give them nicknames that remained with them all of their lives'.

Pete enjoyed playing and watching football, hockey, baseball, tennis, skiing, curling and golf. As a young person, he found work on the farm tedious and tough but it taught him lessons in management, which were put to good use in his jobs with Atlas Steel, Massey-Harris Implement Company, American Standard Plumbing, General Freezer Company, and as volunteer advisor to companies in Nigeria and India.

Pete Goodwillie with daughter Diane and wife Ruth in front of farmhouse, 1988.

This muscular blue eyed, red haired fellow was a good family man who enjoyed his children and grandchildren, in whom he instilled the love of sport. The story goes that he wooed his wife, Ruth Payne by wiggling his prominent Goodwillie ears when sitting in front of her at Welland High School.

Pete's rural roots were often evident. He introduced the grandchildren to Canadian walnuts and hickory nuts, and was often found digging into his 'winter store' of apples kept outside on the apartment veranda in several bushel baskets, covered by many woollen blankets to protect against freezing. His favourite eating apple was the King Tompkin an apple as big as a grapefruit[44] but he also loved apple pie which had to be accompanied by ripe cheddar cheese since: 'an apple pie without cheese is like a kiss without a squeeze'.

Pete told imaginative stories about One-hump and Two-hump the camels, Bushy-tail the squirrel and the farm horse Old Dick. But his life achievement was the research, networking and writing of the 270 page family genealogy, completed in 1986 just before his death in 1988.

The family continues to enjoy apples but its hard to find King Tompkin at the Welland Market. From left Jane Allen, Hugh Goodwillie and Ruth Lechte. (D.Goodwillie)

Joseph Goodwillie and family

Three Goodwillie pioneering brothers thought to be George who moved to Esquesing b. 1804; James lived in Barnet b. 1792; Joseph moved to Welland b. 1795. (Goodwillie)

Pete Goodwillie, the genealogist, visits the Fonthill Ontario grave of Joseph Goodwillie, his great grandfather who started the Quaker Road farm. (Photo by D. Goodwillie 1988)

Above: Grandma Sarah Stover Goodwillie b 1840 d. 1918, Grandpa Hiram Goodwillie b. 1830 d. 1903. (Goodwillie)

Left: Early ancestors: Unknown but thought to be either James and David in Scotland or James and Joseph in Barnet Vermont. Photo taken by B.F. Hale, Photographer, 75 East Main St. Rochester, N.Y. (Cornett)

Left: Mother Luella Page Goodwillie b. 1867 and John Allan Goodwillie b. 1863 Taken about 1918-21. (Cornett)

Right: Aunt Tebe (Phoebe) Goodwillie Hederick: b. 1870 (J.A.'s Sister). Uncle Will Hederick: b. 1870. Undated 1930s? (Cornett)

Others named in the stories

Wedding photo of Iva Goodwillie b. 1891 and George Secord b. 1891 taken 1916. (Cornett)

Iva and George Secord at Family Christmas gathering in Welland in 1948. (Cornett)

From left Grace Goodwillie Northcote, b 1896, Russ Northcote, Mary Goodwillie Haist, b 1893, Perce Haist, b 1891. Photo taken after 1918. (Cornett)

Pete's 1935 Ford with 'rumble seat' From left Dorothy Haist Pierce, b. 1924, Nancy Northcote Shier, b 1931, Joyce Secord Dinnin Shand, b. 1924, Jack Northcote, b. 1924, Jean Secord Cousins b. 1921 Photo taken 1937. (Cornett)

People in the Farm Stories

'Bill' Hugh Allan Goodwillie b.1907 on Old Dick photo taken about 1925. (Cornett)

From left Ruth Goodwillie Cornett b.1901, Jack (Donald Brock) Goodwillie b. 1905. Tim (Harold Hiram) Goodwillie b.1905. Photo taken 1907-08. (Cornett)

John Ross 'Pete' with his two Ruth's: From left Ruth (nee Payne) Goodwillie b. 1911, Pete Goodwillie b.1910, Ruth (nee Goodwillie) Cornett b.1901. (D. Goodwillie c.1987)

Pete with his girlfriend (later wife) Ruth Payne about 1928. (Goodwillie family)

From left Jane Goodwillie Allen b.1953, Hugh Goodwillie b.1943, Diane Goodwillie b1945. (R.Lechte)

From left: Grace (nee Goodwillie) Northcote, b.1900, Jack Cornett, b.1906. Beverley Warner (Haist Pierce family) b1948. Photo taken 1948. (Cornett)

Bob and Beverley (nee Pierce) Warner. 1998. (D. Goodwillie)

Dorothy Pierce and her mother Mary Haist. 1981. (J.R.Goodwillie)

The Goodwillies on the farm taken about 1915-1917 (missing Jack and Bill). Note the old cars. From left Tim, Iva & George Secord, [Mabel Secord?], Grace, Ruth, Mary, & Perce Haist, Pete, Grandma Sarah, Mother Luella, Father John Allan. (Cornett)

The Goodwillie Family at the Turn of the 21st Century

Last Goodwillie gathering in Toronto October 1995. (Goodwillie)

Annual family golf tournament of Goodwillies, Lechte, Allens and Millers (GLAM). Children and grandchildren of John Ross Goodwillie. Standing: Joe Miller, Sally Goodwillie, Brian Allen, Anne Miller, Jon Goodwillie, Dave & Jane Allen, Michael Prosia, Jennifer Allen. Seated: Colby, Diane Goodwillie, Ruth Lechte, Bailey, Hugh Goodwillie. 2004. (Goodwillie)

CHAPTER SIX

The Goodwillie Farm and Surroundings

Stories written by Ruth Goodwillie Cornett, with additions from J.R. 'Pete' Goodwillie and Jane Goodwillie Allen

Home on the Farm

Sunday was really a day of rest, for people and animals. Only necessary work happened, such as feeding the animals and getting the meals. We dressed in our best to go to church and our shoes were cleaned and polished every Saturday night ready for the next day. I still associate shoe polish smell with going to church and Sunday School in the afternoon.

The Goodwillie Farmhouse in 1929. (Cornett)

I was the fifth of a family of eight children. We all lived on a farm about two miles from Welland. There was Grandmother, Mother and Father (Luella and John Allan Goodwillie) and we children, plus several hired men at various times. With eight children to look after, you can imagine how busy our parents were. However they were never too busy that they could not make time for us.

Either Mother or Grandmother was always on hand to answer questions and take an interest in whatever was significant at the moment. There was always someone home when we came in from school. Perhaps this was because in those days there were never many social goings on in the daytime - or at night either for that matter.

Mother was a great worker, manager and hostess, had original ideas and was a wonderful person, not only in the home but for the whole neighbourhood as well. She even acted as doctor's helper for one of the neighbour's son's birth. If anything was needed it was mother who was called on.

Father worked morning, noon and night. He had the farm to look after, a sawmill about five miles away, which he ran in the winter, and during the summer there was the canning factory. He was a busy man but got a lot of enjoyment out of life. He loved the horse races and

Ruth Cornett with brothers and friends. From left: Jack, Arthur and Ken Gaylor, Bill, Ethel Gaylor, Tim at the neighbouring Old Page Farm c 1912. (Cornett)

often took time off to go to them. He entered the sulky horse races at the various County Fairs and often won. He called the sulky a 'bike'.

When Sunday came around, Father was never too tired to take us on a picnic in the summer, or drive 'the company' some place to see the sights. He always loved a joke and was excellent company and a very fine family man as well as a good neighbour. He loved us kids.

We had a wonderful home life and a lot of fun just among ourselves. Oh yes, we had our spats and quarrels but nothing ever lasted over night.

Living at the house with us were also several hired men. Frank Orr was there for years and was almost like a brother. Tom and Nellie Gaylor, an English married couple, had a room at the top of the back stairs. They eventually had a family of their own so moved to a brick house on one corner of the farm until father built a house for them close to our own. The other men slept in the attic which was large and a very pleasant airy place.

There were always a lot of people around and usually fourteen or fifteen sat down for every meal. This was not counting any 'company' that might be on hand as well. I have heard Mother often say that from Easter until after Thanksgiving there were years when we were never without guests. They didn't come just for a day or two but stayed for a week or longer; Aunts and Uncles might stay all summer. They were always made most welcome and fitted into the family routine, doing their share of the work as well.

Stover relatives of Grandma Sarah often visited the farm from Norwich and stayed for several weeks. Photo about 1915-1917. (Cornett)[45]

I think it was sort of like a three-ring circus. There was so much going on all the time people just liked to be at the Farm. It was so quiet at night that sometimes the guests would say they couldn't sleep for listening to the crickets.

Now this is just a sort of prologue. When Father and Mother were married on April 2nd, 1890, none of this was in existence. I'm writing from what I remember and have been told.

Father gradually took over the work from his Father, on the farm. He bought and sold anything he could make a dollar on, maybe even a stack of hay. He finally got the farm producing fruit, berries, pears and so on, and went on from there. Mother said he always had a mortgage to pay off on one thing or another but gradually, with a lot of hard work, made a good home and a happy home for all of us as we came upon the scene.

These are stories perhaps some of you may remember, or maybe you can pass them on to your children and grandchildren – all are true.

The Farmhouse: Our Surroundings

Grandfather and Grandmother bought one hundred and thirty acres on April 10th 1874 from James Swayze. They had two children, John (Father) and Phoebe (Aunt Tebe). Father was born in Bayham Township near Norwich and was just three years old when the family moved to the farm near Welland. As Father grew older he gradually

The original Goodwillie house built in the 1870s was a one-story cottage and seems a rather lonely looking spot-in an old photograph. Hiram standing left and John Allan sitting right. (Cornett)

took over the farm work and when he and Mother married they lived with his parents in the same house.

Aunt Tebe, father's sister, lived with them of course until she and Uncle Will were married in 1897. Uncle Will worked for Father at one time, and later started 'sparking' Aunt Tebe, as Dad put it.

Father bought and sold fruit, shipping it as far away as Winnipeg and Brandon by the carload. In addition he grew potatoes, tomatoes, cabbage, apples, pears, quinces and berries, which he marketed to the surrounding towns and also Buffalo N.Y. He started the factory later.

Building the House

Father and Grandfather rebuilt the original little cottage into a nice two-story frame house and later in the year 1905 that house was remodelled into the present one. Actually only three rooms of the old house were incorporated into the new one, the bay window in the front parlor and Grandma's bedroom were part of it. I was just four years old and the 1905 house is the only home I really remember. There were six children at that time.

We lived in the tenant house next door while the new one was being built a short distance away. There were four bedrooms and each one was full to the brim that summer.

It must have been a hectic time. There were many extra men to feed and house, beside the family. On top of it all, the factory was in full swing. Jack [Donald] was born that year too so Mother couldn't have been feeling much like doing all the extra work she had to contend with.

Carpenters came from town, plumbers from Hamilton and there was the usual quota of visitors to entertain. The rooms were all finished with twelve-inch solid Canadian native chestnut. The dining-living room and the office floors were inlaid with light maple and cherry hardwoods with a beautiful overall design that were the envy and admiration of all who visited.

There was company as usual. I don't know how Mother managed it all. I do remember her being so annoyed with an Aunt that visited with her one child who had the measles. Yes, we all got the measles too. I only think of it as being a very hot summer.

A 1980 visit to the farmhouse

by Jane Goodwillie Allen

Joyce Dinnin and Jean Cousins arranged for a few of the Goodwillies to go on a tour of the old farmhouse. The house had been completely renovated.

I especially remember the kitchen which had a cooking island in the middle, a gorgeous solarium type window looking out the back and a very steep staircase that led upstairs to the many bedrooms. Auntie Ruth commented that the solarium took the place of the back cold storage room where they would keep their fall harvest in the winter. Another feature that had been changed was the size of the front porch, which had been enlarged to encompass the two sides of the house (instead of just the front).

One part of the house that had not changed was the attic. I remember seeing names of some of the nieces carved into the walls there. I think that Jean Cousins and Nancy Shier had done this when they were quite small, and just learning to print their names (approximately five years old)

The house, barn and haystack as photographed in 1975. (Cornett)

The Main Floor of the Quaker Road House

The new house was large, fourteen rooms, with a big finished attic over all. On one side of the front hall were the double parlors. The front room had a big bay window in the front of the house and a fireplace with a high elaborate mantel around it. The back parlor had triple windows facing the front and always was more or less a very formal room, both rooms with wall-to-wall carpet.

Off the left side of the hall was a good sized dining-room and family room combined. This was really where we lived and the centre of activity. Off that room was the 'office'. The floors in these rooms were hardwood, oak inlaid with cherry wood to form a fancy pattern. These floors were different in those days and always kept shining.

The office was a very pleasant room. It had three big windows facing the driveway. Father had his roll-top desk, files and a huge iron safe. Also Grandma's black leather chair sat in the front window with lots of room for us children to sit around her. We loved that room.

The opening of the safe

Memories by 'Pete' Goodwillie

Grace was only nineteen or twenty when she met Russ Northcote of Welland. They were married 30 May 1917. Russ loved cars and was always tinkering and shining his Ford or Chevy touring models. Russ was a draughtsman at the Mean-Morrison plant in Welland, later working his way up to be manager. Through his efforts, many wartime contracts were processed. He was dedicated to his work, had a wonderful sense of humour and great faith in his fellow man. He was a restless individual

The Goodwillie farm roll top desk is still used by John Allan's grandson, Hugh and great grandson Jon Goodwillie.
(Karen Kalashnik)

and always found some mechanical job which needed doing. When his family were young, it was the custom for them to visit the farm on a Sunday afternoon and stay for early tea, as did other members of the family.

One particular Sunday, he and Perce Haist decided they would tackle the big safe mechanism in the office of the house. This was a brute of a safe, solid iron, about three feet square and weighing a couple of tons. It has a large facing door, about ten inches thick, and solid hinges. For several years the combination had not worked and the door was always bolted but never locked. Russ, Perce and Jack Cornett (Ruth's husband) decided to fix the combination. The first Sunday was taken up with exploring the mechanism, as was the next Sunday and many Sundays thereafter. It was a complicated exercise with many suggestions, some trial and error and much laughing and jesting. After many challenging Sundays, the project was finally abandoned. The oiling of hinges and bolts made the door much easier to open and close, but it still could not be locked.

Russ was always kidded about his exploits with his house robber. One Sunday, when he and Grace were visiting the farm, they stayed till dusk before heading home. On arrival at his front door, Russ immediately noticed the back door open and a figure disappearing. He quickly realized he had interrupted a robber who now was making his escape through the orchard in the back yard. Russ took up the chase immediately, but when he suddenly realized he was rapidly gaining on the fleeing figure, he began to wonder what he would do if he caught him. So rather than take the chance of facing a gun, he gave up the chase and was forever after unmercifully joshed about his ability to chase robbers and his lack of nerve on apprehending them.

The Kitchen and Pantry

Adjoining the dining room was a large airy kitchen and a pantry. The latter had cupboards all down one side from floor to ceiling. On the other side were a dry sink, work table, flour bin and sugar bin. Flour and sugar in those days were purchased by the hundred pounds so there had to be a place to store it. The baking utensils hung on one wall. It was a very handy place and a lot of work was done there.

The kitchen itself was a meeting place, a spot for the hired men to sit in the evenings with the main big coal or wood stove, and a hot water tank. In front of one of the windows was a nice rocking chair. We children never ate in the kitchen but it was a very pleasant spot and I used to wish we would do so sometimes. On cold snowy days the windows frosted over making it hard to see outside, but inside, it was oh so nice and warm. And usually there was the aroma of pies being baked and supper not too far away.

Grandma's bedroom was off the kitchen on one side. She had her own washroom so didn't have to go upstairs. There was also a buzzer, which sounded in Dad's room, in case she was sick in the night or needed help. Grandma always had a fifteen-minute sleep, or 'forty winks' after dinner, at noon. Then she was good for the rest of the day.

Off the kitchen on the other side was an outside kitchen, or utility room. The laundry was done there. The butter was churned and eventually a cream separator stood at one side. The whine of the separator every morning was a sure sign everyone should be down for breakfast about 7:00 o'clock and everyone was expected unless they were too ill to make it.

Since the men were up each morning about six o'clock or earlier, feeding the stock, milking the cows and getting ready for the day's work, they were hungry by the time breakfast was ready.

In the winter we always had buckwheat pancakes, maple syrup, sausages and lots of butter, sometimes fried potatoes, fruit and cake. All winter long there was a perpetual crock of yeast buckwheat pancake mix on the table in the outside kitchen. It was what we call a 'starter' now, just keep on adding milk, flour and soda every day after the morning's quota had been used. They were so good, I wish I had some now.

One person stayed in the kitchen making the pancakes until all had their fill, then she ate. Just think of the job to make pancakes

In 2005, the old water pump still remains beside the house. (D. Potter)

for fourteen or more people. The Sunday morning treat was toast, made over an open wood fire on a grill or with a fork.

Water Supply for the House

There was a pump in the outside kitchen. In the summer when there had not been much rain and the big tank upstairs was running low on water, it was our job to pump water from the cisterns to the tank upstairs off the attic. We would stand and pump and pump taking turns until we thought our arms would drop off. How we hated that pump and prayed for rain. In later years a motor was installed.

That big tank off the attic was a very ingenious water system that Father installed to supply the bathroom and taps with running soft water at all times. It worked very well. Our drinking water was obtained from a well with a bucket pump at the front of the house and good water it was too. Naturally we had to carry it inside by the pail full.

Pete's story – fetching water

Although recollections of my father are vague, I do remember the following water pump episode:

On a warm Sunday evening we were at dinner with guests. I was about 8 years old. It was always customary in the summer to have a pitcher of nice cool fresh water on the table for all the meals. As I recall, the youngest was always delegated to get the pitcher filled before sitting down, and during the meal, if more was required. Being the youngest this chore was generally my responsibility, although not always done with genuine willingness, and often under protest, especially if it was raining outside. The pump was some 35 feet from the East entrance. The only alternative, especially in the winter, was to fill the pitcher from a pail in the outer kitchen, which was always kept full for kitchen usage.

On this particular day I was instructed to get the second pitcher full. For some unrecalled reason, I objected quite strenuously and was told in no uncertain terms by my father to refill the pitcher. I reluctantly went to the pump and panted and lingered and delayed the filling. Suddenly, my father arrived on the scene and I was severely reprimanded by word and deed. Needless to say I didn't like the task any better from then on. I must admit, though, that in later years I never objected because the well water was cool and delicious and well worth the effort.

Upstairs

Upstairs in the house there were six nice airy bedrooms, a bathroom, lots of cupboards and a screened balcony off our parent's room.

Mother and Father's room was beautiful. It ran across the whole back of the house with a window or door in each direction, so bright, airy and cool in summer. On the East was a picture window with a built-in seat. This surveyed the country for miles. Many a plan or conference was held there with Mother and many Christmas lists gone over to see that no one was missed.

A couple of times a year Mother would have a seamstress in, and there would be great old times making dresses for all the females in the family. At that time Mother's room was the centre of activity.

The farmhouse in 1906. It would be quite a drop from the attic window on the right. Note the dirt road into the barns and factory behind the house to the left. (Cornett)

What a flurry of laces, beading, lovely materials and so on went into that sewing spree.

The balcony was big enough to contain two double beds and a single cot. I slept there several summers while getting over polio. All the beds were usually in use for we all liked to sleep outside, sometimes until almost Christmas. Oh there were some cold nights with the wind blowing and the canvas curtains flapping and even the odd snowflake falling on my face. The feather tick was so nice and deep and cozy. Except for getting in and out of bed it was a wonderful spot. There were not any electric blankets in those days - and in the early years not even electricity.

Gas and Electricity

Father had drilled for gas as an experiment and got enough for our own use so when the house was built we had gas lights downstairs. They gave a nice steady white light and would go 'pop' when lighted. Gas was also installed in the kitchen stove and later there was a gas-plate in the pantry, just for convenience.

It wasn't long before electricity came out our way, perhaps around 1910, and even a telephone but Father had to supply the poles to bring it in a mile or so to our house.

Not having had gas upstairs, it was wonderful when we didn't have to use coal-oil lamps any more. No one missed the task of cleaning lamps and filling them with oil every morning; not that it was ever one of my chores.

An electric iron was a far cry from the heavy irons that had to be heated on a wood cook-stove too. It was an all day job to iron in the olden days especially with all the long frilly petticoats and dresses.

The Attic

Over all, there was the attic. Sometimes the hired men slept there, sometimes overflow of family, if there was a lot of company on hand, and sometimes it was just for storage. When the grandchildren arrived they made a beeline for this spot. All the boxes of old clothes were dragged out and a great 'getting dressed up' session went on. Edna's high heel shoes were sneaked out too and such a clumping upstairs and down you can't imagine. Mother kept those old things just for the children.

Playing in the Yard

Outside the back door along a cement platform was a woodshed and storehouse. It had been the kitchen from the old house. We had a swing in there and it was a dandy place to play on wet days. In the summer the laundry would be done here before the days of electricity.

The bell in the wood shed tower was rung to bring workers for meals and to alert neighbours about fires. (Cornett)

Every Fall loads of slab wood would be unloaded outside at the back and it was our job to pile the slabs neatly inside the shed at one end for use in the kitchen stove or perhaps the furnace. After the butchering had been done in January there would be tubs of meat stored there, solidly frozen most of the winter.

On top of the woodshed in a little cupola was a big bell which was rung to bring the men in from the fields to meals. In case of fire either at our place or in the neighborhood it would be rung frantically to bring help from anyone within earshot.

In the front of the house was a large front lawn, as well as at the back so there was lots of grass to cut. Everyone took his turn, sometimes one pulling the mower and one pushing it if the grass got too long. Besides doing the cooking, baking, cleaning etc, Mother looked after the flowers and they were always lovely. The 24th of May holiday was a good time to start cleaning up the lawns, perhaps cut the grass for the first time and help Mother tie up rose bushes.

The yard was big enough for baseball, football and in later years a tennis court and it was well used. In the spring, the baseball bat would be brought out and if the lawn was dry and not too soft maybe we would get the tennis court marked. While we younger folk did not use the court much, Mary, Grace and Iva and their boy friends did and we could chase the balls for them. One of the hired men used to occasionally sit on the third floor balcony and tell where the balls had gone if we couldn't find them. The girls didn't like that very much.

There was a large verandah, covered by a Dutchman's Pipe vine, surrounded almost all the east and north sides of the house. It was a lovely spot in summer with lots of rugs, chairs, hammocks and cushions. The City Folk used to sit and rock and say 'This is the nicest spot in the whole country'. It was, too, but we didn't get too much time to use it except evenings and Sundays.

Between the house and the barns was a stretch of lawn with two large maple trees and a gnarled old astrakhan apple tree. The latter was the centre of interest for the small fry during the summer. It had some dandy crotches in which to sit, or we could hide among the leaves while playing hide and seek. It was fairly easy to climb and we missed it when it finally outlived its usefulness for apples or shade.

The Graperies, Orchards and Bush

The farm had many 'graperies' we called them, but vineyards as they are known now. There was an apple orchard where we watched for the first ripe Astrakhan apples, pear trees and berries, in addition to the mixed farming that Father carried on. Oh yes, there was a small woods too at the very back of the farm and a large tulip tree. Early every spring we hunted and found hepaticas, trillium and many Mayflowers.

About half way back to the woods was a small stream, always full of water. The boys used to trap muskrats there. I don't believe they caught too many but they did have a busy time trying to dress the skins and sell them. I believe each skin netted about four dollars and that was something of which to be proud.

There were many happenings at the farm, some good and some not so good. There was the time Dad caught Bill trying to ride or bulldoze one of the cows. Bill had been reading wild west stories and thought he would try his hand at it.

There was the little house we built behind the woodshed, out of old packing cases and odds and ends. It wasn't very big and we had to crawl in on our hands and knees but it was pretty special. I remember eating canned peaches we had swiped from the cellar, from tiny little doll dishes.

The Barns

The alleys to the back of the barn were dark and ran in front of the horse stalls, ten of them. Sometimes if the horses were inside we would scrunch along the wall as far away as we could get, dead scared one of the animals would reach out to nip us. I guess there wasn't a chance but we didn't take any chances either.

The cattle stalls were off at the other side of the barns. When Father decided to go in for thoroughbred cattle he built a good sized

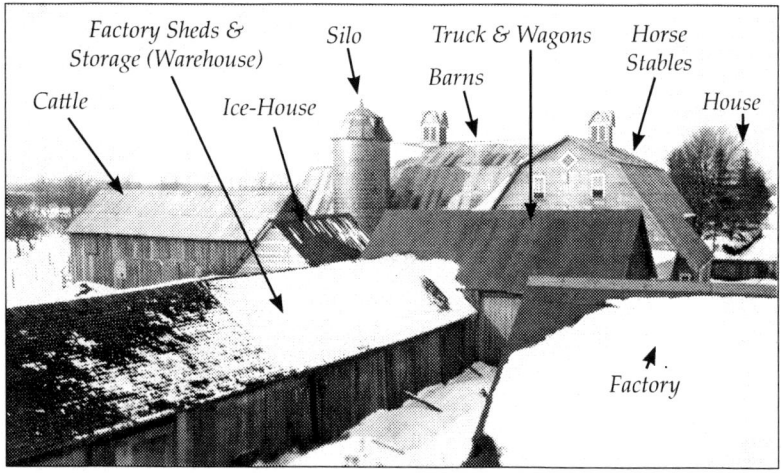

A birdseye view of the factory and farm buildings. (Cornett)

addition to the original barns and eventually a big silo. He had many cows and sold the milk to the dairy in town.

Behind the barns were long sheds where the canned fruit was stored for shipping, and at the back of those was the factory itself. This was a dull place most of the time in winter, but a hive of activity during summer and fall.

A new drive-shed was raised on August 11th, 1894 with thirty-one hands to help raise it. Incidentally this shed burned down in April 1964, after we had left the farm. (Cornett)

This gives you a general layout of the building of the farm. There were so many buildings and all fairly close together that Father was always afraid of fire. Every precaution was taken to avoid such a disaster.

Farm Fun and Children's Adventures

There couldn't be a large family without some really funny things happening. Some were everyday little things that took place on the spur of the moment.

One day a Quaker minister, who was slightly deaf, came to see Grandma. He spent the afternoon and naturally was invited to supper. At that time Aunt Chat - Charity was her real name - was living with us and she also was very deaf.

We were all gathered around the table and each on his best behavior for a Minister's visit was very special. Father, as was usual, asked the visitor to bless the food but Aunt Chat didn't hear. Much to our delight and Mother's horror they both started at once to ask the blessing - and both finished unaware of the other. It was funny and needless to say we kids about burst our buttons to keep from exploding in laughter.

Eva and Grace Mitchell used to visit the farm a lot when they were probably in their early thirties. Father would drive to Thorold with the horse and buggy to bring them up. Eva was full of fun and had a wonderful sense of humor, always had a most infectious laugh and never a dull moment when she was around.

One night Grandma was asking the blessing and all was quiet, Father stretched out his long legs and put his feet in Eva's lap. From the burst of laughter you never would know she'd turn out to be quite a wonderful missionary and travel from Canada's Coast to Coast. I have heard Eva so often tell of the fun she used to have at the farm. She and Dad seemed to have had a running battle of wits most of the time.

Standing from left: A cousin and sister of the missionary Eva, Grace Mitchell shown here with Luella Page Goodwillie. Sitting: an unidentified friend and Lu's granddaughter Jean Secord Cousins. (Cornett)

Farm Entertainment

Since the drive house was fairly new at this time, some of the extra men slept there. Mother and Nellie Gaylor had cleaned and scrubbed the North end, where the good show harness was kept and it was good spot in the summer for the men. There were six beds there. Mary and Iva sometimes put thistles in the beads as a nice (?) surprise for the men, who usually got even in some way.

Some of the men had mouth organs, or a fiddle and in any spare time or evenings there would usually be some music. I remember a phonograph, the first Tim and I had seen. It had a huge horn and we thought that quite an addition to the general confusion.

The first farm radio

A memory of Pete Goodwillie

The forerunner of the radio was the old crystal sets with earphones. The magazines in the 1920s were full of do-it-yourself instructions on how to build the new sets and Bill decided in his teens to make his own set. Forty-foot poles were cut from the backwoods and wires strung up for the aerial. Following the instructions, he was able eventually to build his own working set. The opportunity to listen to KDKA Pittsburg was one of the marvels of our time. It was a game on most clear nights to try and tune in to the station farthest from Welland.

The Goodwillie car in front of the YMCA. Tim goes to the Scout Camp about 1911. (Cornett)

Every advantage was taken for a bit of fun. When the factory was working, the 'Hands' would gather at noon hour for a quick dance or two in the drive-house or when the house was far enough along they would dance in the unfinished rooms.

Children's Mischief

Tim and I, being about five and four years old respectively, were always under foot and no doubt we were in the way most of the time. One day we painted our black and white spotted coach dog. We painted him with every color paint we could find and he was quite attractive to us in his red, green and yellow coat. The poor dog had to be cleaned, no easy task. And so did we. We were in bed real early that night.

One day Tim was climbing around in the woodshed and upset a bag of Paris Green[46] all over himself. It was his hair, his eyes, all over his face and down his neck. This stuff is very poisonous. It was used to kill potato bugs which was another big job to add to the summer's work. Mother and Father were very alarmed for a while fearing Tim might have swallowed some of the stuff but after a good clean-up there were no bad results.

Another day as Father was driving in the lane with a team of horses he happened to glance at the third floor balcony and was horrified. He dropped the reins and dashed into the house, passing Mother without a word. She wondered what was up. He tore upstairs and quietly opening the attic door grabbed Tim with one hand and me with the other. We had been quietly sitting on the edge of the unfinished balcony swinging our legs in outer space. Since there was not yet a railing around the balcony our position was, to say the least, a bit precarious.

Farm Dogs

We had, over the years, various dogs as pets. There was a big black Labrador, Nigger[47], so gentle and always with us. One day Wally, a teacher, gave Mother a tiny pup, just big enough to sit in a teacup. This was Buzz. He was a white poodle and much loved by us all but especially Tim. He could hear the rattle of a candy paper a mile away. He could also sense when he was going to get a bath and disappear into the darkest corner. Before these dogs there was a black and

Mother loved Patsy, the German Shepherd but being a farm dog she was given to a neighbour when the farm was sold. (Cornett)

white spotted coach dog, then a white bull terrier with one brown patch over one eye. This dog was named Slick and would not let another dog come on the place.

One day friends from town drove in the driveway in a lovely rubber-tired buggy but they had a little fox-terrier with them. Slick made one big dive into the rig and that spoiled a nice visit. Slick finally one day attacked a cow and had to be destroyed much to our sorrow.

Then of course the last dog we had before leaving the farm was Patsy, a German Shepherd and a wonderful pet. She was so good with all the children. Contrary to all reports of such dogs, she wouldn't harm one of them. She would bark at the school children as they passed but never went off the lawn. She just seemed to be saying 'hello'. We had to leave Patsy with a good neighbour when we left the farm but she had a good home and lived to a good old age.

Easter Eggs

We had good times in the barn, walking the high beams, jumping in the haymows, or hiding eggs before Easter. Mother always seemed surprised on Easter morning when we appeared with well filled baskets of eggs which we had hidden during the week or so previous to the holiday. It showed the hens had been doing quite well in spite of the fact there were not any eggs in the nests the next day.

I don't why we did this but there must have been some reason for we did it every year. All the other kids did it too. Mother also used to colour eggs and hide them outside for us. Another Easter custom was to see how many eggs you can eat on Easter day. Early Heffner, one of our neighbor pals, could eat twelve at one sitting which we considered great. We were never allowed to glut ourselves like this, one or two at one meal was the limit.

The Local Pond

Jack, Bill and Pete had a boat called the 'Artussa'. It was really only a raft on the pond back of the factory but many an hour they spent on it during the summer. They also learned to swim in that pond before graduating to the canal at the foot of the road.

The S.S. Artusa – a boat to be remembered

Pete Goodwillie's story

The S.S. ARTUSA days were well remembered and they must have been in the early 1920s. We had three ponds on the farm: one up on the 'Page Place' slightly south of the School house in the Pasture field; one about half way back of the barn to the bush and up the hill over the culvert; and one behind the drum shed and garden to the east between our farm and Bill Bailey's place.

As kids, we all liked to play in the two latter ponds in the spring when they were nice and big and no weeds to worry about. Many were the wet feet and pants I got from playing alongside pushing and shoving things in and out of the water and looking for frogs and pollywogs. I guess Jack and Bill conceived the idea of a raft which was duly slapped together and launched on the pond behind the drive shed mainly because it was the closest to the houses and supplies. I think Russ was responsible for the nautical name give to our first -- and subsequent rafts and boats – the S.S. Artusa. I have no idea where the name originated but to this day it is commonly used for all our boats and reference to rafts etc. [Note: internet relates the name to Eastern Europe so possibly it was picked up during WWI or was an area from which migrants came to work on the third Welland Canal]. It was most exciting to cook some eggs at the house and take some bread and jam and have a feed on the raft. What a time: Oh that kids today could only enjoy those carefree days.

The S.S. Artusa at Long Beach-

by Diane Goodwillie

In the early 1950s we had several boats named SS Artusa at the Long Beach Payne cottage. Ruth Payne married Pete Goodwillie and so the Payne Cottage, Castle Erie is now used by the Goodwillies. Its all very confusing. Especially the Goodwillie family cottage "Goodvilla" is now the Dinnin Cottage, a quarter of a mile down the beach from Castle Erie.

For decades our SS Artusa was a wooden flat bottomed boat always painted white with red trim. We rowed to the close point and picked up rocks, looked for minnows and puttered into the narrow channels until the boat's bottom was scraped raw and was no longer seaworthy. The S.S. Artusa then took pride of place as a flower garden beside the cottage porch

The SS Artusa at Long Beach in 1954 with Hugh, cousin Fred Payne, Diane and Pete. (Goodwillie)

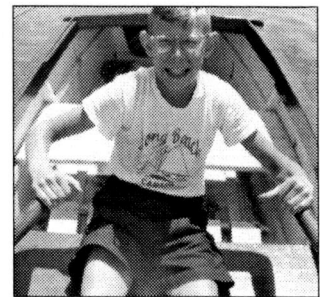
Hugh in his Long Beach t-shirt uses his muscles. (Goodwillie)

In the winter we skated on the farm pond sometimes but mostly we went across the road to Daboll's pond. It was a little bit larger except there were always some water holes along one edge so the cows could drink. We had to watch we didn't get into those holes for the pond was quite deep. Before we could skate, we always had to shovel off the snow and hope the ice had frozen nice and smooth.

There was many a fast and furious hockey game played there. Probably that is where Jack and Bill learned to be so proficient in hockey, or at least that is where they got their start.

Hockey on the farm pond

by Pete Goodwillie

Jack made a name for himself in Guelph College Hockey and played professional hockey with teams in London and Cleveland. In today's world he would have been drafted to play for the National Hockey League. (Toronto Hockey Hall of Fame, Fitzsimmons Coll;ection)

When Bill started as a goal tender, he used the old Eaton's catalogues as pads under his long stockings. This was not very satisfactory, so he decided to make his own pads as he could not afford new ones. Old 100 pound cotton sugar bags were cut and sewn in the shape of pads; then, two-inch ribbings were sewn lengthwise with the old foot pedal Singer sewing machine. The ribbings were then stuffed with horse-hair taken from an old horse collar in the barn. The pads were held in place by skate straps riveted to the sides. These pads were quite good and provided adequate protection for the many shooting sessions on Daboll's pond. Two pair of mitts and an extra sweater completed the goalie uniform. Face masks and helmets were never heard of in those days.

Curling in Welland

by Pete Goodwillie

Other Welland winter games are interesting to note. According to the Port Colborne News, in the 1870s the Canal became very important to local sportsmen. Horse-sled racing, a popular winter pastime from 1875-1890 took place on the frozen canal between the Junction and the old swing bridge where the ice could freeze as thick as 10 inches. In 1876, the canal became the site of the first curling match in Welland's history – some twenty-six years after the first curling club was established back in the town of Leslie, Scotland, the home of Goodwillie ancestors.

The Family Pest

There was one child who always had to sit on a corner where the guests could see little of him. His manners were terrible and he just would not improve. He had to be kept out of sight as much as possible. He was always on hand when the boys brought candy to the girls, and when snapshots were being taken guess who turned up in almost every picture? Yes, it was Jack (Donald Brock). The girls or their beaus tried to bribe him to get lost but with not much luck.

One night he hid behind the sofa, all was well until the candy was presented. That was too much for Jack. He made a quick appearance - and a quicker disappearance with his treat. The girls used to hide the candy, if they had any, but somehow or other it was always found. A box of candy didn't go very far with all of our crowd around and the girls rightly thought they were entitled to some at the very least.

Parties At The Farm

My Father always used to say that he didn't mind how many parties or people we invited to visit us just so long as we helped Mother before, and helped clean up afterwards. Consequently there was always a lot of company and a big party or two each winter.

Iva, Mary and Grace were in High School in town (Welland) and were at the party stage. They had lots of friends coming and going most of the time. When the girls went to dances in town they had to stay over night with friends and walk home the next morning. Everyone walked to the dances and the girls carried their dancing slippers in a bag on their arm and changed at the party.

Sleigh Rides and the Dance

One of the best parties from my point of view was the sleigh ride and dance. Father would send the two hired men and two teams into town for the boys and girls, really young men and women. The sleigh, an ordinary farm box-sleigh, would contain lots of clean hay or straw in the bottom and lots of heavy robes and horse blankets - smelly too sometimes, to keep the young people warm and cozy.

Everyone was dressed in their best and bundled into coats and scarves to keep warm. No one ever dreamed of wearing slacks or sweaters to a party in those days - even for a sleigh-ride party.

During those winters there was lots and lots of snow. Sometimes it was so deep and the main roads so full of snowdrifts that the teams would have to travel through the fields, driving right over fences and all.

Lots of snow in the old days meant good sleigh rides. This photo was taken in the 1930s. (Cornett)

After a good track had been made in the deep snow there would occasionally develop what we called 'pitch-holes'. These holes might be three or four feet deep, maybe between two big snowdrifts or where softer snow had been worn away. When the sleigh would hit these holes there would be a big jerk and everyone would be well shaken up. This only added to the fun.

Once in a while some of the boys would get off and run along side the sleigh to keep warm. There were times when there was an extra big snowbank and the sleigh would tip over sideways. There would then be a big scramble, snow down your neck and up your sleeves. Every one would pitch in to get the sleigh upright again and then on the way once more. No one was ever hurt.

It was a very slow way of travel but with the bells jingling merrily, usually a big round moon to light the way and all the nonsense going on it didn't seem to take half long enough to cover the two miles or more to the farm.

Finally they arrived. Everyone piled out of the sleigh and went into the house to get warm and tidied up ready to dance. The teams were stabled and blanketed and the drivers went to the kitchen to pass the time until the return journey had to be made.

During the day at the farm there had been great scurrying around. The dining-room furniture had all been moved into the kitchen, the chandeliers tied higher so no one would bump his head, and the hardwood floor waxed and a bit of cornmeal sprinkled on to make it very slippery.

The children loved that part for they had a great time sliding and getting the wax worked into the floor. The cornmeal would be swept off and all was ready for the dancing. It was a fairly large room and perhaps thirty or more could dance quite comfortably.

The piano had been moved from the oak parlor to the office doorway so the music would be close enough to hear. There were usually three musicians from town who had come with the crowd.

Piles of sandwiches had been made and carefully covered with damp napkins, jars of pickles were opened and ready and then there were the cakes - every kind you could think of. There were chocolate layer cakes, coconut layer cake, angel, sponge and spice cakes. We children could hardly wait. A big kettle was on the stove and filled with water and the coffee bags all filled and ready to be tossed into the pot. Stacks of plates, cups and so on were all ready for use.

Everything was out of its normal place for a party, and we were all so excited just to be on hand for it.

Soon the musicians took their places and the music was calling all the girls and boys, Father and Mother among them, to dance. At first the boys were slow in asking the girls to dance. They seemed to hate to get started but with a 'Paul Jones' to start and get them well mixed up they were soon all dancing and having a good time.

What is a Paul Jones dance?

from 'Ballroom Dancing' by Alex Moore (Sixth Ed.) www.dance-forums.com

The MC or Leader of the band announces 'Paul Jones' and the band then plays a bright tune such as 'Life on the Ocean Wave' or 'Here we come gathering nuts in May'. The dancers then form two large circles, the men on the inside and facing outwards, and the ladies on the outside and facing inwards, that is, towards the men.

With hands joined the two circles move to the right so that they are moving in opposite directions. When the music stops the man claims the lady directly in front of him and dances. The band should pause for a few seconds to permit the men to take their partners and then play a Waltz, Quickstep, Foxtrot, etc., or occasionally an 'Old Time' dance. After playing about one chorus of music, the band stops, the circle is formed as before, and continued as described above.

The girls looked so nice in pretty dresses with long skirts. And the boys were all in their Sunday best. Jack, Bill, Tim and I were only allowed as far as the kitchen. The drivers were there too so we talked to them and took turns peeking through the swing door into the dining-room to watch the festivities. Eventually of course we tired of that so sneaked a sandwich or two and went off to bed.

Father used to get annoyed with one of the boys. He stamped his feet so hard that the very house would shake, and Father was afraid he would mark the floor so badly it would never be nice afterwards. The dance went on until lunch was served about midnight, then more dancing, and then it was time to go home. It always seemed they had more fun after lunch than before if possible.

The drive back to town was quieter. Everyone was tired. The talk was quiet with a few giggles here and there. Probably a bit of love-making too if the truth was told.

After the crowd left for town those at the farm pitched in to get the dining-room reorganized. The dishes were washed and put away, the furniture moved back to normal and soon you would never have known there had been a party. Of course there were lots of yawns and dragging feet but life had to go on as usual the day after the party and yesterday's clean-up could not be left for the morrow.

A Surprise After the Party

After one of the parties when Mary and Grace went into their bedroom they got a real shock, thinking someone was in their bed. What do you think it was? The boys, who had put their overcoats in that room, had peeked into the clothes closet and found a pair of corsets - the real ones with lots of bone stays and all. They had stuffed them with a pillow, put a skirt on it and tucked it into the bed. Mary and Grace were so embarrassed. They had been in such a hurry getting dressed they hadn't properly put their clothes away and the boys had found them. They were always very careful after that to tidy their room and clothes closet. You never knew who was going to peek.

The next morning the party was really talked over who wore what, what did so and so say, who had a tiff with someone and so it went. It was almost like the party over again for us.

Halloween Party

There was one memorable Halloween party. It was an all girl party, each one coming in costume and masked as well. Each guest was directed by a ghost to an outside cellar door to the basement which was all in darkness. Down the cellar we had arranged a plank over a large pan of water, over which each had to walk. We splashed the water so they would think they were walking over a deep ditch.

One of the girls dressed in a fur coat and with an instrument in her hand which sounded exactly like a cow 'mooing' would then brush against each person. There was lots of squealing. By the time each one arrived and passed through all the hazards, all in pitch dark, and finally reached the light of an upstairs bedroom, by a dusty back stair route, there was lots of chattering. Everyone was in good spirits and ready for whatever should come next.

The party was held in the dining-room as usual, the furniture having been cleared out and the room decorated with imitation black spiders, nets, brooms dressed as ghosts, and lots of cornstalks and pumpkins. We played games and told spooky stories in the dark. When it was time for lunch each person was handed a bundle on a stick, hobo like, and all sat on the floor to eat. Everyone seemed to have a good time and we did too. I think half the fun of a party is getting ready for it and afterwards knowing that the guests had a good time, which makes it all worth while.

Other Parties at the Farm

No one in those days seemed to have birthday parties for children or anyone else. I only remember two birthday parties in all the years when we were young. One was for Tim and we all played football. Birthdays came and went and we just hoped we would be around for another next year.

There were lots of other parties too. The Women's Institute always had a card party each year at our house to raise money. Sometimes there would be twenty-four tables of euchre or five hundred. Twenty five cents each would be charged. If you had small children they came too, sometimes driving everyone crazy with their sliding down the banisters until too tired to keep awake any longer.

Usually once a winter we would have a square dance, orchestra caller and all, "alleman right on the corners all, and swing your partner across the hall". These were real lively parties.

Some sleet and snow storms allowed the neighbours to skate on the Goodwillie front lawn. (Cornett)

One year we had a toboggan party. We went to Fonthill for the afternoon then back to the Farm for a baked bean supper. Did it ever taste good.

Even the grandchildren had parties. Jean had a dance with the room all decorated with streamers and such, and Pete was the Master of Ceremonies as it were.

Mother and Father were so good and never anything too much trouble. I think, or know, they enjoyed the fun as much as we did.

One winter there was a very heavy sleet storm. It froze so hard on top of the snow that we had an impromptu skating party on the front lawn. That was different, and all the neighbors were on hand for the fun, with wieners and coffee afterwards.

I can't begin to tell you of all the different parties. Incidentally of course there were never any cocktails. One sniff of liquor on anyone's breath and out they went. This was the same for public or high school dances. It just wasn't done in the best society. We had great times too.

Picnics

Family picnics either to Port Dalhousie (on Lake Ontario) or to Port Colborne and Crystal Beach (on Lake Erie) were highlights. Someone

This Democrat Wagon c 1906 is being sold for US$5,500.00 by the Montana Driving School as advertised in 2005 on the web.

would drive the family in the wagon to the N.S. and T stop 17 station[48] about a mile up the road. The cars had hard wooden seats, open sides and a long running board on each side to allow passengers easy access to their seats. There was a special picnic car. The trip took about forty minutes to either lake beach. Picnic baskets were loaded with food; watermelons and ice cream were the special treats for the children.

It was nothing for Father to hitch Sox to the carriage on a Sunday and drive fourteen miles to Niagara Falls for a picnic - to entertain the company. Can you guess what a slow trip that must have been? The picnic basket would have contained fried chicken, salads, cakes and pies, so that the women had been busy too. Hot water could be obtained at the picnic park usually.

The Farmer's Picnic at Crystal Beach was the most important of the year. In the early days, the family travelled on the Grand Trunk Railway but later they arrived by horse-drawn vans and still later in the factory Packard truck or the 1912 McLaughlin Buick touring. The roller-skating, the merry-go-round, the Ferris wheel, the miniature train, the roller coaster and all the other entertainments made for great excitement.

The Sunday School Picnic

As there wasn't a Church for many miles and many of the children were missing out on Sunday School, Mother and Mr. & Mrs. Wilson and some of the other neighbors got together and organized one.

Our Sunday School was not in a Church but in our little one-room red school house. The same school house that we attended every day during the week. We learned our bible verses for Sunday and had our classes and sang the hymns and received our Sunday School papers. In the summer we had 'The Picnic'. At Christmas time there was the Sunday School concert. These were local social events of high quality for the surrounding community. What a picnic we had. All the neighbours went to the Sunday School so all the neighbours went to the picnic. All work ceased and men and women took the day off. It was usually held in the good hot weather just after the haying was finished and before time to cut the grain.

The main idea of the picnic of course was going to a lake so sometimes it was held at Port Dalhousie and sometimes at Port Colborne. We lived about the same distance from each lake.

When we went to Port Dalhousie the men usually made arrangements with the Sunday Schools in town. They all got together and hired the street cars to take everyone at the same time. The day I remember best was beautiful. We were to board the cars at the top of the road a mile or so distant, Stop 17.

The street cars were open in those days with benches running from side to side and a step all along the full length of each car on the outside. When it rained it was a bit uncomfortable or even if the wind blew too hard it was not too pleasant but who thought of that? We were on our way to a picnic and a bath in the lake a real event for all.

Since there were many baskets of food Father said he would take them separately in the democrat wagon for there was not enough room in the van for all the neighbors, ourselves and the food too. Father didn't go to the picnic, just to the station. He piled the baskets in the wagon, hitched 'Dick' and went on his way.

Now we were in the big van ahead when suddenly we saw that 'Dick' got scared of something and had started to run away. The wagon was swaying from side to side and almost went into the ditch, first one side and then the other. We just hoped it wouldn't upset. Father was frantically trying to keep the wagon upright and to stop the frightened horse. This he finally did and we drew a breath of relief.

What a catastrophe if that wagon had upset and spilled the food all over the place. A picnic without food wouldn't be much of a picnic at all. I don't suppose we even worried what happened to Father.

Those baskets must have been well packed for not too much spilled out. Father gathered them together and finally got to the street cars in time for us to be on our way. It was a poor start for the day but the rest turned out better.

We arrived at Port Dalhousie safely about noon, a long journey for us. We laughed at nothing and sang most all the way down. On arrival we made a great rush to see the water. Was it rough or smooth? It was smooth, lucky for us we could go in swimming. Of course we couldn't swim but it sounded big.

Did we have time to go in before dinner? 'No'. Well, then the next thing to do was explore the place and the canal, with a large passenger steamer just coming from Toronto. How wonderful it would be to have a ride on that ship. We would go out on the long pier, which extended into the lake, and watch the ship sail out again, until out of sight. If we were lucky a freighter might also arrive or depart. The canal was not as busy in those days as it is now.

There were a few stores not far away, a merry-go-round, some swings, and in the afternoon the dance hall would be in full swing, especially if there were enough older folk on hand to warrant the band playing.

Before we knew it, it was time to eat. What food, not a few sandwiches and a banana. There were platters of cold fried chicken, sliced ham, gloriously pink, pots of baked beans, sliced tomatoes, potato or cabbage salads, deviled eggs, pickles, cakes and pies to defy the imagination and to cap it all, Watermelon and Ice-Cream. Who could eat all that, and who would ever think of a sandwich or bread and butter. It would be such a waste of good stomach space. The tables were really laden with not a single square inch of empty space.

When I think of it now, I wonder if our mothers did enjoy a picnic very much for they must have been working days to get so much food ready, probably cooking and baking with a wood cook-stove too. It was a real children's day in my opinion. Probably the women had a good time while visiting together though and if the children were happy the mothers were too.

When everyone had eaten as much as could be stuffed down and the baskets repacked with the remnants of food there were some games to be played. Who could run after eating so much? However we couldn't go in the water for at least two hours so we might as well try the games. There were prizes for everyone, win or lose.

There were the usual three-legged races, wheelbarrow races, jumping and running races, and so on. When the older folk entered it was fun to watch as well. We rented a bathing house, a big deal at fifteen cents. It was about as big as a telephone booth. There was one hook or nail on which to hang your clothes and a bench or plank to sit on. It was sort of smelly too and damp but where else could one undress and get into that bathing outfit of dress, stockings and cap?

Of course all the girls wore stockings, and some lucky ones even had bathing shoes. We were well covered up. The dress was always to the knees and at most times below them. I don't know how well we could have done any real swimming but we only bobbed up and down in the water and squealed and paddled about. We stayed in as long as we could. We would be about blue with cold but we had to make the most of it. It would maybe our one and only time all summer to be in the lake. Oh we had fun at the farm and sometimes Jack or Bill or Tim or Pete would paddle in a pond - but a lake happened just once a year.

Soon it was time to go home. Everyone had a quick snack out of the noon leftovers. The baskets were repacked, the children rounded up and given a quick slick up and the day was about ended. We trailed to the streetcars very reluctantly, scrambled to get an outside seat if possible and then were off on the return journey. There was not quite so much noise and merry making as on the trip to the picnic. Everyone was tuckered out and tired. The small children went to sleep and the parents talked quietly among themselves. We kids fooled a while but when we finally reached our stop to get off we were mighty glad to see Father there with the team and van to pick us up and go home. We were a dirty tired crowd but had had a wonderful day.

Chores Around the Farm

As we got older we had lots of jobs to do. The worst task, as mentioned earlier, was pumping. This included pumping the water to the tank upstairs during the summer if the water was low and also pumping water out of the cellar in the spring when the cistern happened to overflow. I think it must have developed lots of muscle. As we got old enough we each took our turns at these jobs and we all breathed a sigh of relief when they were done.

It seemed to me in those days, that washing dishes was a monumental task for there were always fourteen or more for every meal as well as additional company most of the time. It seems as I think of it, that Grandma and I spent a lot of time doing those dishes but she used to say 'I don't mind dishes at all.' I thought she was crazy to like doing dishes. I used to complain most heartily on Sunday nights especially, but Grandma used to say 'never mind, someone will do them when you have a beau'. But by that time, I'd forgotten all about it. I don't suppose I did the dishes any oftener that anyone else, it just seemed so since I was the youngest girl and not occupied with a beau.

Sometimes I'd get out of the dishes by practicing my music lesson. To tell the truth I don't know which was worse. You see Sunday nights Iva, Mary and Grace had their boy friends to supper. Quite often there would be two "sittings" there would be so many on hand to be fed. We didn't like to have to wait but there was no alternative. I can still see those luscious cakes, piled high with whipped cream and sprinkled generously with coconut.

The boys took the cows to pasture each morning during the Spring and Fall and fetched them back again at night. It didn't matter, rain or sun it had to be done.

Washing Clothes, Milking and Other Chores

In addition to bookkeeping, one of her (Iva's) weekly chores was to attend to the old wooden rocker washing machine. The clothes had to be soaked overnight and boiled up in the big copper kettle the next morning before being transferred to the rocker washer. They were then wrung out by hand and hung on the clothesline stretched from the house to the barn, summer and winter. Iva contended that when she got married, her father was forced to purchase a new electric machine to replace her.

Mary was more like her mother than the other girls. She was always a tease with a wry sense of humour. She always seemed to be in the centre of some hilarious joke or prank, although in later years, her conservative approach to life was reflected in a dry sense of humour and more subtle witticisms. As a girl, she shared the demanding work of the factory and farm, helping in the cook room, tying & cutting grapes, helping to turn butter in the old wooden barrel-like churn, now an antique in its own right.

The hired men usually did most of the milking though Iva, Mary, Grace and Tim did their share. About all I ever had to do was hold the cow's tail while Mary or Grace milked, or shoo the flies. There was one rather mean cow that Mary hated to milk. It kicked a lot and she was dead scared of it. She used to take a box sit the pail on it and if the cow kicked of course the pail flew but Mary was safe.

The Goodwillie girls with their boyfriends visit the horse trough. (Goodwillie family)

Mary never liked horses too well either. One morning she was coaxed into trying to learn to ride horseback. She was no more up on the horse's back than she slid off over his tail. That was her last attempt to ride. She could hitch the horse and drive - but no riding thank you.

There was lots of grumbling at times and finagling to see who got out of the job but there was lots of fun doing it too. It was a leisurely sort of business for the cows must not be made to run, no matter how big a hurry to get playing ball or other pastime.

The Power of Fire

There seems to have been a lot of very bad thunderstorms in those days but perhaps they seemed worse in the country. We were always terrified of fire at the farm for there really was not much protection and there were so many farm buildings and factory buildings to be concerned about. There were a few close calls but fortunately never anything serious.

Once there was a grass fire that licked up the back of the 'tower' at the factory but this was noticed in time and quickly put out. But it was a scare and blackened shingles on the outside of the tower wall were a permanent reminder.

If a storm happened at night everyone got out of bed, dressed and came downstairs to wait it out. There were some queer costumes at times and a lot of sleepy looking folk.

There were a couple of neighborhood fires. The first one was on a summer afternoon half a mile or so down the road, at Gainers. At the call of our bell all the hands from the factory and neighbors rushed down to help. The house was ablaze and furniture was being carried outside.

There was one memorable incident. Gainers had a large sideboard in the dining-room, full of dishes. Iva and Mary carried the whole thing outdoors. After the fire they went to carry it back inside and couldn't budge it - shows what excitement will do.

Another time the Hutton place, where the Cyopik family was living, burned to the ground. It was at night and made a big blaze. Edna Rosewell and I were up on the top of our house with pails of water to douse sparks as they flew over (About 1926).

The whole Cyopik family was at our place until next day when other arrangements were made for them. The very first fire was on July 17, 1894. The original drive-shed burned down. Father was sure it was a case of arson and had a good idea who did it but didn't do anything about it. There was a load of fruit ready to take to market the next morning and it was tied fast so it couldn't be pulled from the burning shed.

Iva was a baby at the time and I've often heard Mother tell how she ran across the road in her bare feet and nightgown to put Iva in the neighbour's care. The shed was quite close to the house and it was a miracle the house was saved.

A couple of days after George and Iva's wedding there was a terrible thunder storm which knocked out the lights and a chandelier or two. A transformer 50 yards away had been hit by lightning. Father was terrified some of the buildings might have been struck but all was well. Everyone was concerned too about all those cut-glass and silver presents displayed in the back parlor.

Pete's story of a thunderstorm on the farm

The night of the severe thunderstorm which resulted in the transformer being struck on the pole just a few yards from the house was a real nightmare. We (Bill and I) were sleeping on the porch next to our parents' room when the storm came almost without warning, a tremendous flash of lightning and a deafening roar of thunder simultaneously reverberated through the house. The lightning hit the transformer which flared up with fire, sparks, and smoke and the fire seemed to literally flash through the house followed by dense smoke. We were all sure the house had been struck.

Father and Mother leaped out of the bed and ran through the house, inside and out, while we remained stunned and unable to comprehend what had happened. Fortunately while there was plenty of evidence of charred wires, and lots of smoke, no actual fire resulted.

From then on I always had deep respect and fear of thunderstorms, especially during the night. As a matter of fact, during a night storm from then on, everyone in the house always got up, got fully dressed, lit candles or oil lamps and remained tense and alert until the storm passed. Sometimes the storm would return two or three times but each time, although dozy and sleepy, we always went through the same procedure.

Seasons

Each season brought its interest. There were violets to be picked in the Spring, wild strawberries looked for in June and later green apples to picked, and eaten; sometimes just plain kicking your bare toes in the dust or mud. Most of the summer the boys went barefoot if they wanted to.

When the ditches were flooded in the Spring that was a time for floating boats of twigs or leaves down the rushing waters. It made for tricky walking as well, then we could wear high rubber boots - never high enough to keep our feet from getting wet though.

Walnuts, Hickory Nuts and Chestnuts

On the farm were a few hickory nut trees, one black walnut tree and one chestnut tree. The latter didn't have many nuts but they were always religiously searched for and enjoyed. We always had to pick them before the town people found them first.

After the first frost in the Fall we used to go hunting nuts. We really looked for sweet chestnuts and had our favorite spots in which to look, Merritt's woods being the best. We would walk miles, scuffing through the woods looking for the telltale burrs lying on the ground. Wherever there were burrs, some nuts were bound to be scattered nearby. We rarely found more than a cupful but what we found we highly prized. It was just great to be out in the good Fall sunshine and scuffing through the woods.

Farmers are urged to grow native chestnuts in 2005. (Ontario Ministry of Agriculture and Foods)

If we came across hickory nut trees of course we gathered those nuts too but we had a hickory nut tree ourselves so didn't really mind not finding them. Once in a while we would be chased as we were trespassing but usually we just looked in any woods, which seemed to be fair game for whoever would take the time to look for the nuts.

The native sweet chestnut trees are all gone having been killed by a blight.[49] It is too bad for those nuts were delicious, either to eat as we picked them up or taken home and boiled or roasted on the top of the stove or at the fireplace. If they hadn't been pricked before roasting they might explode and fly every which way.

The sweet chestnuts looked sort of like the horse chestnuts you pick up but they were small, about the size of my thimble. The burr in which they grew was covered with very fine prickles and about three inches in diameter. After a good frost the burr would split open and the nuts, three to a burr, would scatter on the ground. Horse chestnuts have burrs too but they are fat and thick, and not nearly so prickly.

Shucking and eating nuts –

by Jane Goodwillie Allen

Dad (Pete Goodwillie) loved his nuts! Every fall we would gather walnuts, hickory nuts and sometimes butternuts. In my early years we would get them from Uncle Jack Ferguson's farm (from my mother's Payne relatives near St. Thomas). Later these were collected from Walnut Hill and other places around the Long Beach cottage. At the

Toronto house (approximately 1965, 11 Ashwood Drive) Dad would keep his stash of nuts in the basement furnace room. It was always such a chore to husk the walnuts. He would dry the nuts for a while and then put on his overalls and gloves to take the green husks off the nuts.

Often Dad and I would go downstairs after dinner and play some ping pong which ultimately led to a nut cracking, picking and finally an eating snack. In the later years it was more difficult to find the hickory nut trees. He may have even gone back to Welland or the Welland market to get these nuts.

His grandchildren, especially Jon and then Brian would disappear to the cottage shed and you could hear the nuts being cracked and fat Canadian walnuts being eaten. I recall a time at the cottage when he worked so hard in the fall to husk the nuts. He left them in the shed over the winter to dry. When he returned the following spring he found that the squirrels had enjoyed a wonderful winter feast and taken all of his walnuts.

Cutting Ice

We are so used to all the modern appliances that refrigerators are just taken for granted. What did they do many years ago? How did they keep food from spoiling in the hot summer months? I'll try to tell you.

In the real Olden Days most everyone had a good cellar - the bare ground pounded hard with use. It was really almost as hard as cement and was carefully swept and kept clean and tidy. The cellar was pitch dark and very cool even on the hottest day. Sometimes there would be an entrance from the outside but mostly you entered by a trap door from the kitchen or pantry above. The cellar usually had a lot of shelves and perhaps an old table. Sometimes butter or cream would be put in a big crock or can and lowered carefully into the well. This method was very good on very hot days but a real nuisance too.

At the farm we eventually had a big ice house. It had to store enough ice for the factory and the house as well. It was quite a big building. It was built of timber and the sides were about a foot thick, hollow and filled with sawdust. You see the sawdust acted as insulation. Father had a sawmill at this time so there was no problem getting any amount of sawdust which was used between the layers of ice as well, to keep them from freezing into one huge block.

At the factory there was a big cooler with sides about two feet thick and dark as a dungeon. All across the top was a place to put the ice. The cooler was large enough to store one hundred crates or more of fruit until it could be duly processed, perhaps a day or two in the busy season. This cooler would take a lot of ice so there had to be a large amount available.

During those long ago winters I am sure we had colder weather than we have today. The cold lasted longer too. Once the snow and cold weather began, long before Christmas, it never let up until maybe the last of March or first of April. The ice in the ponds canals and rivers just keep getting thicker and thicker until perhaps about February it would be fourteen inches or two feet thick. Then the ice-cutting would begin.

We got the ice from Reuter's pond that was about a mile or so from the farm. It was sort of an off-shoot from the canal. The water was clear as crystal and deep so it was perfect for ice-cutting. This water

Sometimes donkeys were used to pull the wagons or sleighs. (Cornett)

was so good that during the summer we never hesitated to put it in a big pitcher of drinking water.

It took about two weeks of good weather to get the ice-house filled to the roof. The hired men would take long saws which were loaded along with huge ice tongs onto the bobsleighs. The teams were hitched to the sleighs, and off they would go to the pond.

The men would saw ice all day, cutting it into great blocks about two feet square. Up and down the saws would go, a fine 'zing' whining through the clear cold air, until finally a big block of ice would float free. Another and another block would be cut until finally there would be enough for a load. When enough blocks had been cut the men would take the big ice tongs and pull the blocks out of the cold water and slide them onto the sleighs, then head for home and the ice house. It was a hard, wet job and all done by hand.

When arriving at the ice-house the ice was unloaded block by block and put in layers with lots of sawdust between. I don't know how many loads it took to fill the ice-house to the top but there were many days of hard work and several teams going back and forth every day.

Sometimes after school or on Saturdays we would tag along for a ride on the sleighs. We thought it lots of fun to jump on and off as the sleighs were moving. The loads were heavy and the teams had to pull for all they were worth. Needless to say they didn't travel very fast. With the bells jingling merrily, the men laughing and teasing us and we running and jumping off and on to keep warm we used to have a very good time.

Usually one trip was all we needed. While waiting for enough blocks to be cut we would maybe skate a little, while keeping well away from that yawing black hole of water from which the ice was being dragged. We were glad to get back to the house, pull off our heavy boots and clothing to get warm again.

It was on one of these jaunts that Harold got his nickname which stuck all his life. The men started to call him 'Timothy Tickle Britches' and from then on Harold Hiram was called 'Tim'.

The ice now stored would last all summer, and until time to cut more. When it came time to be used it would be washed off before being taken into the house or cooler.

Father had an ice-box specially made for the house. There were about eight shelves, wide enough to accommodate the many milk pans, and perhaps five feet long. It was lined between the walls with cork for insulation. The ice was put in a separate compartment at the top. About twice a week, or oftener, the ice-box was filled and that kept milk and other foods very well indeed.

Making Ice Cream

In the summer or on special occasions Mother would make ice-cream the old-fashioned way. She would make a cooked custard, add lots of good rich cream and then put it into the ice-cream freezer. This would be packed around with chipped ice and salt and then one of us would turn the crank. We would turn and turn until finally it would hardly turn at all which was a sure sign the ice-cream was ready to take out. The can would be opened, the dasher removed - and licked by the lucky person helping, then the can would be re-closed and repacked with ice and salt to finish the hardening. This was the best ice-cream imaginable and a far cry from the stuff we buy these days.

One Christmas Jack thought he would add a lot of cherries and make it extra special. He knew all about making it for he had been to Agricultural College [the University of Guelph]. Much to his disgust the cherries were all at the bottom of the can. He took a lot of razzing about knowing how to make ice-cream.

He also had the ideal way to pull the tendons from a turkey: 'put the turkey's feet in the hinge side of a door, close the door partly and pull on the turkey'. However, sad to say, nothing happened!

Well in those days there was a lot of work involved in having some of the nice things of life - like ice. We take for granted our nice shiny refrigerators and deep freezers, maybe in a few years from now we will look back and find they are a thing of the past too.

Courting and Marriages

When George was courting Iva in the summer, he would come by canoe either from Welland or Port Robinson. He would park the canoe at the foot of the road and walk up to the house, a half mile or so. Going canoeing was a very popular pastime in the early 1900s.

Since there wasn't too much privacy around Iva and George would usually go for a walk, weather permitting, down the back lanes. Father was a great tease and used to ask Iva if they were "going to salt the cows". She was very embarrassed and got real annoyed.

At the time before I knew they were engaged, I apparently thought George was coming pretty often. I kept a record of when he came and how often. Iva didn't like that much either but Mother and Dad just laughed. And they did get married in spite of all the teasing.

Marriage at the Farm- Iva's Wedding

Iva and George had a lovely wedding at the farm. Truck loads of hydrangea were brought from the nurseries to decorate the front parlor and to make a bridal bower for the ceremony in the bay window. That was quite an affair, more that a hundred guests, and everything done at home. There were piles of chicken salad and pounds of salted almonds and ice-cream with water ice in the

On the 6th of September, 1916, Iva the eldest Goodwillie married George Secord from Port Robinson whose family lived in a house called the 'Castle' because of its imposing appearance on the south side of the Welland River. (Cornett)[50]

centre. Hugh [Bill] called this cheese and was not having any of that stuff in his ice-cream. The dining-room was set with small tables and all in all it was a big event in our lives with lots of excitement in every direction.

Bank Manager's Quarters

George was the manager of the Imperial Bank branch at Fonthill. After the wedding, George and Iva moved to the apartment above the bank where there was a trapdoor in the bedroom right over the bank vault below. And a handgun was kept nearby to deter any possible bank holdups. Fortunately, they never had to use it.

ONE OF THE MOST interesting weddings of the season was that which took place at three o'clock on Wednesday afternoon at The Hedges, Quaker Road, at the beautiful home of Mr. and Mrs. John Goodwillie when their oldest daughter, Iva Kathleen, became the bride of George Harry Secord, manager of the Imperial Bank, Fonthill, son of Mr. and Mrs. William Secord of Toronto.

The ceremony was performed under an arch of hydrangea and fern, by the Rev. G.K. Bradshaw, pastor of the Welland Methodist Church. The bridal party entered the drawing room while Miss Blanche Secord, sister of the groom, played the wedding march. The bride, who was given away by her father, wore white crepe de chine with taffeta, georgette crepe and veil with pearl trimmings. She carried a shower bouquet of lilies of the valley and roses. The bridesmaid was Miss Mary Goodwillie, who wore roses brocaded crepe de chene and carried sunset roses. Albert White performed the duties of best man. Six bearers of rope of flowers formed the aisle down which the wedding party passed.

September 1916 – Newspaper report of the wedding

CHAPTER SEVEN

Horses, Cars and Roads

Stories written by Ruth Goodwillie Cornett with additions from J.R. 'Pete' Goodwillie and Jane Goodwillie Allen

The Drive Shed at the Farm

A drive-house was at one side of the house on the far side of the driveway. It had an upstairs for storing baskets and odds and ends. In the lower part the cutter, a top buggy, a two-seated carriage nicely upholstered in tan linen and a two seated sleigh called the Gladstone, were kept. The back seat of the Gladstone could either face the front or be flipped over to face the back as well. With a big fur robe tucked around us it was the height of luxury on a cold day. I was always afraid we might hit a pitch-hole and we would go flying off into space, when facing the back, so hung on for dear life. Of course it never happened so one more thing to fuss about needlessly.

Then there was a rubber-tired buggy. It had a very high seat with a bright red stripe around the back, was well upholstered but had no top. It was quite an elegant equipage. When the car took its place, the grandchildren used to pull it up and down the driveway. Each one took his turn being the horse but it seemed as though little Jack (Northcote) was usually

The Gladstone sleigh. (Cornett)

Bill on a carefully groomed horse in front of the drive shed. (Goodwillie family)

the 'horse' most often. It was very light and easy to pull and when sitting up on the high seat was quite exciting for a small child.

There were special cupboards built in one end of the drive house in which all the good shiny harness was stored. This harness was always kept very carefully and all the brasses well polished. It was used on special occasions and when Father showed his horses at the County Fair, which was usually every year. When the horses were combed and brushed, their manes braided with bright ribbons, the harness gleaming, they looked gorgeous. They took many prizes at the Fair.

Father was a good horseman and rightfully proud of his stock. He usually had three to five teams of horses in the barn as well as a driving horse. When he needed to buy a new team of horses he and Mr. Dave Secord, a veterinarian, would drive by sleigh or buggy to Cayuga, Fisherville or Norwich to look at prospects. When they found a well matched pair, they would bring them home with them. A good team used to cost about three hundred and seventy five dollars in the year 1899 and according to a diary Father kept off and on. A team cost over five hundred dollars in 1907.

Gyp – Runaway Racing Horse

Iva and Mary always played together, and usually got into mischief. They were about five and three years old respectively when Father sent the two girls down the road to a neighbor's place on an errand. It was long before anyone had a telephone you see, so small fry were usually sent on any number of errands for the grown-ups.

When the girls got to neighbour Bill's (Bill Bailey) he was nowhere to be seen. But standing in the front yard was the horse from the farm, hitched to a light democrat wagon and just waiting to go some place.

A democrat wagon has a long box on the back and a high seat in front. The farmers used it for light loads, such as taking bags of grain to the mill to be ground into flour or feed and collecting baskets of apples or grapes from the garden and so on. I guess today the farmer would use a half-ton truck or such in its place. They are very scarce around here nowadays.

Bill was nowhere in sight and the two children, being impatient to get back home to their play had an idea. No doubt it was Iva's idea and Mary, being the younger of the two, just went along with it. I must admit Mary wouldn't have been too reluctant at that.

Iva said 'Let's drive the horse'. Without a second thought they climbed into the wagon, got up on the seat, picked up the driving reins which had been twined around the whip, and in a loud clear voice said 'Giddap Gyp'.

Now Gyp was a very intelligent horse, smart, full of pep and loved to race. Lots of times Father would race Gyp at the Country Fair, or just a friendly race along the road. Gyp would really go pretty fast and with his training of course did his best not to let any other horse pass him. When Iva said 'Giddap', Gyp a sort of looked around at her and then slowly started out of the lane and up the road.

I think he knew that she shouldn't be driving and that Bill wasn't there; however Gyp was a horse and used to doing as he was told. When Iva gave the reins another smart slap so they hit his back, he started to trot.

This was not fast enough for the girls so Iva gave another and another slap of the reins and yelled "Giddap, Giddap" at the top of her voice so Gyp got the message and really started to gallop. They went flying up the road.

By this Mary was pretty scared and just hung on for dear life. This was a little more than she had bargained for. In the meantime, just as the girls were getting under way, Bill came out of his house and saw what was happening.

He called to the girls to 'stop' but it was too late. Gyp was really getting under way and both girls were having a glorious time, or rather Iva was, Mary was too scared. Poor Bill, he didn't know what to do. He started to run after them but soon realized that would be hopeless. He would never be able to catch Gyp.

He hurried back to the barn and got another horse, jumped on its back and started to give chase. He thought, 'I can soon catch them for my horse hasn't a wagon to pull'. He had forgotten that Gyp wouldn't let another horse pass him if he could help it, so the race was on.

The girls had been wearing wide straw hats but they soon flew off. The dust from the road rose in a cloud as they went faster and faster. Gyp was really enjoying this game. As the horse came to the home lane he slowed down and tried to turn in, he knew it was home. However Iva would have none of that, this was too much fun. She gave Gyp another smart slap and off they went at a full clip again.

As soon as Bill would get close to the wagon Gyp would put on an extra spurt of speed and run faster. Of course the girls yelling and Iva slapping the reins didn't induce the poor horse to slow down at all. Finally Bill got close enough that he could talk to the girls and promise them some candy. They had driven more that two miles before Bill finally persuaded Iva to stop the horse. I think Gyp sensed that all was not well and it also suited him to call the race off.

Iva and Mary were full of glee - and dust, and just a bit frightened too. They thought that was the best ride they'd ever had but now their fun was short lived. Bill took them home and Father took over.

What do you suppose happened? Yes, a whipping was in order and they were sent to bed without their supper. Bill was also more careful to see that the girls were not around when next he had Gyp hitched and had to leave him for a few minutes.

SOX – the Handsome and Smart Horse

Sox, Father's driving horse, was given that name because he had four white feet that looked as though he had on white socks. Father loved horse racing and when not too busy in the summer he would take an afternoon off and go to the races.

Father was always very proud of all those horses that he had at the farm, sometimes as many as five beautiful matched teams and he was always sure to have a good driving horse for the carriage or buggy. He saw to it that they were well taken care of. Good teams well matched in looks and size were hard to find and very expensive.

Sunday mornings during the nice weather the horses, one or two at a time, were always brought outside and brushed, curried and cleaned after their past week of work. Their coats gleamed after the good brushing and they always seemed to be very proud of themselves when the job was finished.

John Allan loved racing and Sox knew he was the best looking horse around. (Goodwillie)

We had several wagons of various types, besides lumber wagons, bobsleds etc. There was a one-seated wagon with rubber tires and a red band across the back of the seat, quite a swish affair in those days. Then there was a two-seated upholstered carriage used a lot for going to Quaker Church. [most likely just south of Ridgeville[51]]. It was a black buggy with a top which would go up or down, and a plain democrat wagon which had two hard seats, one of which could be removed and the wagon used for light loads, a strictly every-day affair. These wagons were used with the driving horse only. One or another was used almost daily.

There was also everyday harness for the horses and a 'good' harness which had a lot of brass to be polished and kept in good repair. The good harness was used for special occasions and dress up, showing at the County Fair and so on.

There was a little removable seat sometimes put in front of the dashboard to make extra room for a couple of small children in the buggy. We sat with our backs to the horse and many a flick of the horses tail did we get. However if we wanted to ride we had to put up with it without a murmur, or stay at home.

Sox was a very proud animal, he just seemed to know he was extra special. When he was hitched to the rubber-tired buggy he would hold his head high, lift his feet daintily and in general seemed to draw attention to himself – 'look, I'm Sox, admire me.'

When he was hitched to the democrat, a mediocre conveyance and not always free from dust or mud, the horse just sort of slumped along, dragged his feet, drooped his head as much as he could and tried to say: 'I'm not dressed up, don't look at me.' Our High School Principal once said he thought Sox saw himself in the store windows and 'strutted' when he was dressed up.

Everyone in town knew Sox, and at the County Fair sometimes Dad would enter in the races just for fun. He often won too. These were sulky races or as they were called at that time 'bikes'.

Frightening Donkeys and Mad Dogs

Sox was terrified of two donkeys that lived about a mile down the road along the canal. These donkeys were cute little fellows about three feet high and wouldn't hurt a fly. Their owners used to hitch them to a stone boat, a sort of sled for hauling wood etc but most of the time it seemed as though those donkeys were just rambling around loose along the canal bank.

When we wanted to drive to Port Robinson we were never sure we wouldn't see those animals. Sox would lay his ears back, shy away and squat and then take off as though being chased by fiends. With the canal on one side of the narrow road and a deep ditch on the other I was always scared to bits but no harm ever came from these antics.

One time Sox was stolen. Everyone felt badly and the whole countryside was searched frantically to find him. Everyone in town was alerted but not a sign of him.

One day after about a week when finding Sox was thought to be about hopeless, Father was driving across a bridge several miles from home. He thought he heard he heard a whinny from below the bridge. He was startled and got out of the buggy to investigate. Sure enough, there was Sox tied up out of sight below the bridge abutment.

Sox had recognized something about Father, or maybe just hopefully wished someone would find him and he let it be known where he was. There was great rejoicing when he got back home safely, thinner but unhurt. The thief was never found.

Another time, Grace and I had driven some factory hands home after work. We were on our way home. We came to a culvert and do you think Sox would cross it? No Sir!

We had to turn around as best we could and drive another four miles or so to get home. We were very late getting home and everyone was wondering where we were. Grace was especially angry at the extra trip. It didn't bother me for I was just along for the ride.

We found out later there had been a mad dog running back and forth in the culvert. Sox wouldn't cross for fear of drawing attention to himself - and us. We forgave him for giving us the extra drive.

Sox had many excursions and lived a good life. He came home from a short drive one evening, was taken ill and in spite of every care he didn't get better. These things happen on a farm where there are lots of animals and one seems to get, well, not used to it, but learn to take it as part of life. Sox was sorely missed but soon 'Dick' took his place.

Dick – the Faithful Horse

There was a Victoria Day Holiday [24th May] when we were about ten or so. Mother let us hitch Dick, the current driving horse, to the two-seated carriage. Jack, Bill, Edith, a neighbor, and I drove about five miles to the River where we had a picnic.

We tied the horse to a tree well away from a railway trestle going over the river at that point, and then we got out our fishing tackle. There was nothing fancy about it: a pole cut from a tree, with a string with a fish hook on the end, oh yes, a cork for a bobbin to tell if we had a 'bite' and a lead washer for a sinker.

We fished and fished but all day only caught one sizeable fish and it was not one fit to eat. Not having much luck at fishing we decided to go home again. We didn't any of us know too much about driving but we managed all right and got home safely. There wasn't much traffic, perhaps we drove there and back without meeting more than a buggy or two. The roads were dry

Pete Goodwillie on Old Dick in 1925. (Cornett)

and dusty, no pavement. All in all it was a very leisurely drive and we did pay attention to what we were doing during the trip. Dick was a frisky horse but when we were driving he always minded his manners. Probably felt he knew more than we did.

Old Dick to the rescue

by Jane Goodwillie Allen

Pete Goodwillie stories could go on for an hour but he always kept you interested. The story of Old Dick changed over the years, so I'm not sure how much of it is true. The new generation of Goodwillie grandchildren heard an updated version of the Old Dick story that I heard when I was a tot.

Old Dick was a big old work horse that was too old for work around the farm. The Goodwillie kids would ride Old Dick to the Quaker Road school house and on the way you had to be sure to go 'up hill easy, down hill slow and on the level ground Suzie let her go': [Stories were often told with Dad on his back and child sitting on his knees, pretending to ride old Dick as he clomped slowly or took off at a trot.]

The Old Dick story that I liked the best was when this old horse saved the day. One spring day, some children were playing across the road at the edge of a pond when a little boy suddenly fell in a hole and was drowning. Water holes for the cows were found around the pond. Dad ran to get some rope and Old Dick. They tied the rope around the boy and Old Dick pulled the boy out of the pond and saved his life.

Charlie's horse and Pete's first summer job

by Pete Goodwillie

A humorous incident stands out in my memory which occurred in the summer of 1927 [at age 17]. This was the time of great activity around Welland due to the deepening of the Welland Canal, the rebuilding of the aqueduct and the straightening out of the canal through the 'island' at the foot of Quaker and Thorold Rd. and the installation of lift bridges to replace the old hand-operated swing bridges. Jobs were quite plentiful and I was determined not to 'stay on the farm and do nothing' - meaning make no money. I had heard Jack Ostrander [Ossie] had gotten a job over on the Island and I figured I could get one too. So one day late in June or early July I walked over to the canal to get a ride across on the rowboat and headed for the center of activity.

In those days mule teams, scrapers and dumpers and wagons did most of the digging. I recall seeing Ossie drawing a team of mules with one of these scraper dumpers in the area they were rapidly digging out with mule power. I don't recall seeing any bulldozers or tractors or mechanical dirt movers. Actually, most of the dirt was removed by suction dredge (Canada Dredge and others) and a huge dyke system filled behind Reuters and just west of the old canal. I remember during that summer and the next two summers hearing the constant hum and noises from the activity on the island and the pile-driving at the aqueduct.

Anyway, there was no job to be had at the mule-driving area and I was told to go down to the east side of the canal and see a man where the scow was moored. Sure enough I was quickly looked over with no questions asked and told to go

Men and mules working on canal construction, around 1920. (Courtesy of the Welland Historical Museum)

join a group of men who were unloading long steel railroad rails. I was quickly given a handle opposite some other 'loop' gadget in the form of a long handled punch-bar which when lifted, tightened on the rail and allowed it to be lifted - with two other men, on each end - and carried off the barge to a pile on the shore. I worked on this from about 9:30 to 12:00, had a lunch and quickly decided my back was not that strong and my head not that weak so told the boss I didn't want the job. I didn't even arrange to pick up any pay but left by rowboat and headed home.

But I didn't get there.

On the way home I had to pass Gainer's farm which was about 1/4 mile east of ours on Quaker Road. [since purchased for the relocation of the Welland County Fair Grounds]. I decided to stop in and see if 'Charlie' (Gainer) needed any help for the summer. And sure enough he did. I would work from 7 until 6 or 7 and get all my meals there but would sleep at home. My pay would be $30.00 per month (for July and August). It didn't offer the glamorous wages I had thought I would get over on the island but it was the first full-fledged summer job I clearly recall. Up to this time, my summers were always weeding roots, driving the team for the hay fork, stacking grain, pitching stooks in the mow, etc etc.

Embarrassment in Welland

Two incidents of importance took place that summer. Charlie had a real old horse which he didn't use very much except to make hay and go to town or the odd light job or two. I had been warned about this horse's age and infirmity and not to push her - I forget her name - and to be careful it didn't fall. I was told an old horse had extreme difficulty in getting up. This horse apparently slept standing up. Believe it or not!

One day when the weather was inclement and little to do Charlie told me to hitch the horse up to the light democrat and take some grain to Welland to be chopped. This meant 6 or 8 large bags of oats had to be rolled out for easier consumption for the other horses and cattle and was a usual procedure on the farm in those days. Tim did this regularly, too. I also got a few bags of bran to mix with the oats for the pig "slop" [wheat rolled and processed in the mill].

Well, I got my load to the mill and accomplished the job fine and was on my way back to the farm. All this time I was somewhat embarrassed as I was old enough to not exactly feel this was the best job in the world and since I had quite a few high school friends in the city, I thought they might see me and kid me about being an "old farmer" – or even use that hateful nickname that Jack started and rubbed off a bit on me in the first couple of years at the high school – 'haywire'.

Embarrassed and hopeful not to see anyone I knew the old horse plodded along and across the creek bridge heading north up the hill (opposite the present Brass plant) when lo and behold the dumb horse suddenly slipped on the damp brick pavement and fell completely down in the middle of the street. I was mortified. What could I do? Surely the brute would die right there and leave me the ridicule of all of my friends.

The horse struggled vainly. The harness got twisted. Its eyes bulged wildly from its head. I jumped off the wagon and grabbed the bridle and tried to pull and urge the horse to its feet. To no avail. It struggled some more. People started to gather and I felt like running and diving in the creek. Somebody said 'Hi Pete having trouble?' Sure enough there was a 'friend'. By now a couple of hearty souls came to my assistance and with prodding, pulling, urging slapping, we finally got the beast to its feet and continued on our way home. I was sure scared. I told Charlie and he just grunted and said that's too bad, she's getting pretty old.

The End of Charlie's Horse

I suppose the conclusion is also interesting. About 3 weeks after the horse falling incident, Charlie asked me to go rake the hay in the field across the highway. Charlie owned about 20 acres on the west side of the highway (actually the fields

Horses and mules were used with scrapers and dumpers on building the Welland Canal around Alanburg 1870. They were also used for road building and maintenance. (Courtesy Courtesy of the Welland Public Library Local History Collection)

butted up to our own line fences). So I hitched the old horse to the rake and headed to the field to rake the hay which had been cut that morning into windrows.

Charlie had instructed me to rake the hay and tie the horse up under a small tree when it was done, and then start cocking up while he went to the southerly 10 acres and finished the cocking the hay there.

I finished the raking and tied the horse up rather short to an upper limb so that she couldn't back off or leave the shade of the tree. Then I started cocking hay at the top of the hill some 300-400 yards from the horse. Sometime later I was attracted to some people in a passing car yelling and shouting and pointing toward the horse.

And to my amazement the horse had keeled over with its head held up by my short tie and upper limb. I rushed over, released the tie and took a close look. She was dead as a mackerel. And I became scared stiff, thinking Charlie would blame me in some way for it. All I could do was hurry over the hill to the next field and tell Charlie of the incident. I can still see his reactions when I told him. 'Oh, well, she was pretty old' and he continued with his work.

The conclusion to this episode was a dirty trick played on Tim. Charlie decided that a hole would have to be dug beside the carcass and roll the corpse in it and bury it right there under the apple tree and that it would be done after supper. Well, as it happened, Emmy Pitkin and I had planned a big date at the Garden Party in Fonthill for that night and I was desperate. So when I told Tim about it he said he'd help Charlie. And so I got out of a hot hard night's work.

Country Roads

In the winter, after a big snowstorm, farmers were the only ones to clear the roads. It was a co-operative effort. Father at one time organized the neighbors to clean their own roads and soon after a storm the roads would be passable. Each farmer would take his team and break the part of the road allocated to him. Of course there was too much snow for much travelling except by horse and cutter. The roads were only narrow tracks for bob-sleighs since of course no one had an automobile in those days.

In later years when autos had come into use, they were never used in the wintertime. The battery was removed and stored in the

Car on the Beaverdams Road. (Goodwillie family)

basement at the house. The car itself was put up on blocks and the tires removed for storage. There was no way a car could navigate country roads, or city ones either.

In the Spring, after the mud had begun to dry up, the same organized work began. The roads were scraped smooth of the muddy ruts and gradually they would be pounded hard and smooth by the wagon wheels.

When automobiles came into use, of course a different plan had to be made and as you know now the roads are well looked after by the Government.

There was many a time when big snowbanks made driving impossible with a car. During many winters it was just not feasible for me to be home after work unless I walked and that was out too. I would spend most of the winter with Grace and Russ or Mary and Perce who were living in town then.

Pavements are so nice to have now we just couldn't get along otherwise. The first pavement in Welland was of wooden blocks out North Main Street. The pavement was very slippery in wet weather but lasted for years.

From mud to stone to macadam, the roads have progressed in the last fifty years. Do you ever wonder what will happen during the next fifty years?

Father and Mother's wedding date was April second and I've often heard them say that when they started on their honeymoon, in 1890, with a horse and buggy, the snowbanks were high on either side of them but the road was a mass of mud, deep, sticky clay mud.

The Gravelling of Quaker Road

by Pete Goodwillie

The gravelling of part of Quaker Road stands out in my memory and is worth recalling. About 1919 or thereabouts it was decided to gravel the road from the Plank Road [Highway #3 or Niagara St.] westward to the schoolhouse.

I don't know who financed it or whether my father did it on his own for his own benefit.

In any event gravel had to be brought in by team from the Fonthill area some five miles away. The wagon had a bottom consisting of hardwood 2 x 4s or heavier, which were loose on the front and rear axles. The sides and ends were removable and about two feet high. The gravel was hand shoveled into the box wagon and a heavy team drew the gravel to the right and the ends and sides removed and the bottom boards turned until all the gravel fell to the ground below. One load was sufficient for crowning and leveling for that wagon length - about 15 feet. Then they returned for another load.

I don't recall how many loads per day but probably not more than four and it must have been a back breaking job, but with lots of rest riding the empty (or loaded) cart to and from the site. It was a slow and tedious job but the gravel packed down, drained the waters to the side and provided a pretty solid roadbed for the vehicles of that day - mostly horse drawn. It sure made it easier during the wet weather.

Although the road didn't get completely graveled to the school, it was always a relief when coming and going to the school when we could walk on the gravel instead of the dust and mud of the clay road. The balance of the Quaker Road

One of the first seven passenger cars in Welland[52]. In Fireman's Parade, Grandma Sarah enjoys the ride with Goodwillie family and friends. (Cornett)

was not graveled until about 1925 and was done by truck (but hand shoveled on and off).

The First Car

Father purchased an automobile which was of one of the first in the County - a seven passenger McLaughlin-Buick. It had wooden spoke wheels, a hand crank, smooth rubber tyres, carbon acetylene lights and a tool box on the running board. Every time it left the farm it was full to overflowing, for there were lots of 'customers' for a ride every time it went. What a common everyday occurrence it is now to ride in a car, you can't imagine what a thrill it was for all of us in the times sixty years ago.

It was a beautiful car with large brass sidelights, brass headlights, and lots of brass trim around the engine and tyre holder which was on the side running board. The top of the car folded down at the back and had lots of izing-glass curtains to be put on in a hurry if it should rain. The engine had to be cranked to start it and this was a real heavy job, only a man could do it.

Iva was very anxious to learn to drive the car but that cranking bit was beyond her strength, as was the steering. One day she tried to crank and almost had her arm broken, it would 'kick back' if not done properly. All in all that was a man's car only.

In the winter the car was put on blocks to save the tires and the battery was taken into the house. It was usually quite late in the spring before the roads were dried out enough to drive without getting stuck in the mud.

Of course the roads were deep with snow all winter for it was unthought of to have them cleared down to the ground. Besides there were far too many sleighs still in use at that time and the snow was needed for them.

Every horse in the country was frightened to death of an automobile. The horses would rear up on their hind legs and then run away if not properly controlled. Our horses were the same. It took years for them to get really acquainted with the car or truck. The roads being

Donald Brock (Jack)'s first car in front of the Goodwillie drive shed. 1925. (Cornett)

narrow the car would usually be brought to a standstill until the driver had his horse safely past that strange contraption. Lots of times the horse would be led past the car until all was safe again. There were many complaints from the farmers about these big nuisances.

One night we were out for a drive, all bundled up with dusters over our dresses and huge scarves around our hats to keep them from blowing off. That was the standard fashion you know. Well, this one night Mother and I were on the jump seats, the one that folded into floor, when not in use. We met a horse and buggy on a very narrow road. There was a deep ditch on one side and a high bank on the other. That horse about jumped out of its skin; being so close to the car we were sure it would fall on us. Mother opened the car door and jumped out. She rolled into the ditch and long grass and fortunately was not injured. It was no laughing matter but Father always teased her after that about her quick jump. The car was practically at a standstill or it might not have been so funny.

Niagara Falls Picnic

One Sunday, having guests, Father decided we would to on a picnic to Niagara Falls. I was the lucky one to go that day, or was I?

It was a very hot day, the roads were dry with the dust inches deep. No, there weren't any pavements then. We got away from home in

A memorable trip to Niagara Falls. Father, Grace, Mary and Tim wait for the tire to be repaired. (Cornett)

good time, picnic baskets tucked in under our feet and everyone well covered with scarves and dusters. What a cloud of dust was raised as we drove along at all of fifteen miles and hour.

We hadn't gone very far when 'pfzzzzzt' - a flat tire?

Father got out to look and sure enough, flat as a pancake. We all got out and stood around while Dad got the tools out of the box on the running boards, jacked up the car and after much huffing and puffing pulled off the tire. He had a good spare one so put it on, then with more huffing and puffing it had to be pumped up with the air pump. The spares didn't hold air in those days.

Finally we were loaded in again and on our way. We hadn't gone more that a few miles when there was the ominous 'pfz zzzzzt' again. This time there wasn't a spare tire so Father had to put a patch on the first one he had taken off. That was a tedious job but as he always carried patching materials it was just a matter of doing it. Finally that tire was fixed, on, and pumped up, so away we went.

It was almost noon by this time and very very hot. You know we had seven punctures that day - all on the way to the Falls. We finally got there about six o'clock, not any farther than the first power house though. We never did see the Falls.

The tablecloth was spread on the grass and we had our picnic. The men from the power house came out to admire the automobile and in the course of conversation they suggested we have a tour of the building. They took us far below ground into the power house and explained the workings, an experience I've never forgotten.

By this time Father was exhausted and the rest of us pretty hot and tired too. However on our return trip all was well and no further punctures or trouble.

We had many a laugh about that trip which had started out so well - seven punctures in one day was really too much. *[Note: This car was sold about 1919 or 1920 to a band of Gypsies who had heard about the car and wanted transportation].*

Daredevils at Niagara Falls-

[Speech by J.R.Goodwillie to the Niagara Falls Historical Association April, 1982]

One cannot be born in Welland with three generations of Niagara history before him without being consciously and unconsciously absorbed in the influences of the mighty Falls of Niagara and its surrounding area. To comment on Butler's Rangers, War of 1812-14, Upper Canada Rebellion, Welland Canal and the Fenian raids would be sacrilegious? Comparison to the direct and indirect contacts one experienced living only 12 miles form the seventh great wonder of the World.

My living experiences included the run-away scow which broke loose and foundered on the rocks just 300 feet from the Falls. This was on August 6, 1918 and its remains are still there. Two men were miraculously rescued. In 1960 a seven year old boy, Roger Woodward, was swept over the Falls after a boat accident above the rapids. He lived to remember the terrible ordeal and another miraculous rescue by the crew of the Maid of the Mist after sighting the bobbing object in a life jacket.

And then there was the collapse of the Honeymoon Bridge in 1938 after the grinding ice tore the pinions of the bridge loose. Everyone for miles around held bated breath for four days awaiting the collapse of the 840 foot span. The author saw the span the day before it collapsed and the day after. It was a tragic sight laying limp and inert on the ice of the lower gorge. Having crossed the bridge many times, one could not but feel a little sorrowful. Atlas Steels of Welland were able to procure many of the 8 inch spikes used in the planking and convert them into paper envelope openers as souvenirs. I was lucky enough to get one of these. It is in our archives.

One could go on story after story of the legends of Niagara. Some were hand-me-down stories such as the Great Blondin and Farini. Some were boy worship adventures of the Red Hill River Rats. [Editor: These were all Niagara Falls Daredevils] But always the mist and roar of the dropping water mesmerized one watching the awe inspiring natural phenomenon.

It was at Niagara that I tasted my first beer. '44' beer was made legal in 1928. Bill Joy, Tobe Rogers and Emmy Pitkin and the author, after playing softball for Welland went to one of the new 'parlours' and dared each other to the awful tasting beverage. We were 18 years old and didn't dare be seen in Welland consuming alcohol.

CHAPTER EIGHT

Local Happenings: School, Parties and Events

Stories written by Ruth Goodwillie Cornett, with additions from J.R. 'Pete' Goodwillie

School Days

The original 1816 Quaker Road School was built on Robert Garner's property [whose family later married into the Page family]. This property was later sold to Levi Goodwillie. A new building was built opposite in 1862 on Lot 233 on the south side of Quaker Rd. facing west of First Ave. This property had been owned by the Page family. The third S.S. # 5 Quaker Road School was built in 1893 of rusty

Above left the Quaker Road School in the 1920s. Above right: The 1950s expansion showing how the earlier building was utilized. Later this was demolished. Left: A more modern structure was built on the same site and opened in 1995. (Cornett, Michael and the Welland Tribune)

coloured brick with white trim with a white or gray picket fence around it. About 1919 the vacant Page farmhouse was used for an extra classroom. A remodelled and enlarged school opened in 1925. In 1952 two classrooms, an auditorium and storagerooms were added and halls widened. This building was demolished and replaced in 1995 with a $3 million structure housing 342 students from Lloyd Rice Elementary and Quaker Road Schools.

School days, school days,

Dear old golden rule days,

Reading writing and 'rithmetic'

Taught to the rule of the hickory stick........

So goes the old song, our school days didn't have a hickory stick but they did have a wide rubber strap, always a last resort for the teacher and a frisky student.

Local Happenings: School, Parties and Events

In the Fall we would start to school right after Labor Day, walking about a quarter of a mile and thinking it a long way. It seemed much farther in the winter when we had to break a track through the deep snow unless the men had been out with the teams to 'break a track' and clear the roads. We would do our best to shield our faces from the biting wind and be mighty glad when we arrived at the school and found it nice and warm.

In the Spring we plodded through mud and water, jumping the ditches and trying to find a good place to walk without getting our feet wet. Later when the sun had dried the roads we'd look for a smooth place to walk among the ruts. In the late spring we could find and pick violets and later wild strawberries, all of which made our walk more interesting.

Our school was a one-room red brick building, perhaps having about thirty pupils in all. There was a boys' entry and a girls' entry where we hung our coats etc, then the rest of the building was one big room. There were three long high windows down each side of the room with blackboards in between and all across the front.

There were four rows of double desks with aisles between them, about ten desks to a row. The little people sat in the front seats

Students at Quaker Road School. c. 1912. From left standing: Earl Heffner, Edith Wills, Edith McNeil, Miriam Rice. Middle row: W. Weasner, Tim Goodwillie, Birdella Tobias, Bea McCann, Ruth Goodwillie. Seated: Ruth Heffner, Luella Meritt, Ethelwyn Learn, Joe Reuter. (Cornett)

which were small, then the seats gradually got a little bigger until large enough at the back for an adult. You didn't reach these seats until you were in Junior or Senior Fourth class, as a rule.

When a new term started in September it was a big rush to get to school first to grab your favorite spot, the back if possible, or close to the stove, but surely not too close to the front, where the teacher could keep an eye on you.

Sometimes for punishment the teacher would make you sit with a boy or vice-versa and to most of the children that was really a disgrace and so embarrassing.

The teacher had a big desk at the front on a platform just one step higher than the classroom. It gave her a bit of an advantage to see what was going on.

In one corner at the back, taking about one quarter of the space was a whopper of a big furnace. This was much better that the small coal stove that was originally the only heat in the room. Your face burned on one side and your back froze, but each one of us would rather be close to the stove than too far away.

School Work

Probably we were taught about the same subjects as today except that we had to do most of the work ourselves for there were not any extra teaching aids. There was a large globe of the world, some good sized maps for teaching geography and a big dictionary. We bought our own textbooks, a scribbler or pencil which we always prized very highly. We made such promises to ourselves to keep the scribbler nice and tidy but, alas, I'm afraid we failed dismally.

Most of our work was done on a slate, bound in red wool, and with a slate pencil for writing. If we wanted to be mean we would run that pencil up and down on the slate and make a terrible squeaky noise which brought the teacher down on us in a hurry.

We always had a small bottle of soap suds to clean the slate and spent a lot of time shaking that bottle. Sometimes the slate was so slippery with dried soapsuds that the pencil wouldn't even write.

There were eight classes in all, no kindergarten. When we started to school we started right in to work all day long except we got out at three-thirty instead of four o'clock for the first year.

Each class would be called to the front of the room in turn, their spelling heard, more given, arithmetic taught and then reading, geography, Canadian and English history, writing and so on. When our class was finished then another one would be called and so it went all day.

When our work was finished we could always listen to the other classes and perhaps on the side learn some of that work too. When we got into the Senior grades at school we had lots of homework and when we were in Senior Fourth - grade eight to you - we really worked. We had to try entrance examinations for entry into High school.

For the last month or so before these examinations the teacher usually kept us after school for extra lessons - just the entrance class as it was called. If it was warm weather we would study outside under the big maple trees. I don't think we were extra dumb it just seemed to be routine for the teacher to put forth the extra effort.

We had to go into town to write the examinations and that in itself was a real experience. It was our first, shall I say 'adult' experience and so very important. We entered a world of total strangers and were on our own. For anyone who was shy it was murder.

When we finally got to High School the girls were always addressed as 'Miss' which made us feel very dignified and the boys were called by their last name only.

To get back to the Public school, I'm sure the teacher must have worked very hard with all eight classes to look after and in one room too. I can't remember any one of the teachers who was not good to us and always cheerful. Some of them would play outside with us and that we loved.

Sometimes we would be asked to clean the black board after school and we felt really honoured. We did this by pounding the brushes on the side of the school outside. How the chalk dust would fly. I'll bet there is still a spot showing on the bricks outside the old part of that school.

Games at School and Lunch

We had recess of fifteen minutes during the morning and afternoon and it was fun. We played all sorts of games, depending on season. There would be anti-anti-hi-over, here we come gathering nuts in May, Run Sheep Run, Pom Pom Pullaway, Prisoner's Base, Baseball, and Football, just to name a few.

In the winter it was usually Fox and Geese, or Run Deer Run, after we had painstakingly tramped the correct figures in the snow. Sometimes we would make Angels in the snow by lying on our backs and moving our arms and legs in a sideways motion, then carefully getting to our feet so as not to spoil the figure. If there was a really big snowstorm we would build forts and have a snowball fight. The boys were better at this than the girls.

One side of the playground was supposed to be where the boys played and the other was for the girls but most of the time we played together.

When it rained or was too blustery outside the Teacher would let us play Scat in the schoolroom or perhaps Charades which wasn't so noisy.

There was a drive-shed on the girls' side of the school in which we could play too when it rained or wasn't too cold. This was where the people coming to Sunday School used to shelter their horses. You see no one had a car in those days, they either drove a horse and buggy or walked, sometimes several miles.

We were only five minutes walk from home but nevertheless we usually carried our lunch. The girls ate in their cloakroom and the boys in theirs. It was very crowded with coats and hats but that didn't bother us and we didn't really give it a second thought.

If anyone had a hardboiled egg in his lunch you had to watch out for it might be cracked on your head when you weren't looking. It hurt!

School Holidays

There were several holidays during the year to which we looked forward with great anticipation, not counting summer vacation or Christmas of course.

Arbor Day

In the Spring the first Friday in May was called Arbor Day. You will never hear of it any more. In the morning we all worked outside in the school yard, picking up papers, sticks and generally tidying the whole place very nicely. We always worked hard to be finished before noon for the rest of the day was free, then we all planned on going to the woods to study Nature. It usually turned out to be a flower picking day and a good spring outing after a long winter. The teacher of course went along but there was no way she could keep the children together to give any kind of a lesson. I'm sure she enjoyed it as much as we did.

We always came home with bunches of mayflowers, dog-tooth violets, purple violets and lots of trillium, red and white. Nowadays no one is supposed to pick trillium but we picked lots of them and there always seemed just as many the next year. How pleased Mother seemed to be when we proudly presented our bouquets on arrival home. We had had a big day and we didn't need any prodding to go to bed that night.

Valentines Day

You know when I went to school no one ever had valentines bought from the shop, well hardly ever. We always made our own. We thought they were wonderful and it was fun to make them too. We would start weeks ahead of that wonderful day, February Fourteenth.

Friday afternoons were always when we had art lessons. These consisted of mostly drawing squares, balls, fruit or flowers and then we could use watercolors. How we loved to use those water paints. Perhaps it was messing around with water too that we enjoyed, just a bunch of little kids.

Well, several weeks before Valentine's Day all we did in art class was make valentines. We painted hearts, cut out hearts and then wrote verses on them.

> 'Roses are red,
> Violets are blue,
> Sugar is sweet
> And so are you.'

Just a sample of the verses. All in all there were some pretty original cards turned out - good and bad.

Before the big day arrived the teacher would have made a slit in the top of a big box to be the postbox. We 'mailed' our creations in the box, one to each person in the room, well almost, we did have our favorites and perhaps left out a few we didn't care too much about. At three o'clock the magic box was opened and the teacher played postman handing out the cards.

What a big time we had looking over all those cards and counting and re-counting them. If anyone was lucky enough to have received a real 'boughten' card he/she was the centre of attention. Once in a while a mean card was put in but no-one liked that much.

By the time all the cards had been handed out it was four o'clock or nearly so, but away we went home to show our many cards to Mother and Grandma. They were properly admired, in between getting the supper on the table. In a day or so they had been put away until the following year. Perhaps if we were sick in bed a day or so they would be brought out and lovingly gone over again and again.

24th of May

Victoria Day, twenty fourth of May, came hard on the heels of Arbor Day. About a week before that date we would start to chant:

> 'The Twenty-fourth of May is the Queen's birthday,
> if you don't give us a holiday we'll all run away.'

The day before the holiday there was a flag raising ceremony, soon after the morning bell called us to classes, then lessons would begin. We always had to write a composition or essay on the Queen, and the history of the Flag. Then we had to draw and paint a picture of the Union Jack. That Flag was hard to draw correctly but we did our best. Usually we got out of school a half hour early, especially if it was a Friday. The day was always celebrated on the twenty-fourth no matter on what day of the week it fell.

Father always bought for us a few packages of five-cent firecrackers. They would make a little bang and fizz and that was that. However, we had a good time fooling with them, always away from the buildings in case of fire. We had sky-rockets and big noisy firecrackers too but these Father would save for a big surprise. He would put them off on the front lawn after dark with all the neighbors congregating to see the fun. Of course the house was always decorated with flags and lots of bunting on that holiday.

Pete's note about firecrackers

I have a fond memory of my father on firecracker day, the 24th May. As kids we always wanted firecrackers and every year would be the same story. 'I haven't got time.' 'Foolish spending' and the such with off-hand remarks of little or no interest or concern for our wishes. But always on the big day he would go to the desk in the office – or some other hiding place – and bring out a horde of bangers.

Sometimes on the afternoon of the twenty-fourth of May there was a big parade in town and some of us, if not all, would be taken and everyone was in a gay mood. I don't suppose it was much of a parade as they go these days but it was pretty good at that time.

Once I remember it was a lovely warm day but the corn hadn't been planted and we were elected to drop corn while one of the hired men dug the holes and covered it. We were badly used, we thought, but it only took the morning and Father made it up to us some other way. You see Twenty-Fourth of May didn't necessarily mean playing around.

All in all our holiday times were very simple but we had a lot of good times together, usually just at home. We had to make our own fun. There wasn't any television or radio; there was one movie house in town but we rarely went in until we were at high school and very seldom then.

When we were in our early teens sometimes Father would drive in town to the band concert in the park, held every Tuesday night. When we went we just walked up and down listening to the music while the adults visited among friends. It was not very lively but a nice change. We even had an ice-cream cone, or perhaps we would cross the street at intermission to the ice-cream parlor with its round tables and spindly backed chairs.

Frog Hunting

Iva and Mary tell of an excursion they had when very young. Mother took them across the canal to hunt frogs. The Welland Canal was half a mile or so down the road from our house and in those early days there was a bridge over the canal at that point, I don't remember it. Now even the Canal has had its course changed and the old part filled in.

Well, on this day Mother hitched Gyp, the driving horse, to the buggy and the three of them set out. They took pails and the necessary gear. The Welland River, or Creek, as we sometimes called it, was the other side of the Canal and that was where they were headed.

It was a lovely day and they hunted frogs and worked all afternoon catching them. Mother killed and cleaned them, for it was the legs they wanted, for supper. The girls enjoyed the outing and no doubt Mother did too but I don't envy her the job of cleaning those frogs. Mother could do anything and was never hesitant at trying things she had never done before.

24th May – Spring Planting

Twenty-fourth of May was a very big day in our time and I'm really sorry to see it sort of slip away as a National Holiday. Besides being a day to celebrate it was a day on the calendar by which the farmers did their spring planting, and they still do. After that date there is usually very little fear of a frost so the gardens could be put in and outside work got under way at full tilt.

Oh yes, I almost forgot, that was the date we changed from our long heavy winter underwear to summer things. What a relief that was. You have never had to try to fold those long underwear legs under your stockings so there wouldn't be a big bump -- ugh!

In the country there is always something to do, for a child, winter or summer there are various activities, spring and fall overflowing ponds, streams and ditches for rafts and paddling, fruit and nuts and corn and pumpkins -- oh, such a lot of lovely ideas for fun.

School days

Memories by Pete Goodwillie

I do not recall much about the sawmill, the factory at the farm, the happy carefree times I must have enjoyed romping around the barns and sheds and fields. My only playmates were my older brothers since the closest kid of my age was at least ½ mile or more away (Ethel, Ken and Art Gaylor and Doris Wells - Stella Reuter, Gordon Hill, Raymond Dennis, the Weasner kids). The roads were bad. We had no bicycles and I guess we were taught to stay at home and mind our own business.

I recall the occasional dress up requirement in which I had some kind of bloomers to the knee, long black stockings, and a pullover shirt with a big flappy collar. I didn't like it.

Pete on the left played with his older brothers Bill (Hugh Allan), Jack (Donald Brock) and Tim (Harold Hiram) Photo taken in 1912. (Cornett)

School was at S.S.#5 – a one room deal with a pot stove in the corner. Desks were well marked with carved initials of foregone generations – and my own on one of them.

One year I was the janitor and had to sweep out the school after hours and start the fire in the morning from wood in a large woodshed to the rear. I think I inherited this job from Bill or Jack. I don't remember getting any payment – and probably didn't. My father was on the School Board and in 1920 – 22 he went to many meetings to push for an addition as it was getting pretty crowded what with kids from Stop 17 and Thorold Road area. He never lived to see his 'dream' come true about 1925.

The Sunday School Concert

It always seemed that right after Thanksgiving holidays were over the next big event would be Christmas. Well, almost the next big event. The Sunday School Christmas Concert came first and then came Christmas.

The concert sort of got us all warmed up, if that was necessary, for Christmas. There was a lot of excitement and weeks of preparation for the concert. We even worked at decorations for the tree during school hours.

This concert was quite a production. It was held in the school house, where we had Sunday school as well, as I told you before. The first three or four rows of desks and seats were removed in order that a 'stage' could be built -- of planks. Curtains were strung on wires across the front of the platform and along the back and sides of the 'stage'" covering the blackboards.

The curtains were a dark wine red and we thought they looked quite gorgeous. A couple of the bigger boys would be appointed to open and close the curtains on cue during the concert. This was a very responsible job.

For weeks before the concert each child would be busy learning a 'piece', learning songs to either sing alone or in a chorus. The senior girls at school would be taught a 'drill' or two. This was precision marching. The older folk put on several one or two act plays or skits. They were usually quite funny and some unintentionally so. There would be duets, quartette, recitations, choruses and always one tableau.

What is a Tableau ?

Daisy (i.e cousin Daisy Page) had long fair hair so she was chosen to be the figure in this particular tableau. The lights would all be dimmed to make the room as dark as possible, then a tall white Cross was set up on the stage. Daisy, in a white dress and her hair hanging loose around her shoulders sat at the foot of the Cross. When she was all set and in the right position to be most effective someone backstage lighted a magnesium flare. It only lasted about six seconds but it gave a quick clear picture of Daisy sitting there and was most effective.

The picture was quick and bright and startling but the smell of that powder lasted a long while. All the windows and doors had to be opened immediately until the coughing and sneezing died down. There weren't any flashlight bulbs at that time or perhaps they would have given about the same effect. There was usually just the one tableau.

The Concert Program

The Chairman of the programme always had to be someone who could tell a few jokes in between acts or make some witty comment on the past performance. You see sometimes there might be a delay between acts as the next performer got ready for the next item on the program.

Mr. L. B. Duff of the City (Welland), and Editor of the local paper was much in demand and would usually come if invited in time. He had an inexhaustible supply of jokes and everyone enjoyed him.

Grace always gave a recitation or two. She was very good at it and was much in demand for strawberry socials, garden parties and other concerts. She got paid for it too sometimes. Mother used to coach her in her recitations and many is the hour she spent getting just the right tone or inflection into her 'piece'.

When Grace was very small and got up to speak her first "piece" she just stood in front of all the audience tongue-tied. Finally she looked down at Mother and said 'Ma, what's the first of it'. This brought down the house and was brought up to haunt her in her teen-age days.

When Grace started high school she finally rebelled at these recitations. That did stop her from getting her daughter Nancy [Shier, nee Northcote] to stand between her father's knees and speak her 'pieces' at the 'cocoa-teas' on Sunday evenings at the farm.

Before the concerts were ready there were many practice sessions. There was no electricity at that time in the school, just lanterns hanging here and there. The practices for the older folk were always in the evenings, after the chores were all finished. When it was close to the big night we children were allowed to go. At that time, we watched and practiced the choruses and also found where we had to stand and what to do when it came our turn to perform.

By the middle of December, it was usually cold with lots of snow, but there might be a big full moon to help light the darkness. We would all bundle up and walk to the school-house carrying lanterns, the snow squeaking under our feet. When we got there someone would stir up the wood fire to get it warm and in the dusky shadows of the room there would be a lot of poking, laughing and teasing. The serious business of saying our lines would soon begin. The drills planned and executed and the costumes planned.

Grace as a little girl was in demand for public speeches. She is shown here with husband Russ Northcote and grandchildren Blair and Peter Shier. 1959. (Cornett)

Mother had a lot of imagination and was a good sewer. She could make gorgeous costumes out of anything and nothing. When on the stage they looked pretty nice. It was a lot of work for all the women as each had a job to do. I am sure expressing their imaginations and using their ability did something for all of them. The community spirit was very strong and everyone enjoyed the impromptu get-together. You would be surprised at the talent shown too.

When the practice was over we all trekked home through the snow and moonlight. There was no trouble sleeping in those days. There was lots of laughter, lots of work and lots of fun, and no doubt many frustrations. Maybe Tim would get a cold and couldn't take his part in the play, or someone else couldn't do the drill and so on. It was a hurry-up job to get a replacement - but nothing seemed to show when the concert finally took place.

Well, the day of the concert finally rolled around. What a to-do there was. All were excited and rushing here and there. The farm work had to be done in a hurry and last minute touches on costumes finished. Some were sure they didn't know their lines well enough and some had plain stage fright before the evening came.

There was a half-holiday at school. The Christmas tree was set up in one corner near the stage. How tall and wonderful it looked, no lights, just the paper chains and ornaments we had made during school hours, strings of pop-corn and a few parcels tucked among the branches. At night the room soon filled with neighbours from far and near.

The first few rows of seats were reserved for the small children and actors. It seemed really crowded with perhaps seventy-five people in the room.

The admission fee was about twenty-five cents and of course the proceeds went to the Sunday School. Coal-oil lanterns were hung around the walls as high as could be managed and with streamers and red paper bells for decorations the room was a beautiful sight to all of us. We were breathless with the excitement of it all.

Yes, some of the little folk, and older ones too, forgot their lines and had to be prompted. One or two got stage fright and had to be gently led off the stage, but on the whole it was usually a huge success.

The girls in the drills all dressed in blue sailor dresses and wide paper hats were beautiful and didn't miss a turn. The Wilsons sang a quartette or two. Grace did her recitations and so did Daisy as well as her tableau.

There was much shuffling and getting into place for the choruses. Everyone was in the chorus if he could sing or not, large or small. I remember one little girl who couldn't remember the verses but she moved her lips anyway and pretended to be singing. She was much let down when she overheard some of the oldsters talking about it. They had noticed her little ruse. Mary and Iva took parts in the skits, as well as the Heffners and Hills. Some of them were very well acted. Each performance received loud and long applause, and good time was enjoyed by all.

The last item on the program, naturally, was Santa Claus, red suit, bells, pack and all. He always came in at a window back of the tree. There would be a big commotion and suddenly there he was. He would jingle his bells, strut a bit and with a few big "Ho,Ho,Ho's" get down to the serious business of distributing an orange and a bag of hard candy to each child.

We would hold our breath until our name was called then the joy of going to the front for our gift. Once in a while there would be a gift on the tree for a grown-up. It was usually a joke of some kind.

On the whole it was a very satisfying night and one to which we looked forward from one year to the next. The Christmas concert was a very good introduction to the rest of the Christmas holiday.

Christmas At The Farm

Christmas at our house, when we were little, was not so elaborate as it is today. We didn't have a Christmas tree at all until we were grown up. We just hung or stockings by the fireplace on the back of a dining-room chair. We made sure each stocking, long black ones, had name attached to it. We didn't want Santa to make any mistakes you know.

The rooms would have been decorated with red and green paper streamers, red bells of tissue paper would hang over the dining table and in the hallway. Everything looked very gay and festive.

On Christmas morning we would be downstairs early, just to peek and sure enough each stocking would have some nuts, hard candy and a huge orange tucked in the toe. Oranges were a real treat in those days, only enjoyed at that time of year.

Below the stocking would be perhaps a doll for me, a train of cars with a track, not electric, for the boys or games or books of small toys. One year we each received a gorgeous sleigh, with runners eight inches high. We scoured the neighborhood for a nice hill suitable for such a grand sled but ended up in the back yard where there was a slight slope.

Weeks before Christmas we would have pored over Eaton's Catalogue's toy section, hoping against hope for something special, maybe a big rocking horse. No, we never received one. Those pages surely brought pleasure and anticipation to many children in those days.

Later in the morning Santa might arrive. We would have been on the lookout all morning to see him come up the lane to the house. A discreet word having been dropped that he might arrive. This didn't happen every year. We never knew when he was there until we heard a jingling of bells and he would come in through the kitchen door, a big pack on his back. What a lot of excitement, and some hanging back too. There would be more presents until the bag was empty then away he went. We never did follow to see where he went, if we had we'd have discovered perhaps Frank or Grace had been playing Santa's role, dressed in father's long coonskin coat. We were far too busy enjoying our extra gifts.

About this time Father would be in his office with the door closed, busily putting a five dollar bill or more into an envelope for each of us - this in later years as we got bigger. He was usually far too busy for shopping.

One year when we were about six or seven, Tim and I, that is, we knew something big was going on, a big commotion in the front

One Christmas brought a special surprise of a piano. (H.R.Page)

hall and parlor. When all had quieted down, we found the sliding door into the parlors tightly locked but there was a keyhole. On peaking through 'lo and behold', there was a big new piano sitting in the room. Christmas day brought a surprise for some, but not for Tim and I.

There were many good sing songs held around that piano in the years to come. Russ would play and all their gang would sing, 'By the Sea, By the Sea', 'Tipperary', 'Oh You Beautiful Doll' and songs of the 1900s.

Well after Santa left of course there was always a big dinner at the noon hour. Grandma and I would perhaps have seeded all the raisins for the cakes and pies and puddings. We didn't have raisins seeded in packages then or even seedless ones. Grace would have made several different kinds of candy, fudge, fondant and maple cream with Canadian walnuts. The nuts would have been cracked and laboriously picked out of the shells well ahead of time.

Grace always packed a box of candy for an elderly English couple named Wrigglesworth. They lived up the road from home. On Christmas morning she and Mary would walk up and give the candy to them. Iva, Mary and Mother would do the baking and all this work would have been going on in between regular work, for several weeks.

Christmas afternoon was spent by the grown-ups just visiting with whoever happened to be there as guests. Uncle George Page was always on hand, a genial white-haired old gentleman and there might be various Aunts and Uncles or friends from town. That part of it never interested us too much as children. However, one Christmas in about 1911, when I was about ten, the grown-ups set up tables in the evening in the double parlors. They played euchre and we were allowed to play too. There were some cousins from out west and we all had a merry time.

We had new games and books to put in the day and perhaps a new sled to try if there was snow on the ground and there usually was. Maybe we had new skates given to us. They were not like today's skates, the blades were separate and had to be adjusted to your shoe with a key, and they were always falling off. You didn't dream of putting them on before getting to the pond across the road. Sometimes the skates just wouldn't stay on our shoes and we were so frustrated and cold trying to make them stay put. Small children always started out with bob-skates, with two runners, and these also had to put on and adjusted each time at the pond.

When the grandchildren came along Christmas was different again. We had a big tree set up in the front parlour. It was decorated with lights and balls and the usual ornaments, though not so elaborate as now. Mother, Jack and Tim usually helped with the tree decorating on Christmas Eve. On Christmas day everyone would come from various homes, laden with parcels. These were added to the pile already under the tree. The cakes and goodies were taken to the kitchen where everyone had a hand in getting dinner ready. When everyone was present, about twenty or so, dinner would be put on the long dining room table which had been stretched to its full length.

There was always the usual turkey, vegetables, cranberry sauce, pickles, plum pudding, mince pie, homemade candy and nuts, big bowls of them. Needless to say we all did justice to the good food. When we had eaten until we couldn't take one more bite the dishes were cleared away. When they had been washed it was time for the tree.

It had been almost impossible to keep small fry from prying but the big moment had now arrived and the presents would be opened. One parcel at a time was picked from under the tree. Jean usually read the name and Joyce, Dorothy, Jack or Nancy cut the ribbon and delivered it to the right person. When that parcel had been duly investigated another parcel would be given out. It made quite a ceremony but dragged the excitement and shivery Christmas fun so it lasted a nice long time. Everything was "just what we wanted".

Then there was the flitting from person to person to see 'What did you get?' The pile of papers and boxes was gathered together and inspected to see that nothing inadvertently was mixed up or disposed of. Once George lost a sock. He didn't miss it until the next day and of course that was too late. Jean had to knit another one for him.

Once Jack dressed as Santa Clause, red suit, bells, whiskers and all. He thought the little ones would recognize him but they didn't and were mostly quite frightened to see Santa so close up. Usually after a supper of cold turkey, salads, tarts, cakes and homemade ice-cream all the grandchildren went home early. It had been a busy day and way past the children's bedtime. The children were tired and the grownups were quite content to sit and talk over the day's doings.

There wouldn't be another Christmas for three hundred and sixty-five days - what a long time in the future, how far away it seemed. Mother used to say 'as you get older it won't seem such a long time' ... how right she was.

Summers and End of the World War

The ebb and flow of life at the farm went on. The years skipped by with the usual work and play. Mary, Grace and Iva went camping at Port Dover with all their crowd and had a lot of fun. They camped in tents and even had a chaperone. The second year they went was in 1914 and the Great War broke out before they got home.

The Great War, 1914-1918, as it was eventually called was in our time and made many changes in the daily routines. The first big change in everyone's life. Many of Mary and Grace's crowd went off to war. Perce as a Pharmacist went to Siberia, and returned in 1919.

Grandma and our parents of course remembered the Boer War, in fact Dad used to call Jack "Togo", when he was little, after one of the Boer war generals, black I believe. Jack's hair and eyes were very black.

One morning as Grandma finished her breakfast she had a bad stroke. She was in bed about ten days and passed away Oct. 21st 1918, just before the war ended on November 11, 1918. This was the first break in the family since Grandpa died in 1903.

Planes from the First World War and Granny's bedpan

At the age of eight, I remember Grandma at a very dramatic time. In early October of 1918, she had a very severe stroke and her life was prolonged for only two or three more weeks. During her illness, I was delegated one bright afternoon to rush to a neighbour's house to borrow a badly needed bedpan for my ailing grandmother. The urgency was doubly stressed and I set off running up the road, to get the pan. It was obtained post haste and the half-mile return run was started.

About half way home, I was distracted by a sight I had never seen before. Three Air Force b-planes were manoeuvring just above me at about 1000 feet. I had seen the odd single plane before, but never more than one at a time, and here almost on top of me were three diving machines, side-slipping and roaring as if I were their target (An air-training station was located at Beamsville, some thirty miles away, and towards the end of the War, training intensified).

I was scared stiff, but continued running with the pan and got home without being shot down by the planes. I do not remember whether the pan arrived in time or not. Grandma died on 21 October 1918 ... just two weeks before the 11 November Armistice was celebrated. To an eight year old, the combined dramas of the stroke, the bedpan, the planes, the death of a loved one and the great celebrations of the ending of W.W.I made the incident an unforgettable one.

There was one little thing that happened while Grandma was ill, in fact just as she died. She had been completely paralyzed and hadn't moved for ten days or so. Iva was sitting with her when suddenly Grandma sat straight up in bed and with her eyes wide open said 'Hiram, Hiram, oh what beautiful music', then she fell back and was gone.

A couple of weeks later as Mother and I were washing storm windows for Tim to put on we heard whistles blowing and bells ringing in Town. It was a beautiful Fall day as warm as summer, November 11, 1918. On making a telephone call to see what all the noise was about we heard that the war had ended.

What excitement, and how thrilled everyone was. People paraded the streets, bands played and confetti and streamers were knee deep everywhere. It all lasted until well after midnight. People just didn't want to go home. How Grandma would have loved to see that war ended.

Long Beach Cottage: Goodvilla

George and Russ had wanted to have a cottage and were so anxious that Dad finally said if they would buy the lot he would build a cottage for them. That was all they needed. They bought a lot at Long Beach about the year 1919.

The first summer Dad bought a large tent with a wooden floor and izing-glass windows. In fact a family had lived in it all one winter at one time. He had the tent set up on the spot the boys had chosen. They in the meantime had cleared it of grapevines and poison ivy.

The cottage at Long Beach is still used by Goodwillie family members. Above in 1929 and right in 2004.
(Cornett & D. Goodwillie)

That was a great summer. No one around but the people in a cottage next door, the Cat Lady we called her for she had a long shed with many cats in it. I think it was that year (1921) that Payne's also built a cottage farther along the beach.

A long expanse of beach and clear water, many hot sunny days and a few big storms in between times which almost blew that tent to pieces, made life most interesting. It wasn't any fun at the time of those storms but we had many a laugh later. There was a roller skating rink in the park and sometimes on Saturday nights if there was a picnic in the park, there would be skating and dancing too.

In the summer of 1921 Father started the cottage. He planned it by himself and it has often been remarked what a good plan it was. There were five bedrooms and downstairs besides the living area and kitchen he had built one room divided the boys and girls for a bath house. We all changed into bathing suits there and no messing around with wet suits and feet in the other rooms. Now as you know it is another bedroom.

Father never got to enjoy the cottage at all for he wasn't really very well at the time it was built. There have been many changes, at the cottage. The long four car garage building was past its usefulness and torn down to make way for a storage building, or a garage if ever required I guess.

Bathing beauties of 1928 at Long Beach. (Cornett)

The rooms inside the cottage have been lined with panelling, the floors downstairs covered with linoleum and everything more like a city house except not really enough heating for winter.

A bathroom had been built on, at the back before mother passed away and she enjoyed that very much, one of the first conveniences and a far cry from the little house at the end of the old garage. There were many times when one was trapped by incoming visitors and couldn't make one's way to the house without undue notice of one's previous whereabouts. No one cares about this these days but years ago one could even blush, just making a quick sneak in the door.

Life at the cottage became very hectic with the coming of grandchildren . The first few years it was full with five babies. Washing diapers every day and on wet days trying to get them dry, was always a problem. All the cooking was done on a three-burner coal oil stove. The clothes had to be boiled in a big copper boiler.

Grace, Russ, Jack and Nancy had one bedroom; Iva, George Jean and Joyce another, Mary, Perce and Dorothy another. Mother and I took turns going up and had another room. One of us stayed home to carry on with the meals at the farm for the men.

No-one will ever have as much enjoyment of a cottage as was had by the grand children in 1929 when it was all a new experience and not so commonplace as today. From left: Bill Goodwillie, Perce Haist, Jack Northcote, Nancy Northcote (Shier), Jean Secord (Cousins), Ruth Goodwillie (Cornett), Pete Goodwillie, Joyce Secord (Dinnin Shand).(Cornett)

A 30 minute drive from Welland, the Long Beach cottage continues to be a popular place to visit, spring, summer and fall. Grace Northcote, Iva Secord and mother/grandmother Luella Goodwillie with Jean Secord (Cousins) Jack Northcote, and Joyce Secord (Dinnin Shand). 1929? (Cornett)

When the grandchildren were fourteen and up then things got more interesting. The roller skating rink soon turned into a regular dance hall and was open every night with a live band. You see there had gradually been a lot of cottages built and the place was quite popular.

The big event of the day was to go to the dance at night. There was always someone you knew to dance with. You children learned to dance there. You would go and watch the dances then come home and practice the jitterbug mostly.

Poor Nancy (Northcote-Shier) was the toughest and tagged along wherever the older girls went much to their disgust. She came in handy though. Every morning they would go down to the park and Nancy would get under the walkaway around the dance floor and look for any tickets that might have dropped through the cracks. The dances were three for a quarter and quarters were scarce some evenings. In a few years a new dance hall was built with bathing houses beneath so no lost tickets found their way in the girls' direction.

At one time there was a tennis court and everyone played, first a grass court then gravel, or such, then golf took over, now tennis is coming into its own as a popular sport. There isn't a dance hall any more. A big new one that had taken the place of our original old hangout burned several years ago. It never was the same type, and not so much fun, so few of the cottagers got together there.

There was never any rowdyism and all the beach people enjoyed the dancing as well as those from nearby towns. Maybe Morgan's Point dance hall had the better band, if so then everyone would go there but that necessitated a car and it was not always possible.

Before the cottage was built Iva and George rented a house on the point at Morgan's Point. In fact it was the only house there. Jack, Bill, Mabel and I spent one weekend there. It poured rain most of the time. When we went to come home Monday morning the roads were a sea of deep sticky mud. The car slipped and slewed and finally we were mired and couldn't move. We stayed on the road while waiting for the mud to dry or we could be pulled out. George was due at the Bank in Fonthill to work and most anxious but no way could we get unstuck.

Now there was a lull. No one at the cottage during the week except Mother and Mrs. Worram, her housekeeper. When Jack was away I'd go over and spend a week or so to keep them company. The weekends were as busy as ever though, everyone arrived then. There was always a gang, everyone brought friends for the day or weekend. There were a couple of very hot, windless Sundays one year when there were forty-five people on hand for supper. All we did was make sandwiches and cake and wash dishes. You could always tell when it was hot in town for then there were lots of droppers-in, some brought goodies and some didn't.

There were many wicked thunder and wind storms. How the lightning flew and thunder cracked. It looked so much worse over the rough waters of the lake. If the storm was at night everyone came downstairs, dressed, more or less, in some weird looking outfits. Sometimes when the wind blew very hard the windows leaked with the driving water. Then there was a mad scramble to sop up the water and move the cots in the living room away from the drips.

The screened porch always had cushions and mattresses etc to lug inside if the weather looked threatening but it was a very comfortable spot on a summer evening and on Sunday nights for pass around suppers.

Gradually Iva and George took over the cottage. The children grew up and had other interests or were working and no time for the cottage. Dorothy married and lived in London and Ancaster. Jack Northcote and Nancy Shier were more interested in Muskoka. Iva and George Secord bought out the others finishing the cottage co-operative. Now the Dinnin family have taken over.

A cottage is a good place to conduct family business and build ties. Russ Northcote and Jack Cornett used to spend time at house repairs etc, to first one thing and then another. They always said they never did know there was a lake at the front. They had good times chattering together too.

Diane's notes: The swing at the back was always an attraction for adults and kids. Benches made of wooden slats faced each other with a platform between, so four adults (two facing each other) could sit and gently rock. When kids got on it was rocked more vigorously. Many a story was told on that swing. The fact that the Goodwillie (now Dinnin) cottage was close to the Payne cottage, (now Goodwillie) has kept strong family ties between generations. The timber from the Ridgeville forests built a strong house that has provided a lasting family inheritance even if Grandpa John Allan Goodwillie was unable to enjoy it himself.

Jack (Donald Brock) Goodwillie and wife Elma (Tye) at Long Beach cottage c 1960. Note swing on the right. (Cornett)

CHAPTER NINE

Farming and Fruit Canning Factory

Stories written by Ruth Goodwillie Cornett, with additions from J.R. 'Pete' Goodwillie

Community Harvesting and Threshing

Did you ever see a threshing machine work or do you know what it does? During August and early September work on the farm reached its highest point. Everyone was working against time. The crops all seemed to mature at once. If the weather stayed nice and the frost didn't come too soon, it was hoped all would be taken care of in time.

The old factory built about 1890. 1900. (Cornett)

One of the big jobs was to get the wheat and oats threshed and to the mill or in the granaries. It had to be done at just the right time and in good dry weather. Later in the fall there would be corn to put in the silo.

The grain was finally ready once it had been cut with a binding machine, put into sheaves and stacked in windrows in the fields. This made it easier to handle when it came time to bring it in.

When this work had all been done Father would line up a day to do the threshing with the thresher, Mr. Tom Blanchard, and the neighbouring farmers. It was a community effort. Father would help one neighbour by sending men and teams, and the neighbours would help in return when it came to our turn.

There would sometimes be ten or more men and teams on the job. They all arrived about eight o'clock in the morning after doing their own farm chores. If it happened to be a rainy day, the whole thing was called off until a good day came along. We were always glad to see the sun shining.

The day would finally arrive. Quite often the threshing machine had set up the night before to get ready for work, but if not, we would hear a "chug, chug chug" at about six o'clock in the morning. We would then hurry to see if the machine was really coming. Yes, the engine was turning into the lane with the big red threshing machine trundling along behind.

Threshing in 1930-32. (Cornett)

In the old days the engine burned coal. It had a short stubby smokestack and a small coal tender in the back. Since it was a steam engine it had to be fired up early in the morning to get enough steam to run the other machine. The threshing machine would be set up as close to the barn as possible with a long belt that ran to the engine, perhaps thirty feet away.

It was a rather dangerous operation for if sparks should fly from the engine it could set the whole business ablaze. Many a barn had been burned to the ground during the threshing. Father was always very careful and glad when the job was finished.

Mr. Blanchard (the thresher) and his helper would arrive and everything would be set to go. They came in and had a big breakfast, including meat and potatoes. Then they were ready to get to work. The neighbours started to arrive with their teams and went directly to the fields to bring in the sheaves of wheat, or oats.

There were always two men to a wagon, one to drive the horses and stack the sheaves on the rack. If we were lucky one of us might drive the team. I'm afraid we didn't stick with that job for the whole day. It was not as glamorous as it looked especially if the day was a very hot one.

The loaded wagons were driven back to the barn and then each sheaf of wheat, or oats was pitched onto a belt that carried it

Threshing kept everyone busy. (Cornett)

into the threshing machine. There would be a great whirring of machinery and first thing you knew out one side of the machine would come a stream of golden grain, into a big bushel measure which was waiting to catch it. Out of the top of the machine was a great big pipe, on a swivel, and out of it flew the straw, chaff and lots of dust from the stalks of grain.

There would be a steady stream of both all day long: wheat from the bottom and straw from the top. The big pipe would be moved back and forth to make the straw pile even. Before you knew it there was a big stack of lovely golden clean straw to be used for bedding the animals during the rest of the year.

This process went on all day long. One team would draw up and unload and there would be another wagon close behind to take its place when the first was emptied.

In the meantime the grain would be bagged and piled on another wagon to be driven to the flour mill in town. Grain for home use would be dumped in the big granaries until they were piled full of the golden stuff.

At noon, work stopped. The men all went to the house and got washed up for dinner. It was a dirty dusty job in the barn and a hot one in the fields. There was lots of talk and kidding among the men until it came time to eat.

For a couple of days before threshing all the women folk had been busy baking cakes and pies and getting huge roasts of meat ready for this day. The dining-room table was stretched to full length and by the time the men came in everything was in readiness. Big platters of hot roast beef, potatoes, vegetables, pickles, piles of homemade bread, cake and pie, all disappeared like magic.

There was not too much talking. Occasionally someone would make a remark or make a joke but mostly it was a steady chomp, chomp chomp, as the business of eating got under way. It had taken a couple of days to get the meal ready and it was all gone in fifteen minutes.

After dinner the men went out and tended to their horses, feeding and watering them. Then they stretched out under the big maple trees for thirty minutes or so before going back to the fields and the job in hand, until supper-time.

When suppertime came some of the men went home to look after their own work. However there was enough on hand to do justice to the supper prepared for them. If the threshing didn't get finished the first day, and it quite often didn't, the men were all back the next day until the job was finished.

The number of bushels of grain was recorded and compared to the next farmer's. There was always a sort of competition to see who got most grain to the acre. We were always glad to hear the engine go chug chugging out the lane again for another year.

Filling the Corn Silo

The next big job was silo filling which usually took about three days. When this work had to be done, it was much the same procedure for the women folk with lots of food to prepare and serve and dishes to wash.

The corn was cut. The stalks were brought in, put through a cutting machine and then blown into the silo. By the time we had a silo, gasoline engines were available to run the machinery.

The stalks were cut about four or six inches in length. As they were blown into the silo one or two men would be inside to trample and

Silo filling the Fall of 1932. (Cornett)

Birds-eye view of silo filling in 1932. (Cornett)

pack it down evenly. Imagine what a very dirty job this was with all those stalks blowing around. As the silo filled and when it got close to the top the men came back down by ladder on the outside.

Silo filling seemed to require about fifteen men or more, and more teams too. When the corn was ready, about the middle of September, everyone would rally around for the work. It always seemed to be the hottest days of the year. We used to dread it for there was so much to be done and we were always in a hurry to get it all taken care of.

Most men loved to go threshing and silo filling. It was more or less like a picnic and they looked forward to all the good food and the sociability. When the threshing was finished, the corn in the big silo and the hay piled in the mows, we were almost ready for winter once more.

One year we sent wheat down to the Shredded Wheat Factory at Niagara Falls, Ontario. Two of the girls went with the truck at that time, just for the ride. While the wheat was being unloaded, they were taken through the factory to see how shredded wheat biscuits were made. Afterwards, when invited to eat some of the biscuits in a dining room, they thought they had hit the jackpot! Shredded wheat at that time was quite a new cereal. Corn flakes had not even been thought of and oatmeal porridge was the standard cereal. Now look at all the selection you have, with prizes in the bottom too sometimes.

Slaughtering the Meat

Later in the early winter when it was cold, there was the slaughtering to be done. This was a messy few days, which we all dreaded. Dad always managed to be out of it and go to town on some errand. Although we kids always wanted to stay home from school, we were never given that privilege, for which I, for one, was glad.

There was the fat meat to be cut up in squares and rendered into lard; the sausage to be made, cooked and canned as was the sidemeat [from the side of the animal]. The hams were seasoned and put to smoke in the smokehouse then hung in the basement for instant use, which came in handy when unexpected guests arrived. That ham was delicious, far tastier than what we buy now.

There was lots of work in there harvesting season but it was nice to feel productive. And it was a good feeling to know everything was stored and tucked away for the winter months ahead.

The Sawmill

About the year 1897 Father started a sawmill about five miles from home, near Ridgeville. He ran this mill during the winter months. Lumber was sold to the cities and he also built several houses in the town-which he rented for years. Of course he milled all the lumber that went into the new house and it was of the best, oak, sycamore and chestnut. When the Long Beach cottage was built he supplied for that too.

The mill had been in business about ten years before we were big enough to be taken up there. Tim and I were the youngest at that time.

The hired men from the farm would leave early every morning with teams of horses and bob-sleighs, since, during the winter the snow was deep. 'Early' meant that they would have been up and have the horses watered and fed, have their own breakfasts and be on the road by six o'clock. It was a two-hour drive at what would seem a snail's pace these days.

Father would leave later, sometimes, around seven, with a horse and cutter and arrive in time to oversee the work to be done. Mother would have been up early to get the men's breakfasts and pack enough lunch for all of them.

There was a cook-house up at the mill site. If there was lots of logging and sawing, extra men would be taken on and would sleep there. Uncle Ned was the cook, got the meals and did the chores.

It was just a small place but to us it seemed quite a spot. As I remember there was just one big room upstairs with four-poster beds very close together. We were not allowed up there, but we did peek. Twice a week Mother would make huge pans of fried cakes, a dozen pies or more and pans and pans of baked beans. She would either send them up with Father or perhaps hitch the horse to the cutter and take them herself, with someone always along for the ride.

What we loved best was to go in the morning with Father and spend the whole day. There was lots to do and we loved exploring this new territory.

The mill, in the middle of the woods, was mostly just a roof over the machinery part. We took great delight in riding the big log carrier in and out while the log was being cut up into boards. The zing of

The Goodwillie sawmill near Ridgeville in the early 1900s. John Allan in the sleigh. (Goodwillie family)

the big saw as it sliced its way through the log and the movement of the carrier gave us a huge thrill. I think now it must have been a dangerous practice but the men kept a good eye on us at all times.

Occasionally Dad would set us to piling the slabs as they were thrown to one side. We weren't too keen on this part of the day. Sometimes we would explore the surrounding woods and look for watercress in the ice-cold springs of which there were many. We didn't go too far away for the woods seemed very dense and we didn't want to get lost.

There was an added bit of excitement to beware of too. A man in the district not too well mentally paid the mill a visit once in a while. We were afraid of him, but now I know there wasn't any reason to have been. We never did see him but had heard the folks talk of him.

When noon-time came there was a blast of the mill whistle and all work stopped. Everyone washed up and turned to the lunch baskets. The men who lived at the shack of course went inside for their meal but we had our big baskets of food and ate outside in the sunshine. Hot tea was brought to us and we sat in the sun, out of the wind and were as cozy as could be. It was like having a winter picnic and we loved it.

By four or five o'clock we were ready to go home and usually Father was too. The men and teams would leave the same time and the long drive home seemed endless. We were glad to eat supper and go to our beds early.

The men had the horses to feed and rub down and other chores to do as well so it was a good long day for them.

There was never any grumbling about the day's work or the hours put in. There were lots of laughs and jokes and I only remember pleasant relationships. I believe nowadays men wouldn't work like that. The men seemed to enjoy their work and were really interested in what was being done. The pay was good for those days but very little, as we know it now. If you did a good day's work today you didn't have to do better tomorrow. Things sort of went along at an even pace with everyone happy, and no tension.

When there was a blizzard or very bad weather the mill didn't operate. However during the winter there were always lots of odd jobs to be done around the barns. The machinery needed repairs or the animals extra attention or maybe it would be sort of a relaxed lazy day for all.

One year Father took Mother and Iva and Mary to Norwich where they stayed most of the winter. Father and the men took off a stand of timber in that area and worked all winter cutting and hauling logs. Mother got meals for them all. I don't know where they lived as even Mary and Iva were little at that time.

I hardly think the sawmill operated for more than a few years. As all the local timber was cut the operation gradually phased out and then too the factory took up the winter work later on.

The Factory – Early Beginnings

The story about the factory began a long time ago, about 1890, just after Father married Mother. There were only five people living on the farm at that time, Grandfather and Grandmother, Father and Mother and an Aunt Phoebe, Father's only sister, who was not yet

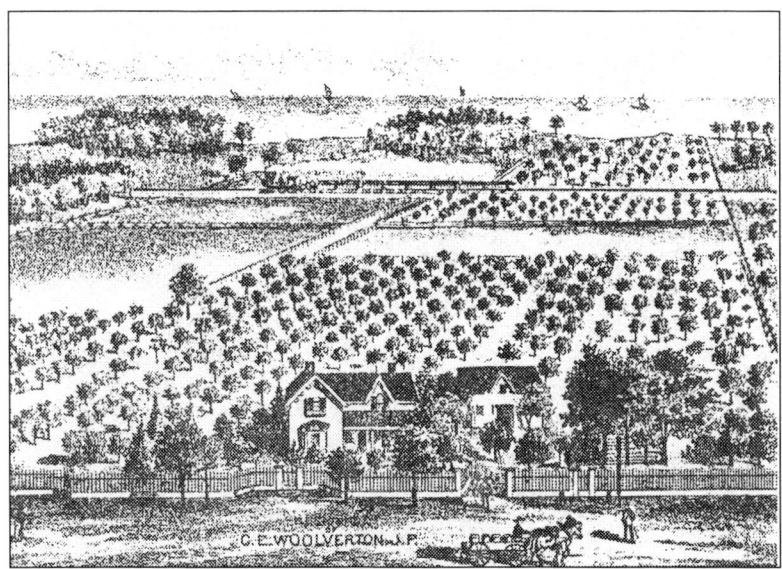

Many fruit farms in the Niagara peninsula started to produce surplus fruit and vegetables in the 1880s and 1890s. Sketch of a Fruit farm in Grimsby (Page)

married. Father, [aged 27 with his Father aged 60], was running the farm as well as a market gardening business among other things. Great Grandfather Joseph who started the farm had died in 1876.

In 1881 large quantities of fruit stocks from Morris Stone and Wellington in Fonthill had been purchased and planted. The farm specialized in pears, plums, apples, grapes, raspberries, red and black currants etc. In order to sell the produce Father was forced to seek broader markets as far away as Fort Erie, Port Colborne, Thorold and St. Catharines. Sometimes he even bought extra fruit from his neighbours and shipped to farther points.

No one had ever heard of trucks in those days, so Father made those long slow tiresome marketing trips with a team and market wagon, at least twice a week. He had to be at his destination when market opened, about seven in the morning, which meant he would be on the road about four o'clock. The team just jogged along at a slow steady pace. However when the fruit was all sold, it was fairly profitable.

In those days raspberries sold for about seven or eight cents a quart, quite a difference from now. The grape vines were said to be the first planted in the Thorold-Pelham area and among the first in the Niagara Peninsula. These grape vines produced excellent quality for over sixty years and were sold to many prominent Italian families in Welland.

Glass sealers, packing boxes and jam pails for the preservation of Goodwillie's fruits. (J.R. Goodwillie)

Farming and Fruit Canning Factory

As the trees and vines came into maturity in 1890 and with an especially good crop of berries, the question arose about what to do with the surplus. Try as he could Father couldn't get them all sold. Everyone, just everyone, had berries. Since nothing must go to waste Dad and Mother decided to preserve the berries and see if there was any market for canned fruit. What a job that was. Everything had to be done on a wood stove in the kitchen and it was so hot!

The fruit was carefully canned in quart glass sealers that Father placed in a suitcase and took as a sample to Toronto where he hoped to make a sale and take some orders. He drove five miles to board the train.

Father was gone a couple of days and the folk at home waited anxiously, wondering how he would make out. When they saw him driving in the lane they ran out to meet him to hear if the news was good or bad. It was a happy homecoming. Father had an order for several dozen cases, on trial, from a big store in Toronto. If the fruit sold well there were prospects of a really big order.

The fruit sold like hotcakes, far beyond any expectations. It was from this small beginning that the Goodwillie Factory originated. The canned fruit was put in pint sized glass jars, and the jam placed

The factory on Quaker Road. (Goodwillie Family)

in small wooden pails with wooden tops nailed to the top edges. These pails of five or six pound capacity were the fore runners of the four pound tin containers and were made like a barrel with wooden staves and wire retainers and a handle to make it look like a small pail. The first jams must have been very heavily sugared to preserve and retain the flavours.

The demand for the canned fruit and jam grew and grew. From this, a small factory was built on the Quaker Road farm a little distance from the house and away from the other farm building. A well had been drilled for extra water and fortunately there was lots of it and wonderfully good water it was.

Father originally grew and canned his own fruits, his slogan or trade mark was 'Home Industry, Picked and Packed the Same Day.' Eventually the demand was so great he was obliged to buy fruit from the neighbours and soon was getting it from the surrounding country. Farmers were growing fruit just for the factory and it was a good business for them too. During the busy season there would be a steady stream of wagons delivering fruit to the factory.

The Expanding Goodwillie Factory

As the business increased there was lots more help required. Some of the men would drive to Welland for women to clean and prepare the fruit. These women were called 'the hands'. I don't know how that name started, maybe because "many hands make light work". Well the work was light but there was lots of it.

In order to bring the 'Hands' out to the factory, two miles or more of clay roads, two large vans were purchased. They were built to specification and seemed quite large to us, but as I look at the pictures now they weren't so impressive. A padded seat ran the full length of each van, on each side. The van had a top and curtains that unrolled and dropped down along the sides for stormy weather. Each one was pulled by a team of horses and driven into town every morning for the women, and back again at night to take them home. If there was any extra room, there would be a mad scramble among us to see who would be lucky enough to make the trip. It was a good bit of fun in those days. We pretended we were in a covered wagon, and really enjoyed the pretence. It was especially nice on the return trip when we had the van to ourselves.

Fruit Harvesting and Canning Work

The real activity of the factory started as soon as strawberries got ripe. There was always lots of excitement and a great deal of comings and goings. The vans of course kept someone busy, noting and checking when farmers brought in fruit and when they received pay. The hired men looked after the rest of the farm and that work went on just the same, factory or no factory. I can still see those huge tubs of cleaned berries with a mountain of white sugar on top ready and waiting to be cooked and bottled. A big luscious strawberry picked from the middle of that pile of sugar was super delicious.

Mother had a lot of extra people to feed and look after, and we children had our jobs to do too. By the time the factory was really in full swing Iva, Mary, Grace, Tim, Jack, Bill, Pete and I were on the job. Mother did have help in the house, but still there was enough work for more than two or three women to manage. Grandma Stover was on hand too and did her share along with everyone else.

On top of all this, we had lots of relatives and city friends coming to visit. As soon as strawberries were canned, or made into jam, cherries, raspberries, plums, peaches and pears followed in a never-ending stream.

Some of us worked along with the 'Hands' and hulled berries, cleaned fruit or worked in the cook-room. The work in the cook-room was a very hot job but I always rather felt a most responsible one too. When you got to work there you had really grown up. Mary and Grace worked there a lot. Iva did the office work.

Those copper kettles were huge to my eyes, with the steam rolling out. Frank Orr supervised the cooking, standing over them watching with a keen eye to know just when the jam was ready to be bottled. I think it was a very primitive factory as factories go nowadays but it did the job. The windows and doors were wide open and there were

White cherries were 'Picked and packed in the same day.' (Label was provided by Beth Lucas, a distant Goodwillie relative living in Chicago)

lots of bees around. It was very hot; no air-conditioning in those days.

You know it was some of Father's strawberry jam that was served to the Prince of Wales, before the first war, as he was on a train tour across Canada. Fruit and jam were shipped to England regularly [jam was a later product than fruit bottling].

Family Work in the Factory

We all worked in the factory as we became old enough. We pulled rubbers (from the glass canning jars) apart, hulled strawberries, put the stuffing in boxes and when we got big enough, we had other jobs as well. Of course, we felt we were killed. Other kids didn't have to that but we did have a good time too. The work was never more than we could do.

Iva did the office work. When she was old enough she had travelled all the way to St. Catharines by streetcar to take a business course.

Mary and Grace worked in the cook-room or any place needed. This of course was when the factory was working during the summer months at the farm.

Grace (born April 1896) helped on the farm, in the canning factory and in the home. Grace was a good elocutionist and was invited to recite at many of the country garden parties, concerts and picnics where entertainment was provided, earning sometimes as much as $5.00 for a performance. She was a cute, dark-haired sparkling girl who was very popular at the entertainments throughout elementary school.

The Factory Work

In those days there were never any strikes and everyone seemed to enjoy the work, and pay, as they worked along to get the job done. There wasn't much work that a woman could do in those days, except housework and most of the women were glad to have a chance to earn some money.

At noon hour the whistle blew and the 'Hands' took their lunches out under the trees, on nice days. It was sort of a picnic for all. When the whistle blew again at one o'clock it was back to work until five and then the drive to town again. As mentioned earlier, when the house was being built they had fun at noon hour dancing in the unfinished rooms until time to get to work again.

There were steel trucks or carts eventually to carry the loaded boxes and crates. A long warehouse and more buildings for storing, all connected by a wide wooden platform. This made an ideal runaway for playing train in between times. We mixed our work with play but were seldom reprimanded for doing so.

In the fall, once the fruit was canned and the jam made, the shipping began. The jars had to be washed, labelled, wrapped and packed, twelve (pints by this time) to a box. The box was wooden and well padded with cardboard fillers so the jars wouldn't get broken in transit.

One of our jobs was to 'fill the boxes', that is put in the bottoms, sides and middle cardboard packing into each box so it would be ready to slip the jars in between and not waste time. It wasn't a hard job but we had to keep enough boxes filled so there wouldn't be any holdup in the packing. We had to be sure that the boxes were ready.

When the whole box-car load of those boxes was piled ahead of us we thought we would be doing that work forever. Eventually we would get them all 'stuffed'. We worked after school, Saturdays and some holidays. I'm afraid we didn't always stick to business too well. We would build houses and so on with the boxes, then work like crazy to catch up again. It was always good when the last box was stuffed and we could look forward to doing something else, but we felt satisfied too.

One day when we were playing hide and seek among the boxes I leaned against a sliding door that was not hooked. The door slowly moved outward and so did I. I fell about fifteen feet and landed on a pile of broken glass. There was great excitement among the women who were washing jars. No doubt I did my quota of yelling. Father gathered me up and carried me to the house but there were no ill effects, just one small cut on my arm. It was a frightening experience and I made sure I kept away from that door afterwards.

The packed boxes were stamped with addresses and ready for shipment. They were delivered, by team, to the railway station either in Welland or Port Robinson - and that was that.

There were times when we had to pull rubbers apart, jar rubbers that is. The rubbers would be stuck together on arrival from the rubber factory and it was much quicker if they had all been separated before reaching the cook-room. It was a very easy job but time consuming when we would rather be out running around.

Selling Peach Pits

The first money I ever really earned was all of eleven dollars for an eleven-quart basket full of peach pits. The nursery at Fonthill used to buy these pits for seed. I thought I was a millionaire.

I had asked some of the women of the factory to put them on one side when peeling peaches so it wasn't too hard a job to sort them from the peelings at the end of the day or after school. It was a slippery sticky mess though. I was so proud of myself I insisted on paying for my music lessons for that quarter which was a lost cause for me.

Farm chores: picking grapes

'Pete' Goodwillie

Grapes were both the bane of my life and the pleasure of harvests. In the spring for many years I had the job of helping tie up the grape vines. Tim had previously gone through and trimmed the grapes but before the buds formed it was necessary to tie the vines to the three wires in such a way as to allow lots of sun into the centres. Unfortunately, this work usually came at Easter time and it was always <u>cold</u>. So cold your fingers nearly dropped off with raw winds and even rain. Seldom was there any warm sun, as it was too early. It was a job no one liked but had to be done come hell or high water and if not completed during the Easter Holidays, then it was Saturdays.

But the pleasure of reaping the harvest was always worth the tortures of the cold. Our graperies were mostly of the Concord and Warden varieties but we also had several vines of Niagaras and Rogers and others. One in particular was a small reddish grape with a large tight bunch and the grapes were sweet as honey. I think we used to harvest about 20-30 tons each year. And every fall the Italian families from Welland would come out on the Sundays and arrange their order with father. I think the prices used to be about $100.00 per ton.

The Farm Factory Moves to Welland

The factory gradually grew and grew as business expanded. Help was harder to get in the country so it seemed more practical to build a new factory in town. This Father did, about the year 1912 or

1913. It was quite a large modern factory, very up-to-date at that time. However, it was not nearly so much fun as the old one. No doubt this was because we were older by that time. I must have been about twelve years old then, for later I used to walk from High School to the factory to get a ride home and the meantime 'stuffed' boxes as usual.

A surprise connection

Another branch of the Goodwillie family lived in Chicago and were successful in business. They were completely unaware of any Canadian Goodwillies until they started seeing the name of Goodwillie preserves on grocery store shelves.

Florence Goodwillie wrote form Boston on 25 February 1916 to John Goodwillie in Welland: "While on a recent trip to St. John, New Brunswick, I noticed on a shelf in a grocery store, some preserves with your name on the label. I bought some home to Boston for a sample but the preserves did not

Envelope from David Goodwillie in Chicago to Goodwillies on Quaker Road. 1916. (Goodwillie)

Farming and Fruit Canning Factory

The Welland Factory had a cream colored brick chimney with black bricks spelling out GOODWILLIE, starting at the top with G. It was a high smoke stack for Welland at that time. (J.R. Goodwillie taken about 1958)

interest me quite as much as the name on the label". Florence advised her cousin, a David L. Goodwillie, who corresponded with the Welland family during 1916 and ordered several shipments of preserves. He commented: "My wife says the nearest to homemade goods you can imagine...now just kindly remember that I want some cases of this year's pack and especially peaches."

During the first World War, Mabel Secord, (Iva's sister-in-law) worked in the factory and a couple of boys from High School as well. They got their final High School examinations by helping during the war, [First World War] supposedly on the farm.

Mother always packed a lunch for us all. This we usually ate in the small office. It certainly wasn't a swish office you see nowadays. There was a roll-top-desk, a table and a cot on which Father often had a nap after lunch. He needed it too for he worked day and night almost, during the rush season.

Sometimes Mabel and I would go outside to the shipping platform to eat. Lots of times while there, a big long troop train would pass through. The boys always waved like crazy and so did we.

Often we thought we were working pretty hard and hard done by. Other kids didn't have to do what we did, they were off having fun someplace. However it wasn't as bad as we thought and we learned a lot as we went along. Work is only work if you make it so. If you work and enjoy it, it isn't hard work. If you don't it seems twice as hard to get the job done, besides it spoils your disposition.

The Factories

Memories of Pete Goodwillie

The factory in Welland was built about 1910-12 and must have been one of the finest in the city at that time. The big smoke chimney was probably 150 feet high made of special refractory buff brick. On the side facing the Canada Forge and Railroad in Black Brick from bottom to top in large letters was the name GOODWILLIE. The chimney was dismantled about 1965.

I have 3 or 4 recollections of the Welland Factory. I well recall going out to Fonthill and Ridgeville to pick up fruit in the old chain drive Packard truck (one of the first five in Welland). We picked up strawberries by the crate full. (36

The Goodwillie truck was in demand for picnics, parades, family outings and factory work. It was an eight ton Packard with chain drive, hard tires and gas lights. About 1910-1920. (Cornett)

quart boxes made one crate). Crate on crate made truckloads which were then taken to the factory for hulling. This is the first job I remember when I was paid for working. Iva was in the office and supervised. I don't recall how much per box for hulling but it seemed like a lot then.

After hulling they were all washed and dumped into a huge tub and pails of sugar added. The taste of those large delicious red sweet strawberries is still in my veins. Later they were emptied into large copper vats where they were cooked and later put in 5 lb tins as jam – or glass as preserves.

Another job was 'the packing boxes'. On the second floor overlooking the railroad track the boxes for packing the glassed fruit and the corrugated paper spaces and liners had to be assembled and made ready for easy packing of the jars – either pints or quarts, 12 or 24 to a box. We used to watch the steam engines and trains go by and delighted in counting the box and gondola cars to each train. Many times we waved to the soldiers on their way to or from training and the wars. This would be in 1917-18.

About the same time, probably a little later I had an accident and suffered a badly crushed big toe. A small truck about five feet long and three feet wide transported the fruit or jams in cases/boxes. The truck had two large twelve inch wheels in the centre and one small roller wheel at each end. When pushing, the front and centre wheels took the weight and it could be moved easily in any direction. Then one particular day I slipped or fell and one wheel went over my left big toe. Boy did it hurt. My father decided I had to go to the Doctor and he bundled me up and drove 'old Dick' with the Democrat to the Doctor. I lost the nail and suffered a lot of pain but no further damage.

It has always been a sad thought that we could not have kept the factory and continued on with the canning business. Unfortunately, Jack and Bill were too young. Iva was married and George was in the bank and apparently not interested. If the boys had been older, or if father had lived another 5 or 10 years, I'm sure the business would have carried on.

I have no recollection of the factory when operating at the farm. Of course I remember some of the stories re-told about the old days but as a kid and later, of course, many hours were spent rummaging around in some of the things left there. For example, we used to play with the two special coach wagons for transporting workers to and from Welland. In later years the birds made a considerable mess of those wagons.

The old water tower was always an interesting place to get into. It had a big wooden tank built up over a square-type covering of two floors with shingle sides on all four facings. There were no windows and only one door. It was used for storing labels etc. These were left over from the operation at the farm and were probably obsolete or excess. I remember about 1923-4 going through this stuff and finding cases of jam with the steel screw wings badly rusted and the jam hardened but still not too bad. There was so much sugar content, I presume that it couldn't really spoil – it just hardened and stiffened. I also found some old #5 wooden pails with the wooden lids intact and the jams also hardened and dried. Foolishly, we never kept any of the old labels (several boxes of them) nor any of the jams.

The Goodwillie Promotional posters were made into t-shirts in 1995 at the most recent gathering of the Quaker Road Goodwillie clan. (T. Mehmood)

At the east end of the factory there were hundreds of these old wooden stave pails nested one into each other and upside down in piles. Fruit was preserved in pint jars and jam was preserved in small wooden pails. There were hundreds of these pails abandoned when the tin pails and glass jars were introduced. There are still a few around to remind us. But I often wished we had kept them all. Every museum in Canada would love to have them.

The buildings used for storage of implements, wood and old wagons became dilapidated and were uncared for with all their valuable relics and antiques. Gradually they were disposed of to use the buildings for farm storage but no one remembers where or how or when.

I've never given it much thought before but you know Father never had us on the payroll. We didn't even consider that we should be paid for any of our work. When we wanted money we asked for it and were usually given more than asked for. How we hated to ask though. It is much better to have an allowance and know how much you can spend.

"Where is factory now?" Well, it ran most successfully for about fifteen years then Father got sick, in the Fall of 1921. He gradually got worse and in January of 1922 he passed away. This was a great blow to everyone as you may imagine. Pete was 12 years old and the older boys still in school.

As there was no-one who could keep the Factory going, it was sold eventually to Martin's Dairy. [which later became the Howard Johnson Dairy and burned down in 1982] The fruit and jams were gradually sold and that was sort of the end of an era.

This is a sad note on which to end a little story but sadness goes with stories too.

CHAPTER TEN

Last Days on the Quaker Road Farm

Father always had violent headaches but in 1921 his symptoms became much worse. I used to drive him to St. Catharines for mineral baths and that is when I learned how to drive a car.

John Allan Goodwillie as a young man. c. 1890. (Goodwillie family)

The baths didn't seem to help and he gradually got worse until in January 1922 he passed away. He had Bright's Disease, [inflammation of the kidneys] which can be cured these days but apparently not at the that time. What a blow!! Since Iva was the only one who knew anything about the office work, Father relied on her. She was so busy, she didn't go to the hospital and Jean was born [fall 1921] at the farm.

Last days on the Quaker Road Farm

The Welland Tribune and Telegraph

An amalgamation on Oct. 1st, 1920, of the Welland Tribune and the Welland Telegraph, each founded in 1863

WELLAND ONT., TUESDAY, JANUARY 17, 1922

Death of a Splendid Man

John Goodwillie Prominent in Business and in Agriculture-

IN THE DEATH of John Goodwillie on Sunday, Welland Country lost a native son, who was in many respects an ideal man. Other men may have worked as hard as he did, other men may have played as hard as he did, but we know of none who combined in such nice proportion hard work and wholehearted play.

He was a man of action. A large farm and one of the best in the country made no light claim upon his labour and his time, but he operated as well a canning business that had won a very enviable place throughout the breadth of Canada. Goodwillie's jam stands in a class by itself. By its own merit it has won its place. Notwithstanding his energy as a worker and his responsibilities as a business man, John Goodwillie was one who took a rich enjoyment out of life. In his amusements he never lost the zest of youth. In his pleasures he was the companion of his family of his boys and girls. He, who in growing years, in growing duties and responsibilities can keep close to his children, gets something real and beautiful out of life.

John Goodwillie was a man liked by everyone, by young and old, by city and country. He stood four-square in all his relationships. He had a kindly and pleasant humour and a keen interest in all about him. Mr. Goodwillie was for four years president of the Welland County Agriculture Society and always took a very deep interest in all phases of the fair, though he was primarily a horseman. He was for many years and until the day of his death a trustee of the Quaker Road School.

On September 25th last he was seized with a bad attack of heart failure and for long his life hung in the balance, but he did regain his feet again and was able to be out and about. On New Year's Day however, Bright's disease developed and from early last week his condition became so grave as to shatter hope. He passed away at nine o'clock on Sunday morning.

Born at Bayham almost 59 years ago, he came to Thorold Township with his father, the late Hiram Goodwillie, when only three years of age, so he has been a resident of the township for over half a century.

He is survived by his widow, four daughters, Mrs. George Secord, of Fonthill; Mrs. N.P. Haist, and Mrs. Russell Northcote, of Welland: Miss Ruth, at home; and four sons, Harold, Donald, Hugh and Ross, all at home. Mrs. Wm. Hedrick of Otterville is a sister. These mourners have the sincere sympathy of many friends in the great loss they have sustained. The funeral is to take place this afternoon with service at his late home at 2 o'clock. Burial will be at Fonthill Cemetery.

Front Page - The Welland Tribune and The Welland Telegraph Tuesday January 17, 1922

After Father's Death

Well, life moved on as it must do. Many an evening Mother spent in the garden those days working to forget, hoeing vegetables or strawberry plants.

Pete was only 12 years old, Jack and Bill were in High school. I had finished school and had been helping Mother for the three years since school. Girls really didn't work out much in those days and Father never thought we should go to work. There was enough to be done at home.

I went and took a business course and got a job at Electo Metals where I worked for eight years until I was married, [1931]. Mother carried on much as usual on the outside. She was never one to show her feelings but I know she must have been very lonely.

What was the Electro-Metals Company

Electro Metals Limited moved to the banks of the third Welland Canal in 1907 Attracted by low cost electricity, an abundance of water to cool furnaces and easy transportation in and out of the Welland plant. It became Canada's first ferroalloys producer. Materials to produce ferroalloys and carbon electrodes were shipped and unloaded using the Welland Canal, CN and NYC railway. Alloy sales were conducted from the Welland office. The success of Electro-Metals established Welland as a specialty steel and iron center. During World War One, Electro Metals supplied the Allies with ferrosilicon for armaments, shrapnel shells and hydrogen for barrage and observation balloons. In 1923, Electro Metals Limited was taken over by Union Carbide and Carbon Company of the United States but the Electro Metallurgical Company of Canada in Welland closed in 2000.[53]

After a few years Tim took over the managing of the farm but Mother always kept a finger on things and advised as things went along. Eventually when the farm was sold, he and his wife Grace [nee

After Father's death, Ruth went to work at Electro Metals. Jack put himself through Agriculture College in Guelph and a Masters degree at Michigan State graduating in 1932. From left: Ruth, Jack and Bill in 1924. (Cornett)

Schooley] lived in a Welland subdivision where Tim had bought and sold property. Beverley Street was named after his sister's daughter [Beverley Warner, nee Pierce]

Iva, Mary and Grace had all been married before Dad passed away and eventually there were five Grandchildren: Jean, Joyce, Dorothy, Jack and Nancy. How life improved with their arrival.

Sunday nights everyone arrived for supper, which Jean started to call 'cocoa tea' because we always had cocoa for the little ones. It was a pleasant time for everyone. Life went along.

Sundays were always very busy days. The boys having been batching all week, a big dinner was always planned for noon. The pies had to be baked fresh that morning, usually four of them. The roast of beef was large and juicy and vegetables by the basket had to prepared. The table was always stretched full length and a small table set up for the children. For supper it was usually stacks of sandwiches, cake and so on, a serve yourself set up.

Pete was a big comfort to Mother when the other boys had gone. He finished High School and went to Queens University, was there the year we were married in 1931. He hitchhiked home for our wedding. Hitchhiking at that time was quite safe. He took a position in Toronto, having the added attraction of Ruth Payne living there. Pete also served in the army in the 1939-45 war but never got overseas. He was slated to go a couple of times but orders were changed at the last moment.

Fruit picking during the war

by Pete Goodwillie

In 1945 as a Sergeant of the RCOC and Kent Regiments, I was camped – in army tents – on the very ground where General Brock, Brant, Governor Simcoe and the US Army had made important history. In September of 1945 the World War of Europe was over. A bomb had been dropped in Japan. The war was coming to an end. Soldiers were being employed in the labour-starved factories and fruit harvesting. On the night the news arrived of the Japanese surrender, I was filling in for a sick Sergeant Major at the Anther [?] Imperial Iron Foundry. Black, hot and tired, I still was exuberant. I would soon get out of my long dreamed discharge and be back with my wife and son, Hugh. A second child was expected momentarily.

On 24th of September 1945, my father-in-law, Douglas Payne, tried desperately to contact me at the Niagara-on-the-

Above: The Secord grandchildren Joyce (Dinnin Shand), left, and Jean (Cousins) loved to visit the farm. 1923-24. (Cornett)

Right: Beverly Crescent in Welland is named after John Allan's great, great grand-daughter Beverley (Pierce) Warner. c. 1949 (Cornett)

Grandmother Luella with Patsy and grandchildren a year before the farm was sold. From left Joyce Dinnin, Luella, Nancy Shier, Jean Secord, Jack Northcote. 1937. (Cornett)

Lake Camp. I had been at Queenston fruit farm supervising a group of soldiers picking the luscious Niagara peaches. That evening I learned I now had a second child, Diane. Who would ever have guessed that some 36-37 years later that same 'girl' would be traipsing all over the area dominated by the Japs shortly before she was born.

The Army officials felt sympathetic to my newly arrived daughter and anxious to reduce their pay-roll. I was given my official discharge. I took the 'Dalhousie City' boat from Port Dalhousie and arrived in Toronto in time to see the new baby being fed.

The Other Boys

Jack quit school and worked at the same plant as I did, for one year. He then decided he wasn't going to get anywhere without more education and finally entered Ontario Agricultural College at Guelph. Here he assumed his right name 'Don'. Jack practically put himself through college by playing hockey. He worked most of his life, eventually becoming the Director of the Dairy Produce Division with the Canadian Department of Agriculture.

Sergeant John Ross Goodwillie was stationed in New Brunswick and rarely got home to visit with wife Ruth Payne and son Hugh who lived with the Payne family on Chatsworth Dr. Toronto. March, 1944. Near the end of the war he was transferred to Niagara on the Lake (Cornett)

Jack and Bill started college together but Bill only went for one year. He decided to go back to farm. He went on the Harvesters Excursion and spent one summer out West on a ranch. One Fall he went on a steamer with Jack but that didn't suit either. It was a terrible trip, cold and ice and a poor introduction to sailing which he didn't like at all. He carried on at the farm but was not too content and was thinking of schooling in New Brunswick or McMaster. One very hot summer

Diane points out to her brother's family the places where she and Ruth Lechte have worked: Papua New Guinea, Solomon Islands, Gilbert Islands, Fiji and the South Pacific generally. 2003. From left standing: Diane, Ruth, Hugh, Sally. Seated: Lynne, Anne, Jon. (K. Rapp)

after working hard in the haying he got pleurisy and was not too well afterwards. The following June he was much worse and passed away in June 1932.

Mother never really did get over Bill's passing. He was such a big strong lovable boy and only twenty-five years old. The strawberries really got a hoeing that year. But life went on.

TB takes its toll in 1932

Hugh Allan 'Bill' Goodwillie
– (Condensed Diary Notes by his little brother 'Pete')

May 24-25, 1932

Willie went down to the Sanitarium to have some x-rays and examinations and the general result is that he has T.B. – a type know as 'galloping consumption' and that it is very doubtful if he will get better. There is just one chance – 'the gold cure'—which he is going to take but the doc says it isn't very satisfactory –just a last resort. He hasn't done any coughing yet. Bill knows he has T.B. but not that he can't get better.

What happens is that his temperature gets higher and higher and he practically burns up and there is also a chance of spinal meningitis as well as it may affect his head. So that accounts for his temperature all along and his losing weight and his sore neck and eyes. But lately his temperature has been almost normal. The doc certainly does not speak hopefully at all but personally I think he's all wet. I've been thinking about it most of the time

Father, John Allan, Grandma Sarah, Mother Lou and son Bill (Hugh Allan) about 1915. (Cornett)

and I just have a feeling that he will get better and I sure hope I'm right.

It's impossible to realize, as he was always such a bearcat for fresh air and exercise and the fact that he looks and acts O.K now. But apparently once it gets going it goes fast as the dickens thus 'galloping'. Anyway he goes to the Sanitarium this week for this cure and will be there for 6 weeks or so.

May 25-June 6:

Bill went to the Sanitarium Friday May 25. On the 28th Bill looked OK to me and seemed quite cheerful but June 6th (a week later) he is much worse. Since he went to the San his temperature has raised till now it is 102 and 103, he sweats terribly and has been very sick at his stomach. He has lost a lot of weight and only weighs 138 lbs. now. His eyes are bothering him a lot.

A terrible little thing happened the other day when in the parlor I noticed a picture against the wall on the floor and thought they had left it there while cleaning and so remarked about it to Ruth and Mother. On investigation the picture had fallen from its place to the floor. Before Dad died mother found a picture fallen in a similar way and of course mother thought of the significance at once. I vaguely remember the picture incident but I do remember the sparrow in the cellar before Dad died and if we find one this time I certainly will believe in such things.

June 7-11

Bill said he felt worse to-nite than he has so far and he certainly looked it. Poor kid he can't be far from the end now surely and I hope he isn't because he suffers a lot but he doesn't complain a bit—I like his 'guts'. To relieve his sickness the docs have drained his spine which relieves the pressure. I guess they'll have to do this often now. He took his second treatment of 'gold' but does no good in fact x-rays of the other day show a worse infection.

I wonder if a bird which flew up against the dining room window twice at supper time to-nite is a sign of impending danger or sorrow. I think I'm the only one who noticed it. In a way I hope it is because Willie is certainly suffering considerable.

June 12-16

I may have a tough week ahead of me. As I write this a big lump comes to my throat and water to my eyes. To add to my worries Ruth's [Payne] birthday is on the 30th and I will have to get a present but what will it be? I always worry about that. What will I use for money? Being her 21st birthday and loving her as I do I would like to make it something nice and distinguished but that's out –there's a depression on. And how I know it.

At age 25 in 1931, Hugh Allan, nicknamed Bill showed potential to take over the Quaker Road farm. Everyone grieved when he died of T.B. in June 1932 ten years after his father had suddenly died. (Cornett)

June 29th (Wed.) 1932

Much as happened since I last wrote. Bill is dead and buried. He died a week ago tomorrow night at 8:15 E.D.S.T. (June 23)

From Sunday till Thursday he was unconscious and in that state he didn't suffer a bit. On Saturday it began to show and he was wandering in his talk so Sunday morning I went down with Ruth [Cornett] and Mother and that was the last time I saw him alive. He was about half-conscious and was talking a lot but we couldn't understand him. The funny part of it was that he looked better but that was because of his higher temp (103 to 104) and his bright shining eyes.

While Mother and Ruth were seeing the Doc I was with him alone and so I tried to tell him that Ruthie Payne and I were in stronger than ever again. All he said was 'are they up at the lake [Long Beach cottage] now?' and that was the last intelligent thing he spoke to me of.

Sunday night Bill regained consciousness for a while and confided to Iva that he thought he wouldn't get better. He put his arms around her neck and drew her down and cried some. He had previously told the nurse he didn't think he'd get better.

June 23, 1932 -- ten years after Dad -- Bill died the same time as he was born around 7 o'clock. And so passed the greatest guy I've every known or will know. It was a mighty sad household that hit the hay on June 23rd.

Relatives came, and friends, telegrams, cards and letters were received. I got the loveliest letter imaginable from Ruth Payne. It was beautiful and almost overcoming. And she had signed 'love' instead of the usual 'sincerely'. It sure was a touching letter.

Friday was another tough day for all concerned. In the morning his body was brought and it came back exactly to the hour just 4 weeks after he walked out to the car to go to the San.

Saturday dawned raining and as the proverb says 'happy is the soul that the rain falls on' so that helped me a bit. It was a sad and most terrible funeral. Everyone had tears. I continually thought of Willie and how he would despise tears and so I kept my chin up as high as possible. But coming back tears fell all the way and I felt terrible and immediately on arrival I went to my room and cried for 15 or 20 minutes.

Pete with his girlfriend Ruth Payne at the Payne Long Beach Cottage. C. 1930. (Goodwillie family collection)

It was also in this state, after the service that Ruth [Payne] came to my room. I was sure surprised to see her. She never saw me cry before and I shame to think of it now but for 5 minutes I couldn't stop. Finally I did and after some time managed to regain myself. We talked a lot. She was perfectly lovely. I can't express how I appreciated it. I have written a few letters telling her a lot I wouldn't tell anyone else.

But I guess that's all. Its all over now and as nearly normal as it can be. The girls come out real often. Aunt Tebe and Uncle Will are here. The berries are in their prime with 60 boxes Monday and over 100 to-day. Tomorrow I go to Toronto for Ruth's birthday and back Friday, so au Revoir.

Selling the Quaker Road Farm

In Father's Will the farm was supposed to be sold, but as long as the boys were still at home it was more economical to keep the farm. Also farm prices were very low and no one had money for much in that period. However in the year 1938 an offer came and it was deemed advisable to make the sale. [about $35,000.00]

It was a real heartbreak for Mother to leave her home of many years. She loved every blade of grass on the place but never made any complaint even though all her memories were tied up in the Farm.

The morning George telephoned to tell her that the sale had been made we both sat down in the back yard and wept. Then Mother got up and went for a long walk back over the farm, alone. She never once showed her heartbreak afterwards. That was the first of May. We had two months to sort, sell, or destroy that which was not wanted. It took us about six weeks to clear the attic. Old pictures to be looked at...will we keep or will we not. It all took time.

Pete married Ruth Payne nine years after Bill died. Their first child born 1943 was named after Bill, (Hugh Allan), 'the greatest guy I've every known'. Here Pete and son Hugh Douglas Goodwillie are at Long Beach, 1944. (Goodwillie family)

Luella Goodwillie moved to 37 Griffith Street Welland after the farm was sold. Later she stayed with daughter Ruth Cornett in Toronto until she died in 1950. Photo taken 1939. (Cornett)

Farm life ended about the end of June 1938. Mother and I stayed at the lake for the summer and well on in October. Then we took a trip out to Camrose, Vancouver and Victoria visiting some relatives. When we got home I found Jack [Cornett] was working in Toronto and we could settle in one spot. We got an apartment and I moved to Toronto.

It is funny how things worked out that way for it just wouldn't have seemed right for me to leave Mother alone at the farm. In the Fall of 1947 Mother came to Toronto and lived with us. We had bought a house [46 Old Mill Drive near Bloor Street] and had lots of room. She lived with us until she passed away in May 1950. George Secord (Iva's husband) died the same year in January.

Now I have told you many of the old time doings, there were many good times, some bad ones, but altogether a good life and lots to remember and cherish. I hope these Memoirs may be of some help in the future when someone asks about Life on the Farm and the Olden Days.

Post Script

Pete married his beloved 'Ruthie' (Payne) in 1941. Other sisters and brothers married and had children and grandchildren and great grandchildren. Ruth Cornett kept in touch with family members and remained the story-teller, aided by her younger brother Pete. Both Pete and his wife Ruthie are buried close to 'Bill' at the Goodwillie Tombstone with his mother, father, grandfather and grandmother in the Fonthill Cemetery, not too far from another section containing two of his sisters (and their husbands) Ruth Cornett and Mary Haist and the grave of the original Quaker Road settlers Joseph and Eliza.

Many of the family members are now scattered and some know little about the farm, but as Ruth Cornett has said: "maybe you can pass these stories on to your children and grandchildren—all are true".

The Goodwillie Packard truck, one of the first in Welland was used for parades and picnics as well as for factory work. (Courtesy Gladys Berg, in Goodwillie)

SECTION THREE

A Brief Family History

A Brief Family History

Year	Event	Other related events and comment
First Nations in Canada and Fife, Scotland		
From 7,000 B.C.	From 7,000 Laurentian people hunted in Ontario. Woodlands people c. 1000 B.C. started using pottery. Algonquian groups were further north.	Stone age Picts occupied Fife from about 7,000 B.C. Gaelic speaking Celts invaded about 400 B.C. Between A.D. 82 and A.D. 208, the Romans invaded Scotland.
0-900 A.D.	By 10th century A.D. mainly Iroquoian speakers in southern Ont. Iroquois Confederacy established 1142 followed by solar eclipse. By 1300 A.D Neutral, Erie, Huron, Petun Nations established. Grew corn, squash, sunflowers, hunted, lived in long houses in fenced villages, used tobacco.	Vikings invaded Fife in the 10th century. Robert the Bruce led a revolt for independence, was crowned king of Scotland in 1306. After years of battle defeated the English in 1314. In 1328 the English finally recognized Scottish independence.
1400-1800	In 1400s lacrosse was played between various First Nations groups By 1640 Neutral Nations wiped out by Iroquois: mainly Seneca & Mohawk. Algonquian groups: Ojibway (Mississauga) migrated south to the Niagara Peninsula.	Golf first played on St. Andrews in 1400s. 1539 First Scottish tennis court built. In 1567, Mary, Queen of Scots, a Catholic, was forced to abdicate the Scottish throne. John Knox in 1560s introduced the Scottish reformation, and the Presbyterian church officially replaced Catholicism. Scottish migration overseas started in mid 1600s.
Scottish links with Goodwillies (S = Scottish; 1,2,3 = generation)		
1590-5	James Goodwillie S1, first known Goodwillie ancestor, born at 'Gaitmill' or Goatmilk, between Kinglassie & Leslie north of Kirkcaldy.	James a (black) smith lived at Goatsmilk all his life. His baptism note is the second entry in Kinglassie Parish Register. Roman relics found at Goatmilk Farm.
1626-27	Son David Goodwillie S2, born in Goatmilk. Baptized 26 Jan 1627.	D.G.had three children Christian 1659 David 1665 Rachael 1671.
cir 1627	Early 1600s family moved from Goatmilk to Tanshall Farm. Sold in 1779. Lived there until 1798.	Goodwillies were yeoman or small tenant farmers on ten acres. New city of Glenrothes developed c.1950. Townhouses on Keith Dr & Tanshall Rd. E. for coal workers in nearby mine replaced Tanshall farm demolished in 1960s.
1627	Heinrich Hellems left Germany. Moved to Pennsylvania. Sons inter-married with Tuscarora people. About 1810, Mattias moved to Welland.	Elizabeth, daughter of Mattias, married Joseph Goodwillie, c.1820. Hellems Ave, Welland named after the family The Welland Canal and a large part of Welland was built on Elizabeth's father's property.

Timeline of Relevant Events

Year	Event	Other related events and comment
1630-75	Jonathon Page with three brothers left England. Moved to Mass. Some Pages went to Ryegate Vermont, near Barnet. Alexander Page at age 20 walked from Ryegate to the Welland area about 1826.	Alexander's grand-daughter Luella Page married John Allan Goodwillie, who successfully developed the Goodwillie Fruit Preservation Factory in Welland. Page Drive, Welland is named after her family.
1665-1745	Grandson David S3 lived in Tanshall. Buried in Kinglassie Church, Fife.	One of oldest stones in Kinglassie Cemetery marks David, wife Elizabeth Dewar and son James.
1709-1782	James, b 1709 S4 in mid 1700s handwrote family history records on parchment.	Smaller grave stone marks James and parents. Tall spire cemetery stone marks James' brother, David S4 & family.
1749 & 51	5th generation S5: Birth of David 1749 & Joseph 1751, American pioneers.	Unemployment and poverty in Scotland after the British Seven Years War with France. Joseph left Scotland at age 22. David studied theology at U. of Edinburgh, became teacher then preacher.
1773, 1788 & 1789	1773 Joseph at age 22 & 1788 David at age 37 left Scotland for America. David went to Barnet 1789 as church minister and remained there for his whole life.	Joseph lived in Mohawk Valley, NY, as a blacksmith & later then joined British Army, then given Loyalist land in Quebec and rejoined brother in Vermont in 1793. In 1790 David married Beatrice Henderson who had come on same ship from Scotland. Given religious duties as well as farm lands in Barnet area.
1777-83	Joseph S5 joined British Army. Prisoner in Saratoga. 1778 and escaped from Albany (Auburn) prison. Garrison duty around Montreal until disbanded 1783.	American Revolution 1775-1783. Joseph was probably a gunsmith. Part of Jessup's Army in Quebec. Remained single. Given Loyalist land in New Carlisle, then married at age c. 34.
1782-1806	James S4 died 1782. In 1788 son David S5 migrated and the Scottish Goodwillie family left Tanshall farm to farm at nearby Macedonia. Mother Mary S4 died 1806.	Goodwillie's were active church members in 1700s as shown in Kinglassie and Leslie Parish Registers.

Quebec and Vermont   C = Canadian 6,7,8 = generation from earliest Scot

Year	Event	Other related events and comment
1784	Joseph went to Paspébiac then received Loyalist land at New Carlisle, 15 km east.	Paspébiac - a name derived from Mi'kmaq describing the sand bay. Became an active centre for fishing in the 1800s.
c.1785	Joseph married Mary Ann Teague, daughter of Jacob who had neighbouring land.	Joseph's future father-in-law, Jacob Teague, fled his farm at Tyron County and joined Butler's Rangers and served at Mal Bay. Other Teague ancestors – Smiths – remain in Gaspé.

A Brief Family History

Year	Event	Other related events and comment
c. 1793	After 9 years in New Carlisle, Joseph & Mary Ann and 3 children moved to Barnet close to older brother Rev.David.	Heard that brother was in Vermont & in 1792 Joseph visited and decided to move his family to farm in northern Vermont.
1795	Birth in Barnet of Joseph C 6 son of Loyalist Joseph S5.	Joseph and Mary Ann had ten children -7 girls & 3 sons. 2 girls & 2 boys migrated to Ont. Between 1818-1826.

Quaker Rd. and Goodwillie Settlers

Year	Event	Other related events and comment
1780-1792	Sales negotiations and treaties with First Nations to surrender land and draw boundaries enabled subdivision and sale of land in the Niagara peninsula after 1792 to British loyalists.	1789 called the Hungry Year after early frosts and crop failure. Free cheap & fertile land attracted British Loyalist, military personnel & African Americans fleeing discrimination as well as other young adventurers. 1792 Fonthill to Port Robinson Rd. named Hurricane Rd. after storm flattened houses and crops.
1791-93	1791 settlers in Niagara district owned approx 300 slaves. An Act of Parliament in 1793 limited slavery in Upper Canada.	Although discriminatory practices continued, Governor Simcoe with civic and religious leaders promoted abolition of slavery and Canada was thought to be a safe place for runaway American slaves.
1796-9	By 1797 Israel Swayze in Beaverdams had planted 200 apple trees on 90 acres. 1799 Quaker Rd. included in Welland County grant of 7,900 acres to Hon Robert Hamilton.	This unregistered land granted as crown land to Hamilton, a wealthy Queenston merchant, although originally land bought from original patentees. Quaker settlers remained loyal to Britain (pacifists during conflict) and moved to area.
1805-10	First known settlement on Quaker Rd. Jacob Gainer arrived in Ont. In 1796 & purchased 100 acres from Hamilton just prior to his marriage. Later this Niagara St. land sold for Welland Exhibition grounds.	Wilderness Indian path. No roads, travel by horse or on foot. Bridgewater (Chipawa) was closest supply town. In France, 1809 Appert won prize for bottling technique for food preservation. In 1810 in UK, Durrand patented the cylindrical tin can.
1812-14	War between America and the British Colony. 1813 Laura Secord risked her life to reveal American plans to the British command.	Niagara peninsula homes were in constant danger of looting and taking men as prisoners by the American invaders. Iroquois and other Nations fought against the Americans.
1816	First Quaker Rd School-north side Lot 174, on the 50 acre property of R.S. Garner.	Later school built on Lot 233 on Page property. R.S. Garner's son L.V. Garner married Jane Page, mother of Luella Page Goodwillie.

Timeline of Relevant Events

Year	Event	Other related events and comment
1818-1823	Joseph C6 moves to Wainfleet from Barnet, Vermont & marries Elizabeth Hellems. In 1823 Goodwillies live in Wainfleet possibly Lot #14 Con 5 (or 6).	Cabinet maker- possibly in Wainfleet, later moved to Welland's Quaker Rd. 6 sons 2 daughters. 1818 letter in family archives from uncle Rev David S5 to Joseph C6 possibly to support land claim or prepare for marriage.
1818-1826	4 Goodwillie youth move from Barnet to within 60 miles of each other in southern Ont.	In 1818 Mary Young to W. Chinguacousy and Joseph to Wainfleet-Welland area. About 1819. Elizabeth Cross to Esquesing via Welland & in 1820s George to Georgetown.
1828-9	Assume the Goodwillies are on Quaker Rd. Farming. Joseph also making furniture & coffins. Welland Canal started 1824 & opened 1829.	Niagara District census shows 2 males over 16 (Joseph & cousin or labourer) and 3 males under 16 (sons) & 1 adult female (wife Eliza) and 1 under 16, (a cousin or helper).
1836	First Goodwillie ownership of Quaker Rd. land. Joseph purchased Lot 227 North side of Quaker Rd. & east of First Ave.	Cost £400 or about $2,000. In 1807 Lot 227 sold by Hon. Robert Hamilton a Queenston Merchant to Isaac Willson who sold it in 1836 to Goodwillie. 1836 crop failures fuelled farmer dissatisfactions and revolts in the next years.
1837-38	Farmers rebellion against political corruption and upper class & religious privileges led by William Lyon Mackenzie.	Two killed in race riots over deportation of American slave Solomon Mosesby. A Black Military Corp helped solve disputes and later those with Welland Canal workers.
1837-8	Original Goodwillie farmhouse burned down c.1837. Joseph elected Rd. representative for Thorold Township - one of three.	First train Hamilton to Niagara Falls over Niagara Falls Suspension bridge. Quaker Road first statute road in Thorold kept in good condition by local farmers.
1840s	Joseph built new house with log beams, plaster 3 inch thick planks. Influx of African Americans via underground railroad. July 1840 skirmish of canal workers quelled by Black troopers from the 'Coloured Corps' stationed at Port Robinson.	Lot 227 house and land sold to Orin Bemis. African Americans competed for jobs with Irish and English immigrants. 1849 Lord Elgin escorted by guard from Black corps' finest men. Corps disbanded in 1850.
1850-51	Death of Joseph's sons: 1850 Alan B. # 5 son & 1851 George Willson Bulien #1 son who was married with child.	G.W. died suddenly. Wife remarried Francis Stokes about 1853. In 1876 Atlas Lot #14 Concession 5 (or 6) Wainfleet Township (100 acres) listed as 'Goodwillis'.
c. 1850-51	Joseph's #4 son Hiram C7 moved to Norwich area & joined by Charles Harmon C7 who married Agnes Smith & continued there till his death in 1898.	In 1851 Joseph first wrote Hiram in Norwich-Tilsonberg area and asked to come back to Quaker Rd. but Hiram did not return until after 1866.

A Brief Family History

Year	Event	Other related events and comment
Moves & Expansion - Goodwillie on Quaker Rd.		
c.1852	Joseph bought West half of Lot 231 & later Lot 232 to make a farm of 130 acres.	Lot 231 bought from James Swayze.
1854-56	Joseph general agent for Welland Herald, a pro Liberal Party paper first published in Fonthill	Last recorded bounty payment 1856 for £12 or $60.00 for wolf-scalps Wild deer seldom seen. By this time most First Nations people moved to Six Nations Reserve near Brantford.
1858-64	1858 Hiram purchased land in Bayham-Norwich age 28. Marries Sarah Stover 29 April 1862. John Allan C8 b 1863 -first child born in Norwich County. 1864 Tremaine (Norwich) map shows 3 properties owned by H. Goodwillie.	Later Norwich land sold to brother Charles Harmon C7. Second letter 1864 at brother Levi's C7 request to Hiram C7 from father Joseph C6 about managing Quaker Rd. farm. By 1877 only one H.Goodwillie property (possibly Harmon's) in Norwich showing on map.
1860-1890	By 1861 estimated 50,000 African Americans moved to Canada.	Between 1860-90, many Blacks returned to families in America after slavery laws changed in the USA.
1861-2	Quaker Rd school moved to Lot 233 on Page farmland SW corner First Ave & Quaker Rd. Planned in 1861 & built in 1862. School 24 x 36 feet &10 ft high. Cost $1,000.00.	Pages and Goodwillies active on school committee. Later school building in 1893 and additions in 1925 & 1952. Demolished & replaced Lloyd Rice & Quaker Rd schools in 1995 on Quaker Rd. School land.
1868 & 1870	New canning methodology developed. 1858 Sealing device for glass jars patented as 'Mason' Jar. 1870 refined to metal screw band sealing glass top to bottom with rubber ring in between. Lightning jar 1892.	Many different companies produced mason jars between 1859 and 1910. Invented in Bennington Vermont the Lightning jar had glass lid or stopper with rubber seal between lid and container with metal spring to keep firmly in place.
1866/7	1867 Canadian Confederacy. Hiram came to Quaker Rd. with wife & son J.A. after 3rd letter from Joseph. Letter refers to apples grapes & cherries already planted.	1867 April 9, Hattie Luella Page born to Jane Page, brought up by grandparents Alex Page on Quaker Rd. and attended Quaker Rd School with John Allan Goodwillie.
1870-74	27 May 1870 signed contract for Quaker Road farm registered between Hiram & Joseph. Shortly after Goodwillie house built farmhouse on Lot 231	Luella Page wrote in Tweedsmuir book that family occupied farmhouse at 209 Quaker Rd from 10 April 1874 to 1938.
c.1871	Edward Morris moved to Pelham and started the Pelham Small Fruit Farm the first venture of its kind in Niagara District.	Later Morris started a nursery and Morris Stone and Wellington ran the Fonthill nurseries. Morris was local manager, Stone had large nursery near Rochester, NY and Wellington conducted sales from Toronto.

Timeline of Relevant Events

Year	Event	Other related events and comment
1873	Death 15 Jan. of Eliza Hellems Goodwillie, buried at Fonthill	Cemetery plot purchased by Levi in 1850. Tribune newspaper obituary says mother of Levi Goodwillie but does not mention other children.
1873	Leslie V. Garner, an auctioneer, hay dealer & manufacturer of carbonated beverages marries Jane Page daughter of Alexander Page, mother of Luella. All grew up on Quaker Rd.	Jane (b. 1849) died after having all her teeth removed in St. Catharines in 1884. Left 2 daughters, Jane & Mary Georgina Garner White born 1882 £250 each. Leslie V died in 1926.
1876	Joseph C6 died 11 October in Crowland (Welland), buried with wife at Fonthill.	Belongings left to John Milton C7 with request to build a monument at his grave. Earlier property settlement for Hiram C7.

H. Goodwillie & Son Farm and Factory

Year	Event	Other related events and comment
1878-9	Farm diary 1867-78 records improved fruit stock planted, growing fruit production and experimentation with marketing.	Hiram became school trustee overseeing school building.
1881	Obtained improved vines and fruit trees under 19 Dec 1881 agreement between Morris, Stone & Wellington Nurserymen & Goodwillie.	Agreement said by 1887 (400) grape vines and by 1893 (832) pear & plum trees became H G's property. Fruit vines said to be first planted in Thorold-Pelham area.
1886	Welland Canning Factory identified in History of Welland County. Excess of fruit & Goodwillie experimentation with preserving under glass.	History of County of Welland says canning factory started by Messrs Bradt & Shepard but no further reference so presumed failed. On Quaker Road used firewood stove to heat and preserve fruit.
1890	John Allan and Luella Page married -honeymooned in Norwich.	Many Stover and C.H. Goodwillie (C7) relatives often visited the Quaker Rd. farm in later years.
1893	1893 a third school was built of red brick.	About 1919-20 vacant Page house used for junior grades until burned down in 1924.
c. 1895	New canning factory built on the Quaker Rd. Farm.	Needed water, ice, gas, electricity and fuel to preserve fruit. Used glass jars which were packed into wooden cartons for shipping.
1897-1910+	Sawmill operated near Ridgeville.	Used farm labourers in off season to work in sawmill, collect timber offcuts and ice for summer factory operations.
1901-3	1903 John bought his first automobile McLaughlin-Buick. Hiram (JA's father) died at almost 73 years old 8 June 1903.	1901 American Can Company formed in the USA. Canadian Canners Ltd established 1903.

A Brief Family History

Year	Event	Other related events and comment
1904-5	Rebuilt and added second floor to existing farm house on Quaker Rd.	Used only three rooms from original house where Bay Window is. Water collected from roof provided flush toilets. 12 inch solid Canadian chestnut walls.
1907	Niagara St Catherines and Toronto (NS&T) Railroad reached Fonthill.	Canadian Canners started to can tomatoes and other fruit later.
1910	Quaker Rd. Women's Institute (W.I.) formed Telephone and Electricity arrived at farm.	Youngest child, John Ross born when W.I. began. Don't know if Luella was charter member but was life-time member. Mrs. Eugene Garner was first president.
1911	Purchase of Packard Truck 3 ton 1st in Welland area. Population of Welland 6,250. Canning factory employed over 100.	The People's Press, Welland May 23, 1911 list H Goodwillie & Son as the oldest house in Canada to pack fruits of canning consistency in glass. They do not make jam at this time.
c.1912	New canning factory with tall smokestack built on railway lines, Burgar St. Welland.	Factory became Martin's Dairy.
1916	Secord-Goodwillie Wedding at Quaker Rd.	Perce Haist went as pharmacist to Siberia during WWI so Mary's wedding delayed until he returned.
1918	Oct 21 Grandma Sarah Stover Goodwillie died. 11 Nov. armistice for World War One.	3 airforce bi-planes sighted over Quaker Rd., Welland. End of war celebrations.
1921	Bought Long Beach land 1919 & started cottage building in 1921.	Used timber from Ridgeville (Pelham) sawmill. John Allan planned it with 5 bedrooms & downstairs bathhouse for girls separate from boys.
1922	John Allan G. died 15 Jan. 1922 of Bright's Disease (kidneys) after heart attack Sept 25 1921 had weakened him.	Post war Depression. Decided to keep the farm & liquidate assets. Sold Welland factory to Martin's Dairy which burned down in spring 1982.
1922	First summer use of Long Beach cottage.	Grace Hederick, daughter of Tebe C 8 & Will, married Peck Newell but Grace C9 died of consumption shortly after their marriage.
1924 - 1925	Remodelled & enlarged the brick Quaker Rd. School costing $15,000.	The wood shed, drive (horse & buggy) shed and outside toilets torn down. First used in 1925.
1926	Quaker Rd. was the first improved Rd. in Thorold Township	1950 the west end was paved.

Timeline of Relevant Events

Year	Event	Other related events and comment
1932	Unexpected death of Hugh Allan 'Bill' Goodwillie who died of TB aged 25.	Bill was interested in farming and possibly would have carried on with the farm.
1938	Farm sold for about $35,000.00.	Goodwillie Driveshed (used as garage) burned down in 1964. Subdivision on farm has Page and Goodwillie Drive.
1941	Pete married Ruth Payne	Worked at Atlas Steel
1950	April 21 Hattie Luella Page Goodwillie died.	Women's Institute Tweedsmuir local history Records completed 1951. Input given by Luella Page before her death.
1952	Quaker school remodelled and opened by Cyopik, Rice, McCoombs all Quaker Rd. families.	Bought additional land from Claude Denis 2.75 acres.
1973	8 bound books, Old Time Stories of the Farm, by Ruth Goodwillie Cornett presented at Christmas to each of her sibling's families.	1975 Ruth reduced size and put some stories into a shorter version which was mimeographed without photos.
1975-1981	First Family tree attempted and 'Life on the Farm Supplement' written by J.R. Goodwillie.	Hand written February 1975 in Lagos, Nigeria when on short term voluntary management assignment for Canadian Executive Services Overseas. Also gave speech April 1982 ? to Niagara Historical Society on history of Goodwillie farm.
1986	200 copies of The Goodwillies 1590-1986: Four Hundred Years of Family History by J.R. Goodwillie.	Revised Second Edition printed (200 copies) & sold for $20.00 in 1988. Out of print as of about 1995.
1988-1998	Nov 8, 1988 J.R. 'Pete' Goodwillie died. Ruth (nee Goodwillie) Cornett died 21 June 1994. Wife Ruth (nee Payne) Goodwillie died 27 Oct. 1998.	All buried at Fonthill Cemetery, Thorold Township. Jack & Ruth Cornett grave near those of Perce & Mary Haist (NE) and Joseph & Elizabeth Goodwillie (near gate). Goodwillie family plot with Bill, John Allan, Luella, Hiram and Sarah in different (SE) location.
1995	Opening of new Quaker Rd. School.	Brick from original school saved before demolition. $3 million for new school which will cater to 342 students from Lloyd Rice and Quaker Rd. Schools.
2005	'Life on Quaker Road' published by Trafford Publishing. www.trafford.com	Carol Diane Goodwillie added to stories of Ruth Cornett and family history of her father John Ross 'Pete' Goodwillie.

First Genealogy Record (Page 1)

> David Goodwillie *My Father* was Babtised October
> The fifteen on Thousand Six Houndred
> And sixtie five years his eag 80
> Elizabeth *My Mother* Deuar was Babtised September
> on Thousand Six Houndred and
> Sovoitie foure years
> James Goodwillie and Marie Davidson was
> Married December the twentie first on thousand
> seven houndred and fortie Eightyears 1748
> David Goodwillie was born December 26 on thousand
> seven houndred and fortie Nine years 1749
> and was babtised the thretie first of December
> on thousand seven houndred and fortie Nine years
> by Mr John Erskin munester
> Joseph Goodwillie was born Aprill the third day
> on thousand seven houndred and fiftie on and
> was babtised on the sevent of Aprill 1751
> David Goodwillie my eldest son and Joseph Goodwillie
> my second son was both Babtised by Mr John
> Erskin Munister of the Asodet Congration
> at Leslie
> Elizabeth Goodwillie my eldest daughter was born
> the fift day of July on thousand seven houndred
> and fiftie three years and was Babtised by
> Mr James Rey minister of the at Kinkaldie

This 'parchment covered' record was handwritten by James Goodwillie (1709-1782) and identifies David, James, Joseph and Elizabeth. (Goodwillie)

Family Genealogy Charts

First Five Generations of Goodwillies Born in Scotland

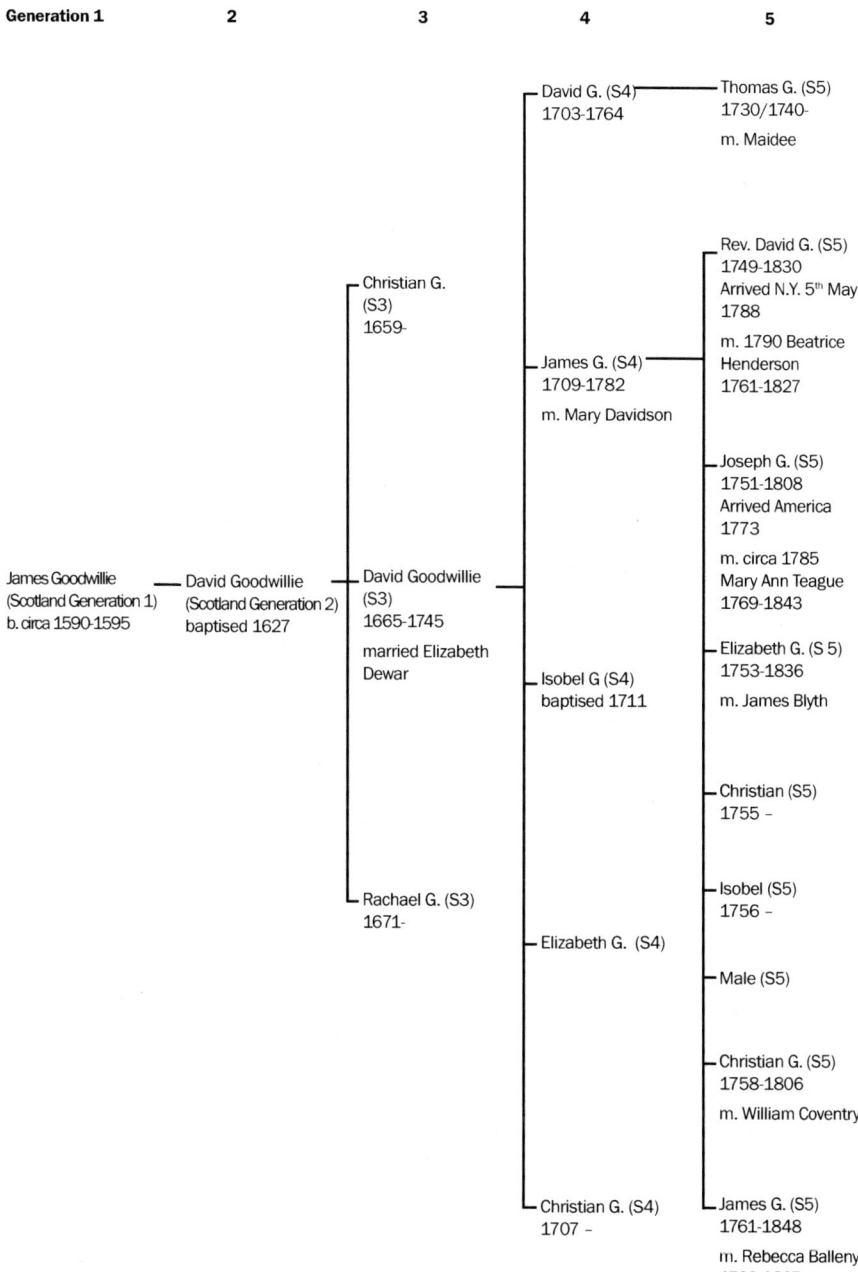

A Brief Family History

Goodwillie Emigrants from Scotland to North America

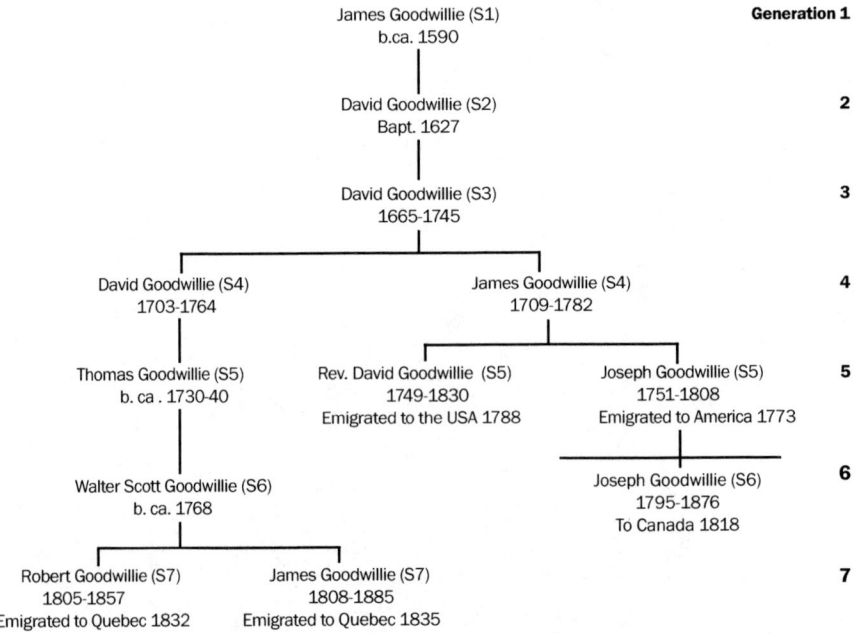

Transcript of Handwritten Genealogy

Entries taken from old book with parchment covers written by James Goodwillie. Note the spelling. It it thought that the first Chirstan must have died within the first year and the name was re-applied to the fourth daughter.

David Goodwillie My father was Baptised October the fiften on Thousand Six Houndred and sixty five years his eag: 80.

Elizabeth Dewar My Mother was Baptised Septmber on Thousand Six Houndred and Seventy foure years.

James Goodwillie and Marie Davidson was Marred December the tuentie sixt on thousand and fortie eight years 1748.

David Goodwillie was born December 26 on thousand seven houndred and fortie nine years 1749 and was babtised the thretie first of December on thousand Seven houndred and fortrie Nine years by Mr. John Erskin Minister.

Joseph Goodwillie was Born Aprill third day on thousand seven houndred and fiftie on and was baptized on the sevent of April 1751.

David Goodwillie my eldest son and Joseph Goodwillie my second son was both Baptised by Mr. John Erskin Minister of the Associt Congration at Lesslie.

1. Elizabeth Goodwillie my eldest daughter was born the fift day of Jully on thousan seven houndred and fiftie three years and was Baptised by Mr James Ley Minister of the Associt, Kirkaldie.

2. Chirstan Goodwillie my second daughter was Born the eight of march on Thousand seven houndred and fiftie five and was Baptise by Mr. William Brown Minister.

3. Isbelel Goodwillie my third daughter was Born the tuentie second day of November on thousnd seven houndred and fiftie six years and was Baptised att Lesslie by Mr John Wilson Minister in Meffe.

First Genealogy Record (Page 2)

Second page of the 'parchment' record identifying Chirstan (Christian), Isabel and James Goodwillie. (Goodwillie)

4. Chirstan Goodwillie was born the tuentie six day of Jully on Thousand seven houndred and fiftie eight years and was Baptised forsaid day by Mr James Thomson Minister of the Associt Congration att Kirkaldy which is my fourt Daughter.

3. James Goodwillie was born the sixtin day of Jully on thousand seven houndred and sixtie on years and was Baptised by Mr. Simon Demperson minister of the Associat Congration of Lesslie on the eightin day of the forsaid Mounth.

A Brief Family History

Descendants of Joseph and Mary Ann Teague Goodwillie (C5)

Generation 5 — **6** — **7** — **8** — **9**

Joseph Goodwillie
1751-1808
m. 1785
Mary Ann Teague
1769-1843

- Mary 1786-1872, m. Thomas Young
- Margaret 1788-1873, m. Henry Somers
- James 1792-1884, unm.
- Joseph 1795-1876, m. Elizabeth Hellems 1803-1873
  - George W.B. 1823-1851, m. Margaret Hilton
  - Charles Harmon 1826-1898, m. Agnes Smith
  - Levi 1828-1895, m. 1. Elizabeth Merell 2. Martha Thompson
  - Hiram 1830-1903, m. Sarah Stover 1840-1918
    - John Allan 1863-1922, m. Luella Page 1867-1950
      - Iva Kathleen 1891-1968
      - Mary Myrtle 1893-1984
      - Sarah Grace 1896-1964
      - Harold Hiram 1900-1965
      - Ruth 1901-1994
      - Donald Brock 1905-1972
      - Hugh Allan 1907-1932
      - John Ross 1910-1988
    - Phoebe 1870-1946, m. Will Hederick 1870-1941
      - Grace Hederick 1901-1923, m. A.E. Newelll
  - Allan B. 1832-1850, unm
  - Caroline 1834-1913, m. James Fisher Mitchell
  - Lydia 1837-, m. Joe Stark
  - John Milton 1844-1919, m. Mary Dobbie
- Elizabeth 1797-1871, m. Alexander Cross
- Christian 1799-1879, m. Wm. Allen
- Isobel 1800- inf
- Nancy 1802-1889, unm.
- George 1804-1871, m. 1. Rebecca Freeman 2. Elizabeth Forbes
- Mary 1807-1826, unm.

Family Genealogy Charts

Descendants of John Allan and Luella Page Goodwillie (C8)

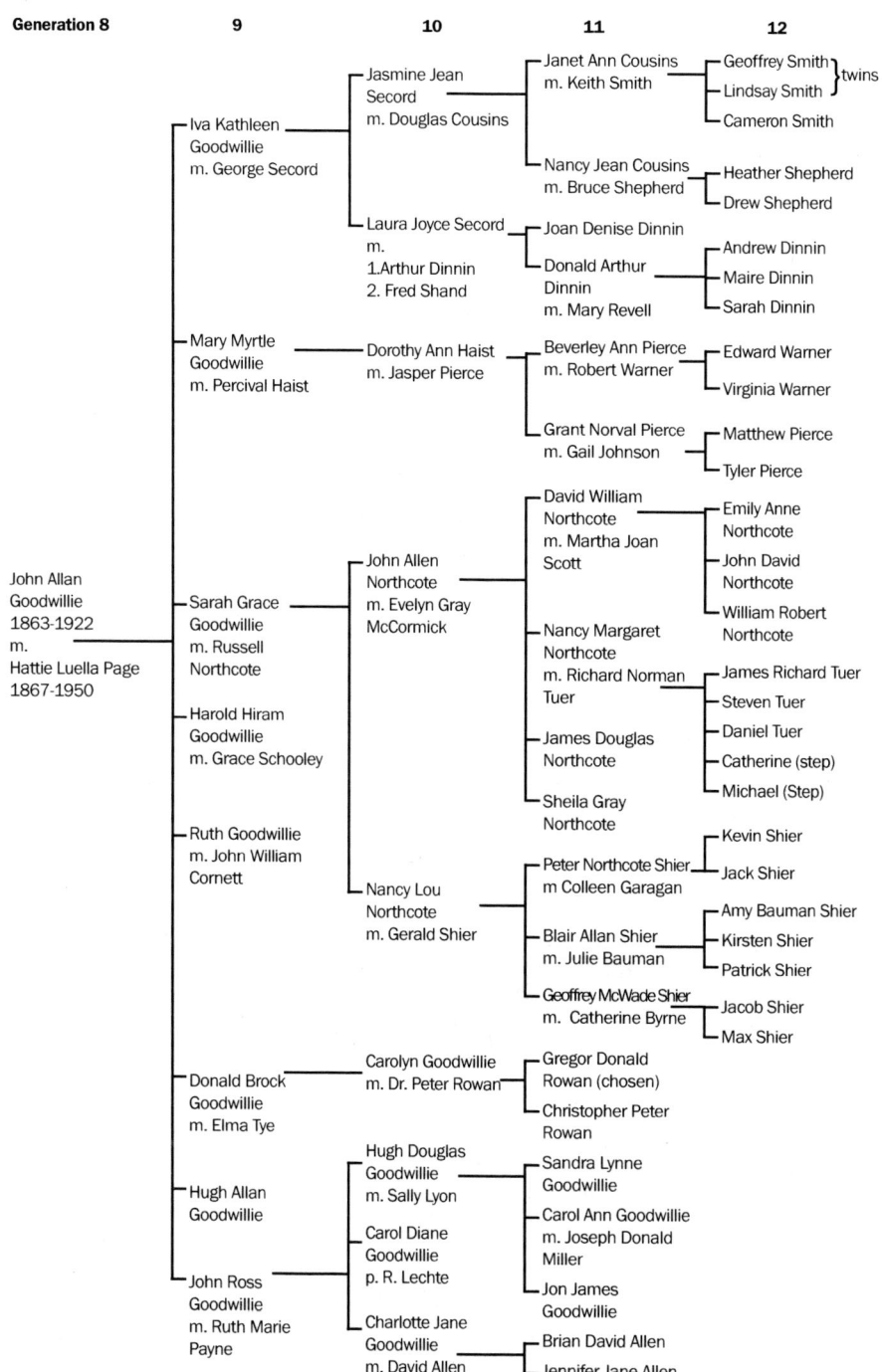

- 231 -

Endnotes

1. 'Algonquin' or 'Algonkin' is used in reference to the tribe, but 'Algonquian' either refers to the Algonquin language or to the group of tribes that speak related dialects. Similarly 'Iroquois' refers to members of the Confederation and 'Iroquoian' to those with language links. Ref. Algonquin website.
2. 'Ojibway' or 'Ojibwe' and 'Chippewa' are not only the same tribe, but the same word pronounced a little differently due to accent. If an 'o' is placed in front of Chippewa (o'chippewa), the relationship becomes apparent. Ref. The First Nations website
3. See websites: Iroquois History and Attiwandarons & Petuns.
4. Johanson. 1982. & Iroquois History Website.
5. Johansen. 1982. & First Nations Website.
6. Michael 1967: p.4.
7. First Nations History Website.
8. Falls Thunder Alley Website 2005.
9. Michael 1967: p. 6.
10. Lopez, Pineylore website & Conway. 1994: p.7-10.
11. Conway 1994: p.20.
12. Jefferson Davis c.1903.
13. Berserker according to the Oxford dictionary is a wild Norse warrior, who fought on the battlefield with a frenzied fury.
14. Michael 1967: pg. 136.
15. Wayne Cook Collection, Historical Plaques of Canada, www.waynecook.com 2004.
16. Fitzgibbon was in charge of a volunteer company known as the 'Green Tigers' on the move constantly and never sleeping in the same place twice but located at the nearby Beaverdams encampment.
17. Michael 1967: p.43-51.
18. Wayne Cook Collection, Historical Plaques of Canada, www.waynecook.com 2004.
19. Courtesy of the Norwich and District Archives Oxford County, Ontario, in the Mott Special Family Files.
20. Michael 1967:p.28.
21. Father was Michael Stover born in Duchess County, NY 1804 and Mother was Phoebe Carmon born 1812. The eight children born between 1845 and 1853 were in order of birth: Euphriam, James, Michael R, Harriet, Charity Ann (Chat), Edward Charles, Sarah, Mary (Mate)
22. Michael 1967: p.123.
23. "Joseph Brant, chief of the Mohawks, bought Sophia and she subsequently worked for the Brant family, travelling with them as they divided their time between Mohawk, Ancaster and Preston. Sophia remained with Brant for twelve or thirteen years until he sold her to Samuel Hatt in Ancaster for one hundred dollars. After gaining her freedom in 1834, she married Robert Pooley and the couple resided in Waterloo." Guelph & Wellington County Museum Website & Dictionary of Canadian Biography Online 'Catharine Brant'.
24. Hill 1981: p.65-80.
25. Page 1876: III.
26. United Empire Loyalists' Association 1984: P. 248
27. D.Hill 1981. in Burtniak et al (ed.) p.65-80
28. Rice, A.B. Ed. 1887.
29. Michael 1967: p. 24 & 27.
30. This pioneer story was recorded by Mrs. Wilson Ransom, Grand-daughter of the Quaker Road Joseph's sister whose husband worked for two years as carpenter then purchased a bush farm in 1822 on Lot 15 3rd line West Chinguacousy, Ontario between Brampton and Georgetown as per Goodwillie 1986: p. 93.
31. Goodwillie 1986: pg xv & 252, and Lower 1860
32. Goodwillie 1984 ed. Bousfield & Toffoli: p86-87

Endnotes

33. Annett 1983.
34. The marriage date is unknown but considered to be about 1785 as the first child, Mary was born June 22, 1786.
35. For example Mary Ann Teague's sister married into the Smith family and moved to Hopetown Quebec where descendants still exist.
36. Annett. 1983.
37. Goodwillie House 26 Goodwillie Road, Barnet Center, Vermont can be visited by appointment through the Barnet Historical Society.
38. The original settler, Heinrich Hellems, migrated from Germany to New York in 1627 and later moved to Pennsylvania where several of his sons married Tuscaroroa Indian maidens. It is said that the Indians never raided the in-laws because of these marriages. Goodwillie 1986: 118
39. Lot 227 was part of 7900 acres purchased by Hon Robert Hamilton. It was then registered as a Crown Grant. Lot 227 was parcelled and sold in 1807 to Isaac Willson who sold it for 400 pounds or approximately $2,000 to Joseph Goodwillie in 1836. – from Michael 1967 p 14 & Goodwillie 1986 . p 120.
40. In the Women's Institute Tweedsmuir Records, Luella Page stated the Goodwillie family occupied the Goodwillie homestead comprised of 130 acres from 10 April 1874 when Hiram bought the property from James Swayze.
41. Goodwillie 1986: p 133.
42. The DeCew Generating Station began work in 1897 and opened its transmission of power to Hamilton, November 12, 1898.
43. Current families include Cousins, Smith, Shepherd, Dinnin, Pierce, Warner, Northcote, Tuer, Shier, Rowan, Allen, Miller and Goodwillie. From left standing: Keith Smith, Sally Lyon Goodwillie, Florence Lyon, Lynne Goodwillie, Joyce Secord Dinnin, Bev Warner, Doug Cousins, Don Dinnin, Mary Dinnin, Joan Dinnin, Dave Allen, Nancy Cousins Shepherd, Bob Warner, Dorothy Haist Pierce, Jab Pierce
Middle Row: Hugh Goodwillie, Geoffrey Smith, Bruce Shepherd, Jean Secord Cousin, Ruth Goodwillie Cornett, Janet Cousins Smith with Cameron, Ruth Payne Goodwillie with Jennifer Allen, Jane Goodwillie Allen, Diane Goodwillie
In front: Ted Warner, Art Dinnin, Jon Goodwillie, Lindsay Smith, Brian Allen, Ginny Warner.
44. Apple Website: King of Tompkin stock came from New York prior to 1804. It is a large, smooth skinned yellow apple with orange red blush. The flesh is yellowish, coarse, crisp, tender.
45. People in photo are from left: Aunt Mate Siple, Uncle Jim Storer, Aunt Eunice Stover, Uncle Charlie Siple, Grandma Stover Goodwillie.
46. Paris green is a toxic copper based yellow green salt used as an insecticide or to kill plant fungi.
47. This name is not meant to be offensive. Naming their pet Nigger reflects the language and attitude of the day and lack of awareness of the implied prejudice.
48. Niagara, St. Catharines and Toronto electric line operated from lake to lake and was used extensively until about 1930.
49. Some varieties of native chestnuts continue to be grown but they are highly susceptible to the blight which started about 1935 and was particularly damaging from 1965-75. Ontario Ministry of Agriculture and Food
50. From left: Millie Chapman, Russ Northcote, Muriel Crow, Louis Neumaster, Ruth [Cornett], George Secord, Iva [Secord], Albert Wright, Mary [Haist], Mabel Secord, Perce Haist, Lila Kattmier, Charlie Sommerville, Blanche Secord.
51. Due to a split between the orthodox Quakers and followers of Elias Hicks two meeting houses in Pelham Township existed within a mile of each other. The orthodox meeting house moved to the corner of Haist and Quaker Roads and the original centre built in 1875 at the corner of Welland Road and Effingham Street became a Hicksite Quaker meeting place. It later became a Women's Institute Hall. The first monthly meeting of the Society of Friends in Canada was held here 10 February 1799. Welland Tribune 16 April 1974.
52. From left: John Allan Goodwillie, Tim, Grace, Aunt Annie Whitehead, Luella, Grace Hederick, Ruth, Grandma. Date unknown.
53. From Welland Library Website. Electro Metals Company, Welland.

Notes and References on Illustrations and Graphics

Photos and Graphics supplied by the Goodwillie Family from books by Ruth Cornett and J.R. Goodwillie Other photos supplied by Diane Goodwillie, Diane. Potter, Ruth Lechte. Alan L. Brown, Talat Mehmood, Karen Kalashnik, Kim Rapp, Adrienne Roy, Sandra Stokes. Other materials supplied as follows:

Map & sketch of Iroquoian and Algonquin Settlements. Roberta O'Brien. *The Pre History of South Central Ontario*. Ontario Ministry of Culture and Recreation 1980. p.16, 17

Iroquoian longhouse. Germantown *Grade Three Indian Project*. Germantown Elementary School, SD #60. Illinois.

Government Plaques. Photos used with permission from Alan L. Brown. # 68 & 36.

Neutral Sketches by Neil Reichelt. Courtesy Earl Plato in *Our People Live* p.184, 45, 196

Grasshopper Graphic by T. S. Sechrist. University of Colorado Bulletin 542S.1999.

Mrs Varina Jefferson Davis, Photo in Public Domain.

George Harlow White Birch Bark Teepee and Chippawa Indians 1876? Rama Indian Reserve, [near Simcoe] Ontario. Courtesy Toronto Public Library, (John Ross Robertson Collection).

Canada Post 10c stamp 'The Iroquoians'

Plaque # 129 # 58 Wayne Cook Collection, Ontario. Historical Plaques of Canada 2004.

Harriet Tubman Public Domain & in Daniel G. Hill. The Freedom-Seekers: Blacks in Early Canada, Agincourt, Ont. The Book Society of Canada. 1981,

Map of the Freedom Trail and posters. Grant Smith. Niagara Falls Review, Niagara Falls, Ontario.

Advertisements for public sale of slaves courtesy Levi Coffin House.

Map of Underground Railroad. Pocantico Hills School. *Harriet Tubman and the Underground Railroad*. New York. 1998.

Sketch map 1784 Loyalist town lots by Committee of Anglophone Social Action (CASA).

The Rev David's house and Map showing Vermont and Barnet. Barnet Historical Society.

Family photograph of Donald Brock 'Jack' Goodwillie. Fitzsimmons Collection, Hockey Hall of Fame. Toronto.

Democrat Wagon. Courtesy of Fraser School of Driving 255 Boulder Rd. Deer Lodge, Montana 5972.

Chestnuts. Reproduced by permission of the Ontario Ministry of Agriculture and Foods.

Welland Canal around Alanburg 1870. Welland Public Library, David Michener Collection. Courtesy of the Welland Public Library Local History Collection.

Men and mules Welland canal construction. Courtesy of the Welland Historical Museum.

Piano drawing. W.H. Eckhardt St. Catherines Agency for the Heintzman Piano and Sketch of a fruit farm in Grimsby. Welland County Atlas. H.R.Page. 1876.

References and Further Reading

Algonquian Information by Norm Leveillee www.normlev.net/ancestry/algonquian/ accessed July 2005.

Annett, Ken. *New Carlisle in Infancy, The 1785 Plans of William Vondenvelden. Gaspe of Yesterday.* Voume 2. Spec. 82-11-23, Number 072. 1983.

Apples Website. All About Apples. www.allaboutapples.com accessed July 2005.

Arsenault, Bona. *Les Régistres de Carleton 1773-1900.* Bibliothèque du Québec. 4 Sept 1983.

Attiwandarons & Petuns www.kwic.com/~pagodavista/schoolhouse/rec/petun.htm Accessed July 2005.

Barnet Historical Society, Goodwillie House, 26 Goodwillie Road, Barnet Center, VT Barnet Public Library, PO Box 34, Barnet, VT 05821. E-mail Address: barnet_pub@vols.state.vt.us Telephone 1-802-633-4436.

Bradford, Sarah. *Scenes in the life of Harriet Tubman.* Auburn, New York: W.J. Moses, printer, 1869 reprinted Applewood Books, 1993.

Brown Alan L. Ontario Plaques Photographs and Information. posted www.ontarioplaques.com.

Canadian Heritage Gallery. www.canadianheritage.org. copyright 2001.

Chestnuts. Website Ministry of Agriculture www.ontariosoilcrop.org/AmericanChestnut.htm.

Coffin, Levi. *Reminiscence of Levi Coffin: The Reputed President of the Underground Railroad.* New York Augustus M. Kelley Publishers. 1968. In Bial Raymond. *The Underground Railroad,* Houghton Mifflin Company. Boston. 1995.

Cook, Wayne. *Ontario. Historical Plaques of Canada* www.waynecook.com 2004.

Committee for Anglophone Social Action (CASA) The Loyalists, Part II by Gisele Gallibois, Kevin Renouf, Eva MacWhirter. Gaspe, Quebec. c. 2000.

Conway, Ruby. *Tales of Tennessee Southern Hospitality in the Village of Port Colborne.* 172 Tennessee Ave, Port Colborne, Ontario L3K 2S1. 1994.

Cornett, Ruth. Unpublished, Old Time Stories of the Farm. Toronto. 1973.

Dictionary of Canadian Biography Online *Catharine Brant* www.biographi.ca/ accessed July 2005.

DeCew Falls Hydro Electric Plant 1898. IEEE History Center. www.ieee.org/organizations/history_center/decew.html accessed July 2005.

First Nations Issues of Consequence. Dill, Jordan S. Website: www.dickshovel.com accessed July 2005.

Flowers, A.D. *Loyalists of the Bay Chaleur.* 1973.

Gallibois, Renouf, MacWhirter. The Life and Times of Our Ancestors, The Loyalists, Part II, published by the Committee for Anglophone Social Action (CASA) Gaspesia. c.2002.

Garrett, Raymond and Related Families. Web publication. Chandler QC G0C 1K0 Canada. www.rocher-perce.org/garrett/ Accessed 2005.

Genealogy Information: www.accessgenealogy.com accessed July 2005.

Germantown Grade Three Indian Project School Germantown Elementary SD #60 Illinois, USA www.germantown.k12.il.us Phone 618-523-4253.

References and Further Reading

Goodwillie, John Ross. 'A Transient Loyalist' in Arthur Bousfield and Garry Toffoli *Loyalist Vignettes and Sketches*, Bicentennial Project by the Governor Simcoe Branch, The United Empire Loyalists' Association of Canada. 1984. p.86-87.

Goodwillie, John Ross. *The Goodwillies 1590-1986, Four Hundred Years of Family History*. Toronto. 1986. Revised 1988.

Goodwillie, Winnifred Constance. *History of the Goodwillie Family: Years 1595-1940*. Mimeo. c.1940.

Green, Gretchen. Molly Brant, Catharine Brant, and Their Daughters: A Study in Colonial Acculturation. *Ontario History*. 1989.Vol. LXXXI, No. 3.1989:236.

Guelph and Wellington County Museum. www.guelph.ca/museum/BlackHistory. Accessed July 2005.

Haudenosaunee Official Website of the Six Nations of Seneca, Cayuga, Onondaga, Oneida, Mohawk and Tuscarora. www.sixnations.org accessed July 2005.

Herriott, Ted. *The Canadian Heritage Label Collection* Purpleville Publishing, 6291 Dorman Rd. Suite 19, Mississauga L4V 1H2. 1982.

Hill, Daniel. *The Freedom Seekers: Blacks in Early Canada* Agincourt. The Books Society of Canada. 1981.

Hill, Daniel. Early Black Settlements in the Niagara Peninsula Immigration and Settlement in the Niagara Peninsula. In Burtniak, John & Dirks, Patricia. ed. *Proceedings of the Third Annual Niagara Peninsula History Conference*. Brock University. April 1981. p.65-80.

Horan, James D. *The McKenny-Hall Portrait Gallery of American Indians*. Crown Publishers, Inc. New York. 1972.

Iroquois History. www.tolatsga.org/iro.html accessed July 2005.

Jefferson Davis, Varina. *The Grasshopper War*. White-Evans-Penfold Co. Buffalo, New York. 1903.

Johansen Bruce Elliott & Mann, Barbara Alice.eds. *Encyclopedia of the Haudenosaunee (Iroquois Confederacy)*. Westport, Conn. and London. 2000.

Johansen, Bruce E. *Forgotten Founders*. Gambit Inc. Ipswich Mass ISBN 0-87645-111-3. Iroquois Indians Website, Greenwood Press, 2000. ISBN 0-313-30880-2. www.Iroquoisindians.freeweb-hosting.com/webdoc34.htm 1982.

Larke, Stan. Remarkable pioneer was involved in community in Guelph Mercury. C5 11 Jan, 2003, 08 Mar. 2003.

Léveillée, Norm. Kessinnimek - Roots - Recines. www.leveillee.net/ancestry/index . accessed August 2005.

Lewis, Bill. *A History of the City of Welland*. Welland. Volume 1, 1997. Volume 2, 2000 Volume 3, 2003.

Lopez, Lillian Arnold. The Grasshopper War. In *Pineylore: The History and Folklore of the New Jersey Pinelands* at www.pineylore.org Accessed July 2005.

Lower, Mark Anthony. *A Dictionary of Family Names of the U.K.* London. 1879.

McCall Smith, Alexander. *In the Company of Cheerful Ladies*. ISBN 034911742X. Polygon. London. 2004.

Meyler, David & Peter Meyler. A Stolen Life: Searching for Richard Pierpoint, ISBN: 1896219551. Natural Heritage Books. Toronto. 1999.

Michael, Betti. *History of Thorold Township 1793 – 1967.* Armath Associates Limited and Reeve and Council of the Township of Thorold. 1967.

Mississauga Indians. Quebec History. Marianopolis College Website. 2004. http://www2.marianopolis.edu/quebechistory/encyclopedia/MissisaugaIndians.htm.

References and Further Reading

Mississauga Indians History. The Bureau of American Ethnology in *The* Handbook of American Indians North of Mexico. 1907.

Mississauga Nations Centre http://www.newcreditfirstnation.com/past2.htm RR#6, HAGERSVILLE, ONTARIO, N0A 1H0, PHONE - (905) 768-1133, FAX - (905) 768-1225.

Moses Mott's Journey: the Norwich Settlement to, Compiled by the Norwich & District Historical Society, Norwich & District Archives, Oxford County. 91 Stover St. N., RR#3, Norwich, Ontario N0J 1PO Canada, Phone: 1-519-863-3638. 1855.

New Carlisle Information: Municipality of New Carlisle 138 boul. Gerard-D-Levesque C.P. 40, New Carlisle (Quebec) G0C 1Z0 Phone 1-418-752-3141 newcarlisle@globetrotter.net Also Travels with Marty to the Town of New Carlisle www.easternshores.qc.ca/nchs/town.html visited July 2005.

Niagara Falls Thunder Alley. *Chronicles of our Early Settlers 1600-1900* Rick Berketa. www.niagarafrontier.com 2005.

Niagara Falls Information. Tammemagi, Hans and Allyson. *Exploring Niagara: The Complete Guide to Niagara Falls Vicinity*. Oakhill Publishing House. St. Catharines, Ontario. oakhill@vaxxine.com. 1997.

Norwich and District Historical Society. www.norwichdhs.ca. accessed March 2005.

Ontario Ministry of Agriculture and Food. Sweet Chestnut Orchards by Todd Leuty. Agroforesty Specialist OMAF. 4 April 2000 reviewed 29 July 2003.

O'Brien, Roberta. *The Pre History of South Central Ontario* Ministry of Culture and Recreation. 1980.

Page, H.R. *Illustrated Historical Atlas of the Counties of Lincoln and Welland Ontario*. Toronto. Office of the Minister of Agriculture. 2002 Edition ISBN 0-9698979-8-7, Wlson's Publishing Company Ltd. Stirling Ontario. K0K 3E0. (1876) 2002.

Plato, Earl. *Our People Live*. 344 South Mill, Ridgeway On L0S 1N0. Self Published. 2000.

Ranson, Mrs. Wilson. *The Pioneer Story*. Grand daughter of the Quaker Road Joseph's sister on farming in West Chinguacousy. In Goodwillie, J.R. The Goodwillies 1590-1986, p.93.

Rice, A.R. Ed. *The History of the County of Welland. Its Past and Present*. Welland Tribune Printing prepared by the Historical Publishing Company Composed of E.R. Langs of Brantford, and their successor J.J. Sidey. 1887.

Seneca Indian Website. www.senecaindians.com 2003. Accessed July 2005.

Styran, Roberta M. & Taylor, Robert. *Mr. Merritt's Ditch, A Welland Canals Album*. Boston Mills Press Book, Erin Ontario. 1992.

Thwaites, R.G. *The Jesuit Relations 1641-42*, Volume xxx. p.187-237 and xxxiii p.95, 97. Cleveland, Ohio. 1895-1901.

United Empire Loyalists' Association of Canada. *Loyal She Remains, A Pictoral History of Ontario*. William Koene, Co-ordinator. Editors: Mary Beacock Fryer & Charles Humber. ISBN 0-9691566-2-6. Southam Murray Printing. Toronto. 1984.

Vermont Historical Society. Website www.vermonthistory.org accessed July 2005.

Welland Public Library Local History Site. Website www.welland.library.on.ca/industry Accessed July 2005.

Welland Historical Museum, 65 Hooker St. Welland L3C5G9. www.niagara.com/whmchin/index.

Welland Tribune Newspaper. *Ancient Quaker Church Serves Railroad Club*. 16 April 1974.

Women's Institute Tweedsmuir Records. Quaker Rd. Branch. Started by Marion Bald Venables and completed by Mrs. H.L. Rice and Mrs. Hamilton Gainer, Luella (Page) Goodwillie. Document held at the Welland Historical Museum. Unpublished. Prepared Nov 7, 1951.

Index

A

African Americans 19, 20, 32-38, 220, 222
Albany, New York 14, 49
Algonquin Nation and Algonquian Language 11, 13, 15, 218
Allan, Brian David 124
Allen, Brian David 231
Allen, Jennifer Jane 75, 231
Allen (Goodwillie), Jane 75, 77, 81, 231
  Stories by 75, 89, 123, 138
American Civil War 19, 33
American Revolution 17-21, 49, 219-220
Apples
  Astrikans 98
  King Tompkin 77
Attawandaron. See also Neutral Nation

B

Baie de Chaleur 51
Barnet, Vermont 37-38, 55-57, 220
Beaverdams 14, 22, 143, 220
Bemis, Orin 58, 221
Beverly Crescent 44, 67, 82
Black Military Corp.
  See Coloured Company
Blanchard, Tom 179, 180
Brant, Joseph 21, 32
Brébeuf, Father 12
Burial Ground 14, 19
Burthen, Sophia 32, 232
Butler, Colonel John 33
Butler's Rangers 149, 219

C

Canning Factory 67, 187-201
Canning Industry 45, 46, 61, 63, 65, 178, 187-201, 188, 189, 198, 203, 222, 223, 224
  Jars 194
Canning Work 191, 192
Cartier, Jacques 51
Caughnawaga or Kahnawake 16
Cherry label 192
Chestnuts 88, 123, 224
Chicago 192, 196

Chippewa Nation 11, 14, 21
Christmas 166-170
Coloured Company 35, 221
Cornett, Jack 74-75, 82, 91, 177, 214, 231
Cornett (Goodwillie), Ruth 68, 72-76, 81, 85, 89, 174, 191, 203, 205, 210, 211, 214, 215, 230
Cousins (Secord), Jean 75, 80, 89, 100, 113, 174, 175, 202, 205, 206, 207, 231
Cox, Lieutenant Governor Nicholas 52-55
Crystal Beach 15, 113, 114
Curling 107
Cyopik family 121

D

D'everado, Morris, Stone & Wellington. See Morris
DeCew 22, 233
Delaware Nation 11, 17
Democrat wagon 63, 65, 114, 132, 140, 190
Dinnin Cottage. See also Goodwillie Cottage
Dinnin later Shand (Secord), Joyce 75, 80, 89, 169, 174, 175, 205, 206, 207, 231
Dogs on the Farm 102, 103, 136, 207

E

Edinburgh 47-48
Electro-Metallurgical Company 74, 204

F

Faragalli family 68
Fifeshire 47-48, 50, 218
Firecrackers 159
Fires 57-58, 70, 120, 121, 201, 221, 223
First Avenue (Page Road) 45, 60, 69, 151, 222
Fonthill Cemetery 78, 215, 223
Fonthill Nursery 62. See Morris
Fonthill town 8, 37, 62, 64, 113, 129, 145, 188, 198, 203, 222
Fort George, Ontario 25

G

Gainer family 58, 60, 120, 140, 143, 220
Garner, Leslie V. 70, 220, 223
Garner, R.S. 60, 220
Gaspé, Québec 51
Gaylor family 85, 86, 101, 161
Georgetown 8, 37, 38, 40
German Flats, Mohawk River 54
Glenrothes, Fife, Scotland 49, 50, 218
Goatsmilk Farm, Scotland 50, 218
Golf 47, 83, 218
Goodwillie, Charles Harmon 37, 59, 61, 221, 222
Goodwillie, David & Florence, Chicago 196, 197
Goodwillie, David (ancestor) 218, 226-229
Goodwillie, David (Rev.) & Beatrice 37, 55, 56, 219, 227-229
Goodwillie, Diane 75, 81, 105, 207, 208, 231
Goodwillie, Donald Brock 'Jack' 45, 67, 81, 88, 104, 106, 107, 110, 117, 127, 137, 147, 161, 162, 169, 170, 174, 176, 177, 191, 199, 203, 205, 207, 214, 230-231
Goodwillie, George Willson Bulien 59, 78, 221, 230
Goodwillie, Harold Hiram 'Tim' 67, 79, 81, 82, 85, 101, 102, 110, 112, 117, 119, 126, 143, 148, 153, 161, 165, 167, 169, 172, 191, 203, 204, 230-231
Goodwillie, Hiram 25, 61-65, 79, 87, 171, 187, 203, 221-224, 230
Goodwillie, Hugh Allan 'Bill' 67, 68, 81, 90, 98, 104, 105, 106, 110, 117, 121, 129, 131, 137, 161, 162, 176, 191, 199, 203, 205, 208-213, 225, 230-231
Goodwillie, Hugh Douglas 74, 77, 81, 105, 206, 208, 213, 231
Goodwillie, James 50, 57, 78, 79, 226-229

Index

Goodwillie, John Allan 61–70, 79, 82, 85, 87–90, 93, 93–96, 98–102, 110–116, 122, 125, 127, 128, 131, 132, 133, 134, 144, 146, 147, 148, 159, 160, 167, 173, 177, 179, 180, 184–189, 192, 195–197, 201–203, 209, 222, 230–231
Goodwillie, John Ross 'Pete' 45, 67, 68, 76, 78, 81, 82, 93, 101, 104, 105, 106, 107, 113, 117, 121, 123, 137, 138, 141, 144, 149, 159, 161, 191, 195, 198, 201, 203, 205, 208, 209, 212, 215, 230–231
Goodwillie, Jon James 75, 90, 124, 208, 231
Goodwillie, Joseph, Loyalist 37, 49, 54, 56, 78, 79, 227–228
Goodwillie, Joseph Jr. 56–61, 78, 220–223, 228, 230
Goodwillie, Levi 58, 223, 230
Goodwillie (Page), Luella 69, 70, 79, 82, 85–89, 94–114, 121, 122, 127, 128, 144–147, 157–160, 164, 168, 169, 170, 172, 174, 175, 176, 185, 187, 189, 191, 197, 204, 205, 207, 209, 210, 211, 213, 214, 222, 225, 230–231
Goodwillie (Payne), Ruth 75, 76, 81, 105, 206, 208, 211, 212, 215, 225, 231
Goodwillie (Stover), Grandma Stories 25–27, 28–31, 40–43
Goodwillie (Stover), Sarah 25, 37, 61, 72–73, 79, 82, 86–88, 100, 118, 168, 171–172, 187–188, 209, 222
Goodwillie (Teague), Mary Ann 54, 56, 219, 230
Goodwillie Cottage 105, 172–177
Goodwillie Drive 45, 60
Goodwillie Name 47
Grand Trunk Railway 114
Grasshopper War, Legend of the 17–21
Grimsby 14, 15, 187

H

Hagar, Azubah & Jonathon 27
Hagar, Frank 27
Haist, Perce 82, 91, 170, 174, 224, 231
Haist (Goodwillie), Mary 73, 80, 82, 97, 101, 108, 111, 118, 119, 120, 129, 132, 133, 144, 148, 160, 166, 168, 170, 174, 187, 191, 193, 203, 205, 215, 224, 231
Haldimand, Governor 52, 54
Hamilton, Hon Robert 220
Hamilton House, New Carlisle 52, 53
Hederick, Grace 224, 230
Hederick, Phoebe 59, 79, 87, 88, 187, 224, 230
Hederick, Will 88, 224, 230
Hellems 44, 218, 221
Hellems, Mathias 56, 218
Hellems (later Goodwillie), Elizabeth 56, 58, 215, 218–219, 223
Hellems Avenue 45, 56
Hockey 106
Hungry Years 1789 25
Huron Nation 10, 12, 15, 18, 20, 218

I

Ice cream 127, 128
Indian Stories 18–31
Indigenous Language Groups
Algonquian 11
Iroquoian 11
Iroquois/Indian Trail 14, 19, 24
Iroquois Confederation of, Nation 12, 15, 17, 18, 21, 218, 222

J

Jam & Jam Pails 65, 188, 190–192, 199
Jefferson Davis, Mrs Varina 18, 19
Jessup's Corps or Rangers 49, 51, 219

K

Keith Drive 50, 218
Kinglassie Church, Fife, Scotland 47, 50, 218
Kirkaldy, Scotland 47, 50, 218

L

Lace 73
Lacrosse 28, 218
Land Rights of First Nations 16, 20
Lechte, Ruth 77, 208, 231
Lenni Lanape Delaware Nation 11, 17
Lévesque, René 51
Lévesque, Rte. Gérard 53
Long Beach 8, 66, 184, 213, 224
Loyalists 16, 20, 32, 37, 51, 52, 54, 69

M

MacDonagh, Father, Port Robinson 36
MacDuff Clan 47
Mackenzie, William Lyon 221
Maps 8, 10, 36, 37, 43, 48, 55, 60
Martin's Dairy 201, 224
Masterman Ready 28–31
McLaughlin-Buick 114, 145–149, 223
Merritt, Mayor William 34
Mi'kmaq Nation 11, 51, 219
Mississauga Nation 11, 16
Mitchell, Eva & Grace 100
Mohawk Nation 12, 15, 21, 32, 218
Montreal 49, 55
Morris, Edward & D'everado, Morris, Stone & Wellington Nursery 62, 188, 222–223
Mott, Moses 23

N

Neutral Nation 10, 12, 13, 14, 15, 218
New Carlisle 51–55, 219
Niagara Falls 15, 24, 38, 59, 114, 147, 149, 150, 183
Niagara Peninsula 187, 188, 206, 233
Northcote, Jack 80, 130, 174, 175, 177, 205, 207, 231
Northcote, Russ 90, 91, 104, 144, 164, 168, 172, 174, 177, 231
Northcote (Goodwillie), Grace 64, 73, 80, 82, 90, 97, 108, 111, 118, 119, 136, 144, 148, 163, 164, 166, 167, 168, 170, 174, 175, 191, 193, 203, 205, 230–231
Norwich 8, 23, 37, 38, 58, 61, 131, 187, 221, 222, 223
Norwich & District Archives 23
NS&T Railroad 114, 224
Nursery Business in Fonthill 62, 188, 194, 222

O

O'Hara, Felix 52–53
O'Hara, Oliver, court case 55
Ojibway or Chippewa Nation 11, 218
Otterville 38, 203

Index

P

Packard truck 114, 198, 215, 224
Page, Alexander 60, 69, 70, 222
Page, George 45, 60
Page, Jonathon 60, 219
Page, Luella 69–70. See also Goodwillie (Page), Luella
Page (later Garner), Jane 222, 223
Page (Young), Edith 69–70
Page Drive 45, 60
Paspébiac 51, 53, 54, 219
Paul Jones dance 110
Payne, Fred 105
Payne, Ruth. See also Goodwillie (Payne), Ruth
Payne Cottage 105, 173, 212
Peaches 64, 194, 200
Piano 167–168
Pierce, Bev. See Warner
Pierce (Haist), Dorothy 80, 82, 169, 174, 177, 205
Plaques 14
Polio 73–74
Port Colborne 15, 18, 19, 107, 115, 188
Port Dalhousie 113, 115, 116, 207
Port Robinson 36, 136, 194, 221
Prince of Wales, Albert 65, 192
Pritchard, Azariah, court case 55
Pumpkin Story 25–27

Q

Quakers 36, 72, 100, 233
Quaker Church 72, 84, 135, 233
Quaker Road 139, 140, 144, 145, 151, 189, 190, 200, 202, 213, 215, 233
Quaker Road School 70, 138, 151–157, 162, 203, 222, 223, 225
Queenston 14, 16, 21, 22, 33

R

Radio 101
Rattlesnake 40
Rebellion of 1837 35, 57, 221
Ridgeville 135, 177, 185, 198
Ridgeville Sawmill 85, 161, 184, 187, 223
Ridgeway 15

S

S.S. Artusa 104, 105
Saratoga, Battle of 49, 219
Sawmill. See Ridgeville Sawmill
School Days. See Quaker Road School
Secord, George Harry 80, 82, 121, 128, 129, 170, 172, 174, 176, 177, 199, 214
Secord, Laura 22
Secord (Goodwillie), Iva 73, 80, 82, 97, 101, 108, 118, 119, 120, 121, 128, 129, 132, 133, 160, 166, 168, 170, 171, 174, 175, 176, 177, 187, 191, 192, 199, 202, 203, 205, 212, 224, 230–231
Seneca Nations 12, 15, 218
Shadd (later Cary), Mary Ann 33
Shier (Northcote), Nancy 80, 89, 164, 169, 174, 175, 177, 205, 207
Simcoe, Governor & Elizabeth 33
Six Nations. See Iroquois Confederation
Slavery
  Black 32–36
  Indigenous 32, 35
Smith (Cousins), Janet 75, 231
Southern Comfort. See also Humberstone Club, Port Colbourne
St. Andrew's Golf Club 47
St. Catharines 14, 22, 24, 34, 35, 37, 188, 192, 202, 233
Stover, Frederick 37
Stover family 61, 86
Sunday School 84
Sunday School Concert 162–166
Sunday School Picnic 114–118
Swayze, Israel 220
Swayze, James 87, 222

T

Tableau 163
Tanshall, Fife, Scotland 49, 218, 219
Tanshall Rd 218
Teague, Andrew 54
Teague, Jacob 52, 54
Tennis 97, 218
Thorold Road 139

Thorold township 16, 25, 45, 46, 162, 188, 203, 221
Threshing 179, 180
Toronto 19, 124, 189, 207, 214, 233
Tuberculosis (TB) 68, 209–213, 225
Tubman, Harriet 34
Tweedsmuir Records. See Women's Institute

U

Underground Railroad 34, 35, 36, 221

V

Valentines Day 157
Vermont 40, 69, 221–222. See also Barnet, Vermont
Vineyards 45, 62, 98, 188, 195

W

Wainfleet 37, 57
Walnuts, Hickory nuts 77, 122–124, 168
Warner, Bob 82
Warner (Pierce), Beverley 67, 82, 205, 206, 231
War of 1812-14 17, 21, 24, 35
Welland 38, 44–46, 57, 61, 70, 74, 77, 78, 85, 87, 107, 140, 149, 150, 163, 190, 195, 196, 198, 203, 204, 205, 214, 233
Welland, Joseph's move to 57–59, 188, 215
Welland Canal 34, 35, 57, 105, 139, 149, 160, 204, 221
Welland County Historical Atlas 59–60, 187
Welland Tribune (Herald) 57, 203, 222
Willson, Isaac 58, 221
Wolves and wild animals 22, 39–43, 222
Women's Institute 222, 224, 225
World War I 105, 170–172, 224

Y

YMCA 101

ISBN 1412070244-4